Le Weekend

Arthur Eperon is one of the most experienced and best known travel writers in Europe. Since leaving the RAF in 1945 he has worked as a journalist in various capacities often involving travel. He has concentrated on travel writing for the past fifteen years and contributed to many publications including *The Times, Daily Telegraph, New York Times, Woman's Own, Popular Motoring* and the *TV Times*. He has appeared on radio and television and for five years was closely involved in Thames Television's programme *Wish you were here*. He has an intimate and extensive knowledge of France and its food and wine, as a result of innumerable visits there over the last thirty years. In 1974 he won the Prix de Provinces de France, the annual French award for travel writing.

Le

Arthur Eperon

Weekend

line drawings by Ken Smith

Pan Original
Pan Books London and Sydney

Also by Arthur Eperon
in Pan Books

Travellers' Britain
Travellers' France
Encore Travellers' France
Travellers' Italy

First published 1984 by Pan Books Ltd,
Cavaye Place, London SW10 9PG
© Arthur Eperon 1984
hardcover ISBN 0 330 28420 7
paperback ISBN 0 330 28202 6
Photoset by Parker Typesetting Service, Leicester
Printed in Great Britain by
Collins, Glasgow

CONTENTS

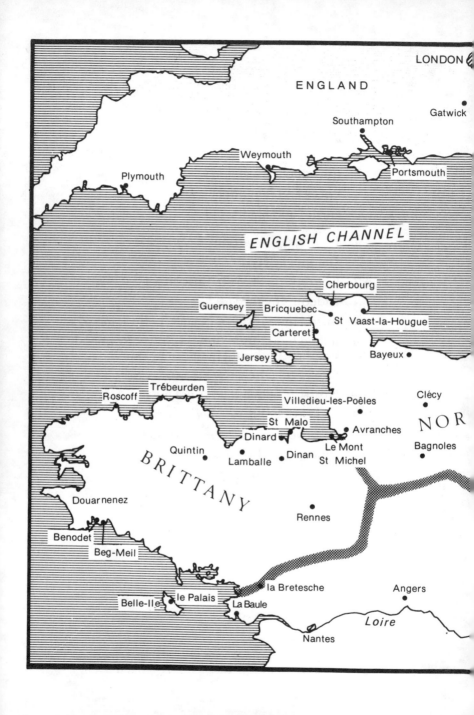

Ramsgate
Dover
Folkstone
aven
Wissant
Boulogne
Le Touquet
Montreuil
le Crotoy
Arras
aléry-en-Caux
Dieppe
Somme
vre
Yvetot
Villequier
les Andelys
uville
Seine
ANDY
as du Pin
PARIS
Fontainbleau
FRANCE
Orléans
Tours

Zeebrugge
Ostend
Bruges
Antwerp
Dunkerque
Calais
St Omer
BRUSSELS
BELGIUM
NORD PAS DE CALAIS
PICARDY
Laon
Compiegne
Reims
Epernay
Chalons-s-Marne
Troyes

0   100 km

INTRODUCTION -
STOLEN WEEKENDS

In Dieppe they have long told the story of a romantic Englishman who planned a stolen weekend over there with a girl from Paris.

On the ferry from Newhaven he fell among rugby players. At Dieppe they crossed the quai Henry IV to the convenient and lively Tout Va Bien café – the All Goes Well – for a quick Pernod before the rugby players went off to Rouen for their match.

Alas, all did not go well. The front row got into a ruck with a gendarme and practised passing with his helmet down the dockside. A vanload of police reserves rounded them up and put them back on the boat just as it was sailing. They included in the package the romantic Englishman who was sitting outside the next café quietly awaiting his Parisienne. Glumly he sailed to Newhaven and caught the next boat back. But the bird had flown.

To me that is a very sad story. A weekend in France on your own can be very pleasant; a weekend with the right companion can be near to heaven.

We live in the heart of Kent and it is easier for us to go to Boulogne than to Dorset. I suppose that we have been across to North France and Belgium between twelve and twenty times a year for thirty-five years, and we even go across to celebrate Barbara's birthday.

It started for me just after the Second World War. As a revolting young newspaper reporter, making routine phone calls on a bright spring Friday, with a dull weekend's desk work ahead, I suddenly picked up my raincoat and toothbrush and made for France.

Back in the office on Monday morning, complete with hangover and duty-free Scotch, I awaited the wrath of the editor to fall upon me.

Nothing happened. No one had missed me. And that taught me two lessons – that I was not, after all, indispensable, and that

a short break in spring, autumn or even midwinter just when
you feel like going is often more satisfying than a week or two in
summer carefully planned.

It is rewarding to fly to Rome, Madrid, Amsterdam or Vienna
for a weekend, but hardly relaxing, and you won't get much
time there. For real relaxation, I want a short journey to an hotel
or inn where I can meet local people, drink good wine at
reasonable prices, eat very good food – a place where 'Monsieur le Patron mange ici', and preferably where he or his wife
does the cooking. I want to be able to get up and go, to jump
into a car, or on to a train, catch a boat and be there. And that
means Northern France or Belgium.

When I wrote the original version of Le Weekend in 1974, a
few connoisseurs were taking short breaks in France and very
few people indeed went over for the day. The first man I knew
who made regular car trips was the owner of the Duck Inn at Pett
Bottom in Kent, who drove his old Le Mans Bentley to Boulogne
market to buy fresh cheese, mussels, scallops, John Dory and
vegetables for his restaurant. Perhaps he still does.

Since then there has been a revolution in short holidays to
France, and day trippers sometimes threaten to flood nearer
ports like Calais and Boulogne. More ferry companies, with
competing short-stay bargains in low season, have made my
hobby something of a fashion. The ferries have improved
enormously. You can even dance your way to France in a disco
on some boats.

The hypermarkets and supermarkets in and around the
French ports have thrived on British visitors, and sometimes
you can hardly hear a word of French in the drinks section.
Luckily these massive stores absorb most of the British shoppers or I should never get near some of my little family-run
favourites. We thought we were pretty adventurous years ago
to take a quick trip to France in December to eat and drink well,
stock up with duty-free brandy, wine, perfume and little Christmas presents and make a modest profit on the trip. Now tens of
thousands do the same, and hundreds of thousands of children
in the south-east of England must have been to France for the
day with school parties.

But this does not mean that France has been spoiled for short
holidays. There are some wonderful places to hide away within
a few miles of the ports and some splendid places to stay and to
eat. Village inns, manor houses converted into small hotels,

beautifully furnished old châteaux where you feel like a family friend rather than an hotel guest – North France and Brittany are as rich in all of them as they are short of terrible super-efficient businessmen's hotels like cabinets for filing people away for the night.

There are smaller seaside resorts to hide away for weekends, and there are whole areas of superb countryside, with tiny hamlets, genuine village inns, old farmhouses and older churches, just behind the busy ports and coast resorts – areas known to few French. British motorists heading for the motorways and the mad dash to the Mediterranean have never dreamed that they exist.

Behind Calais are silent, wooded hills and lush valleys with wandering trout streams and narrow rough lanes. Along the valley of the river Course, south of Dèsvres, are hamlets and inns unknown even to some people of Boulogne. Follow the river Canche on the small roads through the Villages Fleuris and you are in a different world from the main roads across the river. Follow the little roads beside the Authie river and you could be in France of the last century – only 20 km from the lively resort of Berck Plage. I doubt if one in a hundred British drivers beating up and down the abominable N1 or the motorways which are creeping nearer to Calais has heard of the river Aa, but it runs through delightful countryside and villages where you can forget about motorway lag and eat heartily for a song.

You can find the same hideaway hamlets behind Dieppe in the unknown countryside of Caux, where black and white timbered farm cottages vastly outnumber modern bungalows, along the tiny roads of the Calvados country south of Caen and much the same distance from Cherbourg, Le Havre and St Malo – a land of old estates with châteaux, some of which have become hotels, and again south of this in the neat, fertile countryside of l'Orne. As for Brittany – however much the Parisians and the British may pack the charming and interesting coast resorts and fishing villages, you can find peace and even solitude a few miles inland. In high season, France is a country where it pays to stay just inland and make sorties to the beach rather than the other way round.

Of course, not everyone wants to hide away. I think that if you choose a little remote hotel in a quiet village, it is best to go with your wife, your husband or someone you know well. Although swinging and dancing are not essential for a successful weekend, I still think that it is arrogant of a man to take a girl he does not know very well to a secluded place where there is little to do but each other. A man so sure of his abilities that he thinks he can entertain a girl night and day with his charm, conversation and prowess deserves a lesson.

But even in this permissive age of sex equality, there is still something deliciously immoral in dropping routine and stealing a weekend away with a member of the opposition, even if it is your wife or husband. You could, of course, go to Paris simply for the smell of baked bread and Gauloises, the view from the Eiffel Tower over the rooftops of Montmartre or the more general view from the new Pompidou centre. But solitude is expensive over there. Single rooms cost almost as much as double rooms in the few hotels that have them and it is not without cause that hotel rooms with a double bed are still called 'French style' in many lands. I hate to waste a double room on myself. I am more parsimonious about space than money.

A writer friend of mine once accompanied me to France, taking with him a charming girl to whom he was not technically married and who therefore had a different name on her passport. Instead of accepting the fact that it didn't really matter, he insisted upon taking the hotel manager aside and explaining it all.

The manager sent the girl and the baggage upstairs and took us into the bar for a drink.

'Mr Blank,' he said quietly, 'quite a number of gentlemen appear at my hotel with ladies who have different names on their documents. We in hotels are used to it. In fact, we rather prefer it that way. If a gentleman brings his wife they will have a Martini as apéritif and a bottle of Beaujolais with dinner. If the girl is his mistress he will, of course, buy her champagne before dinner, perhaps fine Château Margaux or even an Haut Brion with dinner, and after, they will drink Remy Martin. It is much better for business.'

The Victorians seemed to travel largely to study church architecture, and there is a hangover in modern guide books. Even the green Michelin dotes on it. I wonder sometimes just how many people are *quite* so interested in the details of capitals, pinnacles, liernes and tiercerons as in the general effect of a beautiful building.

But we all have our tastes and mine in Normandy and Pas-de-Calais is history. It is part of English history, too, from William the Conqueror, known locally as the Bastard, sailing from Le Tréport in 1066, to the day before D-Day in 1944 when British paras dropped at Benouville near Caen, took a vital canal bridge, liberated the local pub and held them for twenty-four hours until the Highland Division arrived from the beachhead, led by a piper who in peacetime was a Devon printer. It is the sidelights of history which amuse me – the individualists and eccentrics, the colourful scenes and odd situations. You meet up with our history in many hidden corners. There's the Promenade Beaulieu overlooking Jardin Vert at Angoulême where in 1806 France's General Resnier, already seventy-three, took off in a wing-flapping machine he had invented. He hoped to have found a way for Napoleon's troops to invade England but he ended in the river.

Between Guines and Ardres, 10 km south of Calais, I like to stop and muse among valley farmfields with the distinguished name of Camp du Drap d'Or (Field of the Cloth of Gold). In 1520, when the English owned Calais, the little sleepy town of Guines was Henry VIII's front line headquarters and Francis I of France was installed in Ardres. They met here in an ostentatious display of pomp and wealth. They were supposed to be negotiating an alliance but they tried to better each other in every detail, from dress and décor of their tents to food and sport. Henry had 5000 followers from his court, dressed in velvet, satin and gold. Francis used 6000 workmen to prepare the site. It was history's greatest picnic. Henry's organiser, Cardinal Wolsey, sent over, among other items, 2014 sheep, 700 conger eels, 26 dozen heron and four bushels of mustard. The kings jousted every day but one, and on that day the wind was high, so they wrestled. Francis threw Henry flat on his back. They still swore eternal peace, but Henry went straight to a meeting with France's main enemy, the Emperor Charles V, and soon signed a treaty with him against France.

At the Grand Hôtel Clement in Ardres I have had many a good meal but never heron – nor lamb with mustard. What a party it must have been in 1520.

I have read some harsh attacks on the food of North France and Normandy in recent years by devotees of Nouvelle Cuisine – in fashion until recently but thankfully now in decline. Nouvelle Cuisine came in with the general panic about extra fat killing us. It was a worthy idea and has left behind some splendid dishes which have enriched even French cuisine.

Perhaps 'enriched' is the wrong word, for the basic idea is to leave out the traditional cream, flour and butter whenever possible, to thicken sauces by boiling down (which the best French chefs have always done) or by using cottage cheese or yoghurt, which can spoil the flavour. The trouble is that some devotees of this fashion have become fanatics. They serve meat which is not so much 'rare' as virtually raw, with nearly raw carrots and potatoes. Raspberry vinegar is almost compulsory in most dishes. Worst is my special dislike the Nouvelle Cuisine magret de canard. I just don't fancy raw duck breasts. However, Barbara does.

To me the cooking of Normandy is a delight. The fish is fresh from the little fishing harbours or the large market of Boulogne. Meat is from lush meadows through which flow streams jumping with fresh trout and rich in crayfish. From these pastures come superb butter, milk, cream and an abundance of cheeses unrivalled even in the rest of France. With such riches, not even the most fashionable chef is going to omit cream, butter and succulent cheeses from his favourite recipes. Old-fashioned French cooking is very much alive and well in Normandy.

Nevertheless, when I was young, the trenchermen of Normandy did overdo it. Little inns would have bowls of fresh cream on the table and diners would ladle it into their soups. People did tend towards plumpness, but they walked miles a day instead of sitting in cars, and lived as long as lean men who probably suffered from fear of their bosses, fear of their wives, and ulcers.

I have never claimed to be a true gastronome. Anyway, I cannot afford to be. For it is an expensive hobby. When I took over writing the RAC's wine guides from one of Britain's greatest experts I was billed as 'one of the world's greatest consumers'. I have cherished that description over the years of food and wine, and have the figure to prove it. In this book I have recommended restaurants and hotels right through the price range from those offering gastronomic meals for special celebrations to little places for cheap last suppers when your francs are running out. I have suggested smaller hotels of character, mostly family-run, where you should find fair beds and a good welcome, as well as beautiful châteaux hotels where you will feel like an old French aristocrat. But I have missed out the comfortable but featureless boxes with so little character where you have to inspect the small change on your bedside table when you wake up to recall which country you are in.

The typical French hotel does not exist. In the USA hotel chains brag that their hotels are the same in every city. They call it 'reliability'. French hotels have variety, individuality and sometimes downright eccentricity. The few 'chain' hotels are aimed at businessmen and conferences.

I have picked hotels for value, and some for interest and atmosphere. French prices like all others have risen with inflation but French meals are still the best overall value in the world, even in terms of the fallen pound. You may not get the same standard of hotel bedroom for the price of one on a Spanish package tour, but you will be a guest, not a room number, and most people go to France for atmosphere and food. Equivalent rooms are still much cheaper than in Britain, and you really get what you pay for. Even in France you cannot have Jaguar service at Mini prices, nor gastronomic meals at a Relais Routiers. Most Relais Routiers meals are wonderful value, especially those with a 'casserole' award for good regional cooking. You may well get huge tureens of soup, bowls of pâté and vegetables left on the table for you to help yourself. But I have had some shocking bedrooms – washbasins and shelves falling off walls, lino and rugs in holes, damp patches on walls. That has been my own fault for not inspecting the bedroom before I hired it. Sometimes there are twenty rooms with pleasant comfort and a couple of rough attic rooms for late arrivals. Incidentally while checking your bedroom look in the cupboards for pillows (*oreillers*). The French are careless about pillows and it is no good looking for them at midnight. A friend of mine ordered a pillow before dinner and it arrived with his breakfast.

Logis de France keep up their excellent standards overall but can be booked up ahead in midsummer. All family-run, they claim to treat you like a paying guest, and those which fall down on the promise soon get thrown out of the group. But I have found as many family-run hotels of the same standard and welcome which do not belong to Logis as those which do. France Accueil hotels claim, 'Our guests are our friends. We are attentive to the 1001 details which make a stay a happy one.' They are sometimes better and dearer than Logis. I shall also write about the three châteaux-style hotel organisations in a later chapter.

I have suggested some smaller resorts for weekends or for hiding away, some lively places to swing away half the night, good places for families, some package arrangements to save money and trouble, a few good camp and caravan sites, places within range of Paris, and overnight stops near the ports or on nearby routes for people going longer distances.

If heading further, do leave plenty of time to catch your ferry on the way back. Insurance companies say that more than half the accidents to British motorists abroad are within fifty miles or so of the ports – enthusiasts either rushing south to the sun or staying too long on beaches and rushing for the ferry. Leave time for a last pleasant meal. Leaving France without one is rather like going to a gastronomic banquet and leaving before the last two or three courses.

Prices and reminders

Prices given are correct as far as possible until the end of 1983. Inflation in France is unpredictable, as in Britain, and it is impossible to tell how much they might rise in 1984.

Menu prices are quoted for meals. You can, of course, choose 'à la carte' and just one main dish or two dishes if you wish. There is an increasing tendency in French tourist areas – places like Honfleur, Dinan, Dinard – to insist that you take half-board even for a night – bed, breakfast and dinner or lunch. This is especially so in high season. So if you want to find your own little restaurant, check this before you accept your bedroom. And *do* look at your bedroom before you take it. Rooms can vary within the same hotel. I am amazed how many readers do not look at their rooms. It is normal to do so in France.

In high season, hotels will not usually hold a room after 6 p.m. unless you telephone to say you are on your way.

Room prices quoted are for double rooms without breakfast. A French breakfast costs from about 8F to 20F (luxury hotel). Half-board prices are normally per person, per night for two nights or more, sharing a room.

Check the menu card outside to see if prices are *service, taxe compris* (STC) – service and VAT included. In some restaurants the cheaper menus are STC, dearer menus are not; these will be about 15 per cent higher.

Speed limits in France are 60 kph (38 mph) in town; 90 kph (56 mph) outside town; 130 kph (81 mph) on dual carriageways. Fines for exceeding them are now a *minimum* of around £60, rising according to your speed, and you must pay on the spot. So don't exceed the limits.

You must convert your lights to dip the other way for driving on the right. According to the type of light, you can use plastic clip-on converters or paper stick-ons. You must carry a red triangle to display in emergencies.

Parking laws are now strictly enforced. The parking clock system operates in most towns, so get yourself a *disque* from a tobacconist and prop it against your windscreen with the time when you parked indicated.

Ferries and flights

To France

Hoverspeed (hovercraft) Dover–Boulogne/Calais (35 mins)

Folkestone–Boulogne (Sealink, 1 hr 50 mins)

Dover–Boulogne (P&O, 1 hr 50 mins)

Dover–Calais (Townsend, Sealink, 1 hr 15 mins, 1 hr 40 mins)

Folkestone–Calais (Sealink, 1 hr 40 mins)

Dover–Dunkirk (Sealink, 2 hrs 20 mins)

Newhaven–Dieppe (Sealink, 4 hrs)

Ramsgate–Dunkirk (Sally Line, 2 hrs 30 mins)

Portsmouth–Le Havre/Cherbourg (Townsend, 5½ hrs, 4 hrs)

Southampton–Le Havre (Townsend, P&O, 6½ hrs, 8 hrs)

Southampton–Cherbourg (Townsend, 5 hrs)

Weymouth–Cherbourg (Sealink, 4 hrs)

Portsmouth–St Malo (Brittany Ferries, 8½ hrs)

Plymouth–Roscoff (Brittany Ferries, 6 hrs)

By air

Brit Air (agent Air France, 158 New Bond St, London W1; 01 499 9511): Gatwick–Caen/Le Havre/Morlaix/Quimper/Rennes

Lucas Air (agent Gatwick Handling Reservations Desk, Gatwick Airport, Horley, Surrey; 0293 513631) Gatwick–Deauville

Brymon Airways (City Airport, Crown Hill, Plymouth, 0752 707023) Plymouth–Brest/Morlaix

To Belgium

Dover–Zeebrugge (Townsend, 4 hrs, 4½ hrs)

Felixtowe–Zeebrugge (Townsend, 5 hrs day, longer by night)

Dover/Folkestone–Ostend (Sealink, 3 hrs 30 mins, 4 hrs 15 mins)

Hull-Zeebrugge (North Sea Ferries)

1 Boulogne, Montreuil, Calais

Boulogne is still the port of my teenage memories – crowded, chaotic, lively bars, beguiling little shops, cheap restaurants, fishing boats selling their catch on the quay. It is usually fun, never relaxing.

The snag is that now too many other Britons like it. Around two million invade it every year and sometimes they all seem to be there at once.

A few years ago, the boats disgorged GB cars so impatient to hurry south that they barely stopped at traffic lights. Only a few of us mingled with the French in shops, bars and restaurants. Now even the drivers stop to take on supplies before hurrying to the motorways, and you must wriggle round bewildered British schoolchildren as well as determined British shoppers, to make headway. It is rather ironic that the spot where Julius Caesar took off to invade England in 55 BC and Napoleon and Hitler built thousands of boats for similar operations should now be inundated with English schoolchildren and shoppers laden with loot bags. At least they pay for their loot, which is more than the people of Boulogne used to do in earlier centuries when they popped over the Channel on lucrative visits to our fishing towns to collect money, supplies and such souvenirs as church silver and women.

By early evening, most day visitors have completed their circuit of Auchen hypermarket (3 km along route N42), been round Nouvelles Galeries and Prisunic stores on rue Victor Hugo, chosen their cheese from 200 varieties at Philippe Olivier's wonder-shop on ruc Thiers, had a snack at Hamiot opposite the fish market or a bargain meal at Chez Jules in place Dalton or a jar in a bar, and are off home.

If you want to see Boulogne it's better to shop early, then make for Ville Haute, the historic and interesting old walled town up the hill, and hide at lunchtime in one of the lesser-known restaurants, tasting a plate of mussels, prawns or sole, which will have come straight from the fish market, with a bottle of Muscadet, dry white, and dreaming of the serious meal you will take in the evening.

If you are on a day trip, of course, early shopping means taking an early boat from England. If you can do it, your day will be much better value for money.

You can drive to Ville Haute up

Grande Rue, but parking up there is impossible. So, if you are fit enough to climb a long, fairly steep hill, park down below alongside the fish market on quai Gambetta or in the second-storey car park beside the supermarket in boulevard Daunou. Then walk up rue Faidherbe beside Hamiot's snack bar.

Most of Boulogne's best shops are in this street or in the smaller streets at right angles – nearly all little shops selling most things you might want from dresses and shoes to cream gateaux and charcuterie. I shall tell you about them and the fish market in Chapter 14, on shopping and souvenirs.

You will see a church on the right, St Nicolas, facing into place Dalton, the market square. An amusing market is held on Wednesday and Saturday mornings, spreading down Grande Rue. Stalls are packed with butter, pâté and cheeses direct from farms, chickens, cider, colourful vegetables and more colourful flowers.

At the old town walls, turn right along the boulevard to Porte des Degrés, a gate shut from Henry VIII's siege in 1544 until 1895, and now open only to pedestrians. Mount the ramparts and walk along them to the castle and on to Porte des Dunes.

It is incredible that Haute Ville survives. In 1940 Hitler parked invasion barges in Boulogne harbour while he contemplated Dover's cliffs from the same clifftop at nearby Cap Gris Nez as Napoleon did in 1801. So the RAF bombed the port 400 times, almost entirely destroying the town down the hill but missing Haute Ville. As an RAF participant, I will not deny that luck played a part.

The castle was built on Roman foundations in the 13th century and strengthened by Louis XIV's great military architect Vauban, so that in 1940 Hitler's 2nd Panzer Division failed to take it. The French walked out with flying colours as their country surrendered.

Prince Louis Napoleon, future Napoleon III, was imprisoned here in 1840 after an abortive landing from England to try to oust King Louis Philippe, the friend of Queen Victoria, known mostly to us for the name of a shirt. And after the First World War the body of the British Unknown Soldier lay here in state on its way to be buried in Westminster Abbey.

The superb Italian dome of the cathedral of Notre-Dame which dominates Boulogne was decorated by Vatican craftsmen. It has been aptly called a synthesis of the Pantheon in Rome, Les Invalides in Paris and London's St Paul's. The present cathedral is built on the site of other churches dating back to 636 AD. Legend says a statue of the Virgin, standing in an open boat, was pushed ashore by angels. Louis XI pronounced it a true Madonna in 1477 and pilgrims soon arrived to start Boulogne's tourist boom. Fourteen French kings, five kings of England and many murderers and evil-doers prayed here for absolution from their sins.

Various statues were burned or stolen through the centuries. The latest, by local lad Paul Graf in 1924 in 12th-century style, weighs 26,500 pounds. Each August it is carried in procession, followed by fishermen, farmers and girls in traditional headgear.

Early cathedral treasures disappeared when our Henry VIII took Boulogne, looted it of anything movable, then sold the town for 200,000 gold ducats back to Henry II of France – notorious for his savagery in torturing and killing Protestants, but rating a bust on the old town's ramparts for ridding Boulogne of English visitors. Some citizens must wish they had a hero to do the same – but not the shopkeepers or restaurateurs.

In the cathedral crypt, Edward II of England married Isabelle, daughter of Phillip IV of France in 1308. Their son Edward III claimed the French throne and started the Hundred Years' War. An expensive wedding.

The centre of Haute Ville, with a 13th-century belfry tower and an 18th-century house called ostentatiously Imperial Palace because Napoleon used it, is called place Godefroy de Bouillon, after a local hero who led the First Crusade. He was made King of Jerusalem but refused to 'wear a crown of gold where my Saviour wore a crown of thorns'. He called himself Defender of the Holy Sepulchre.

There are seventeen towers round the old walls. Leaving by Porte des Dunes, you see Gayette tower with a wall-plaque to another failed invader of England. Pilatre de Rozier was the first human to fly in the Montgolfier balloon over Paris in 1783. Two years later he tried to cross the Channel from this tower. Alas, at 1900 feet his balloon collapsed. He is buried in nearby Wimille churchyard. In the hilly Guines forest, south of Calais and south-east of Boulogne, is a column on a remote hillside to the men who made it – Frenchman Colonel Blanchard and American Dr Jeffries, who crossed from Dover in the same year, 129 years before Blériot's first plane crossing.

Boulogne was for long a beach resort. The big sandy beach beyond the casino is not brilliant for bathing but in summer useful snack bars are set up selling anything from hot dogs to fried fish or fish soup. Beach bathing started in 1789 and lured colonies of Britons to live in Boulogne. It was also a refuge for our bankrupt aristocrats, avoiding creditors, those crossed in love, and couples 'living in sin' in times when such liaisons meant self-imposed exile except for princes and dukes.

Dickens came for the sea air and wrote much of *Bleak House* and *Hard Times* in Boulogne. A young actress called Ellen Ternan also inspired him to deep breathing.

After 1863, with Napoleon III on the throne, Parisian aristrocats came for the casino gambling. You can still have a flutter in the new casino – or, more profitably, dance, watch a show or swim in its heated pool.

Napoleon I spent three frustrating years in Boulogne preparing to invade England. He built 2000 flat-bottomed boats and a premature victory column in local bronze to his Grande Armée. You can see it by going along the N1 road north from Calais, then taking the D96 left. By climbing a mere 265 steps you have a splendid panorama; some days even the white cliffs of Dover are visible. Napoleon's statue on top looks the same way. A kilometre west is a stone marking the spot in 1804 where Napoleon sat on a throne with 100,000 troops in an arc on surrounding slopes and distributed 2000 decorations of the Legion d' Honneur to officers and troops. He did nothing by halves. More spectacular than either is the Calvaire des Marins – a huge cross dedicated to sailors lost in shipwrecks or wars, just off the D940 coast road.

Southward, backed by a forest and with a good golf course, is **Hardelot**, with a fine beach and snob appeal, and further south my favourite little lively resort of Le Touquet. North, towards Cap Gris Nez, with views of England, is **Wimereux**, with a beach of shingle, sand, low-tide rock pools and seaweed loved by children. Beside it stands the Atlantic hotel, famous for spit-roast fish and meat. I saw Michel Hamiot build it from a little hotel with beachside charcoal grill into a pricey world famous two-star Michelin hotel with a huge gas grill. Alas, as I tasted a superb chausson of crab recently, I learned that the Hamiot family may sell it. La Ronde!

There is a nice drive back to Boulogne on little roads – the white roads of those indispensable yellow Michelin maps – past Souverain Moulin and through Boulogne forest with

shady walks, lanes, picnic tables and inns. The château of **Souverain Moulin** is closed, but you can visit its chapel, decorated with works of the greatest modern tapestry artist, Jean Lurcat.

Behind Boulogne and Calais are some wonderful country hideaways among green hills, deep valleys, woods, tiny hamlets – the charming village of Le Waast, for instance, 15 km from Boulogne. Take the white roads north-east to the **Guines forest**, or west to **Licques** and **St Omer**, where you can take a short boat trip along tree-lined canals or drive through Boulogne forest to the **forest of Dèsvres**.

My favourite run is to drive on the D341 to the outskirts of Dèsvres, where the famous porcelain is made, and turn right down the little D127 following the valley of the river. It is a secret lush land where even the pubs seem to hide away: a place of peace and beauty even in midsummer. There is a trout farm where you can fish, riding stables, meadows for picnics and strange little hamlets like **Estrée** and **Estrelles**, divided by the tiny river yet not speaking to each other since the Wars of Religion of the 16th and 17th centuries, when Estrée was Catholic, Estrelles was Protestant. They have all of 250 inhabitants each, separate schools, mayors, fête days, churches and burial grounds. You can tell the Catholic churchyard by its ornate tombs. Their joint war memorial stands on the bridge. Names of the fallen of Estrée point to that village, their neighbours' losses point the other way.

Though sometimes crowded midsummer, the old walled medieval town of **Montreuil-sur-Mer** is a delight. It just grows on you. Like Rye in Sussex, it has not been *sur mer* for centuries, but its 700-year-old ramparts overlook the whole surrounding country and you have lovely views as you walk around them on grass pathways and under trees. In a tower of its castle of stone and brick is a simple old board listing the local knights killed fighting Henry V at Agincourt. It's a formidable list.

In the narrow streets below are lovely old buildings like the ancient Benedictine abbey of St Saulve and the flamboyant 15th-century chapel with fine rich furnishings, ancient houses and little shops, tiny squares like the shaded place Darnetal where the fountain plays beside the war memorial and my dear friend Robert Bureau still smilingly serves delightful meals in Darnetal restaurant.

Beside the square is one of the most amusing antique shops I have seen round the world. Two massive stone dogs from some château gates have stood outside for years, awaiting a buyer. One day I shall have them for my garden.

The road downhill to the huge market square passes the Hôtel de France and separate restaurant, Relais du Roy. Both have reopened lately.

Years ago, when the hotel was in decay, I walked along its rumpy corridors past empty rooms and a toilet with a suite of ornate cast iron with flowery motif and chattering pipes to my huge bedroom overlooking a courtyard. Down there, one wall was covered with a massive flaking mural showing an 18th-century gentleman stepping into a post-chaise. It was the Yorkshire parson, the author Laurence Sterne, starting his *Sentimental Journey through France and Italy* by distributing *sous* to the poor.

'They order these things better in France,' he wrote. And generations have used the phrase to refer to hotels and meals. In fact, he was talking about begging.

Montreuil's Saturday market offers most things from cabbages to clothes and furniture – a huge market on the old scale. Overlooking it in bronze on a horse is Sir Douglas Haig, British army commander of the First World War, whose headquarters were at Château de Beaurepaire, 6 km along the N39. Montreuil was headquarters, too, of Napoleon's Marshal Ney, and in 1944 of the Nazi anti-invasion commander. In the attic of the delightful 200-year-old Château de Montreuil, a superb little hotel, are relief maps of the coast and a noticeboard ordering everyone entering to give the Nazi salute. I prefer to *bow* as I enter Christian Germain's shrine of great cooking. But that is another story, for another chapter (see page 120).

Montreuil is only 14 km from **Le Touquet**, 24 km from the charming old town of **Hesdin** and its pleasant forest. If you drive there, use the prettier white road north of the river Canche.

North-east of Montreuil to **Hucqueliers** and **Fruges** are more attractive villages, pretty farms and simple, old-style inns, and south is the attractive valley of the river Authie. Montreuil is altogether a splendid base for a weekend.

Calais had a raw deal from French governments after the war. The money for rebuilding went into Boulogne and Dunkirque. Sometimes I think that Paris believes that Calais is still English – and that goes for French guidebooks, too. I have many friends there but I do not find it has the same atmosphere or interest as Boulogne, nor is it so good for eating or shopping. Mind you, there are more good little restaurants than previously, and British visitors who do their shopping around place d'Armes, the square fairly near the ferry terminal, often do not realise that the main shops which local people use are past the railway station and the town hall up the hill (see Chapter 14, on shopping).

Calais is two towns: the ferry port 38 km from Britain, geared for the lucrative trade brought by British motorists and by tens of thousands of Britons on a day's shopping trip, and the manufacturing centre and industrial port where boats from most of the world land cargoes.

There is little left of its violent history. The only reminders of English possession from 1347 to 1558 are shop windows full of local lace, an art brought here from Nottingham, and Rodin's evocative statue of the burghers of Calais outside the town hall – tribute to the six men who offered their lives to Edward III of England after an eight months' siege if he would spare the other townsfolk. Edward was persuaded by his queen to spare the lot.

Oh yes, the church where Charles de Gaulle married a local girl in 1921 is in English perpendicular style. Incidentally there used to be a little hotel in the neighbouring resort of Wissant where they claimed that Charles de Gaulle would stay incognito. He could perform some clever tricks, but I don't think that of remaining unrecognised was one of them.

Last century Britons hid in Calais from their creditors. Nelson's Lady Hamilton came in 1815 to die in poverty and misery. Beau Brummel, arbiter of fashion and manners, uncrowned king of Bath and Tunbridge Wells, stayed here fifteen years to avoid his creditors but kept up his way of life until he got a job as vice-consul in Caen in Normandy.

In a bunker which was German navy headquarters 1940–44 is a little wartime museum, and on the tiny island in the harbour the Green Jackets (the Rifle Brigade) made a last stand against the Nazis in 1940 to give others time to escape to England.

One of the worst jobs in the British diplomatic service must be vice-consul at Calais. It is not only the exit port for Distressed British Citizens being sent home by boat but the consul's sleep can be disturbed nightly by drunken British citizens in trouble with the police or stranded day-trippers who have lost their tickets and purses.

One vice-consul told me of the wide range of distressed citizens who passed through his office – genuine cases of worthy people stripped of everything by muggers on the Paris Métro; strange cases of old ladies who have lived a stainless life in Sevenoaks suddenly taking a holiday in Monte Carlo and blowing their all at the casino; many cases of unwise motorists who have not insured their cars fully against major breakdowns and get stranded anywhere from the Dordogne to the Pyrenees. But the majority in these days when you can get money abroad on credit cards are young hitch-hikers.

'The young do not seem to realise that you may be able to hitch-hike to Katmandu but you simply cannot hitch a lift across the Channel, the consul told me. 'The ferry companies do like you to have a ticket.'

The boat-missers are the biggest headache. Most are drunk. 'We used to give them a ticket for the next day's boat and enough francs for bed and breakfast, all to be repaid in Britain, of course. But most of them went straight back to a bar and spent their bed-and-breakfast money. Some even sold their tickets. So now we give them a chit for a bed and breakfast and they must report for their tickets next morning.

'We used to have trouble with miners' outings – on the way back from taking fraternal greetings to French miners of the north, I believe. I think that the French miners were rather hospitable. Now rugby clubs are a problem. You know, the police of Calais understand the British very well and tolerate our eccentricities. But one thing they will not tolerate is young gentlemen playing rugby football with their hats at 1 a.m. They go to gaol.'

His biggest dislike was for self-styled VIPs who knew everyone at the Foreign Office. 'One fellow breezed in here one morning and said: "Terrible trouble, old boy . . . left my wallet and cards at home . . . let me have 500 quid, there's a good chap. Everyone at the FO knows me, so I'll see you all right." I had to tell him that I was not allowed to compete with the banks and that if he waited an hour his bank in London would be open, so he would be able to telephone for cash. He got quite nasty, said he would report me to the Foreign

Minister himself. I never heard any more. Anyway, the chap was driving a Mercedes.'

Many Britons do not know that Calais has a big sand beach. Fewer know that there is a good open market in place Crêvecoeur on Thursday and Saturday mornings, with fish direct from boats and food from farms. Very few indeed know the delightful countryside you can find by taking the D127 to Guines and exploring the lanes in the triangle between the N43, N1 and N42. Even my wife Barbara, an experienced travel writer and expert on France, was amazed by the peace and charm of this area when I showed it to her last year. It is a world apart from the ports and main roads. The D127 follows a canal and in **Guines** you should turn right into the little main square to see a tiny French town square seemingly kept as a film set of the First World War period. The little old Lion d'Or bar-restaurant is splendid value. You can eat well, too, in Ardres, and on the road you pass the Field of the Cloth of Gold where Henry VIII met Francis I and Henry took his undignified tumble.

Ardres is a delightful little town, excellent for a good meal on a trip to Calais, better for an overnight with time for a really good dinner. I was drinking with Barbara in a little bar by the church where locals go recently when I asked for the toilets. La Patronne said that, for madam, there was one behind the bar; for me, there was the church wall opposite. It had been used for 500 years, she said. Ardres is my old France. But I have known it for a mere fifty years.

Through the forests of Guines and Tournehem, there is another nice run to **St Omer**, a pleasant town where waterways, 300-year-old merchants' houses, and the ancient shops and cafés in Grande Place tilting all ways still lure artists. A good place for a weekend, too.

Poor **Dunkerque** took a terrible bashing in 1940 and has been rebuilt for shipping and industry, not beauty. But it was linked to Paris, Lille, Brussels and Germany by motorway (A25) long before other Channel ports and is now France's third biggest port. It is for long-distance drivers, not weekend relaxers. The ferry terminal is a fair bus-ride from town.

England owned it under Cromwell but Charles II sold it to Louis XIV for five million *livres* and must have regretted it. It became headquarters of Jean Bart, whose corsair squadron captured 3000 ships and 30,000 prisoners, destroying Holland's commerce. He is buried in St Eloi church, one of the few old buildings left.

Malo-les-Bains, seaside suburb with a long sand beach, casino and promenade restaurants, is very pleasant.

Hotels and Restaurants

Boulogne (postal address 62200 Pas-de-Calais)

Hotels
Faidherbe, 12 rue Faidherbe, (21) 31.60.93: refurnished, very pleasant, some noise; breakfast only; rooms 120-180F.

Metropole, 51 rue Thiers, (21) 31.54.30: no restaurant; central; useful overnight hotel; simply furnished, good service and French breakfast; traffic noise; rooms 100-200F; shut mid-December to early January.

De la Plage, 124 St Beuve, (21) 31.45.35: locals use the restaurant, which is good value; opposite the dock and useful overnight. Try lotte (monkfish) in saffron, moules marinières (very good). Menu 52F, 65F, 108F; rooms 83-109F. Shut Mondays; Sunday evenings except in summer.

Restaurants
La Matelote, 80 bd St Beuve, (21) 30.17.97: Michelin starred; best and dearest fish restaurant in area. Interesting and imaginative meals served in elegant room. Tony Lestienne has a light touch with a hint of Nouvelle Cuisine (orange vinegar dressing on his foie gras salad, the dreaded raspberry vinegar in sauces). We like his turbot fillets in crayfish sauce, his scallops cooked *en papillote* (wrapped), and his delicious desserts, some unusual like mint sorbet with hot chocolate sauce. Carte only, around 180-200F. Shut Sundays evenings; Mondays.

La Charlotte, 11 rue Dover, (21) 30.13.08: tiny restaurant next door to Alfred's, which we used when Alfred's was full or too crowded, is now nearly always full and crowded; success deserved, but book and expect all British fellow eaters. Excellent fish dishes, some almost eccentric; blanquette of turbot with asparagus; curried turbot with fresh fruit; bouchée (small vol-au-vent) stuffed with scallops gratin; salmon on spinach purée. Menu 70F, 110F (fish). Quercy red wine 33F. Shut Sundays.

Alfred, 24 pl. Dalton, (21) 31.53.16: we're a little worried about our old favourite after a few bad reports from readers; one even criticised the famous shellfish platter. My friends are still fans, and locals still use it. Typical old-style bistro with red-checked tablecloths, tight-packed tables, bustle, slow service when crowded; that is a bistro. Menu 75F, 100F, 150F; good 35F housewine. Shut Tuesdays.

Chez Jules, pl. Dalton, (21) 31.54.12: favourite of young locals now discovered by young Britons; pleasant inside; excellent value; try farandol boulonnaise (plate of various fish). Menu 60F; snacks. Shuts around 1-2 a.m.

La Liègeoise, 10 rue A. Monsigny, (21) 31.61.15: once famous, out of favour recently, but now young Alain Delpierre from Paris and Le Flambard at Lille has given it new life. Interesting and very good dishes from local fresh fish; try hot oysters in langoustine mousse. Menu 75-115F; shut Sunday evenings; Fridays; January 15 to 31.

Chez Zizine, 22 rue Amiral Bruix, (21) 31.43.24: still looks run down – part of the act, but overdone; still local favourite for fish, but prices getting high for best fish dishes. 40F menu excellent value. Shut Sundays.

Chez Pitch, 10 rue Coquelin, (21) 31.45.64: two rooms – bright, cheerful brasserie, cosier restaurant; quick cheap meals, dish of the day 25-27F, or menu 49F, 65F. Housewine 27F. Friendly, quick, useful. Shut Sundays. Also has rooms 70-80F.

Union de la Marine, quai Gambetta, (21) 31.38.83: big, cheap, cheerful; opposite fish dock; first-floor restaurant overlooks port. Menu 35F, 55F. Vin du patron 18F. Shut Thursdays except July and August.

In **Haute Ville** –

An-Bascaille-La, 16 pl. Godefroy de Bouillon, (21) 80.57.30: friendly, cheap, good cooking, useful; some dishes of French West Indies; open all day until midnight. Menu 45-70F. Patron's wine (red, white or rosé) 25F. Shut Tuesdays.

At **La Capelle-les-Boulogne**, 7 km on N42 –

Auberge de la Forêt, 33 Route Nationale, (21) 31.82.05: Philippe Lebrun cooks very well; good country dishes and some ambitious (artichokes stuffed with crab); choice limited to give freshly cooked food. Menu 68F, 100F; wine from 32F. Shut Mondays.

At **Le Portel**, 5 km SE, fishing village and beach for Boulogne families –

Au Grand Large, 1 rue du Maréchal Foch, (21) 31.71.51: little old-style restaurant where I have eaten superb local fish for years. Renowned platter of shellfish and mussels (stuffed, in cream or marinières); fish soup Thursdays and Saturdays. Good value. Menu 50F, 96F. Housewine 29F. Shut January.

At **Wimereux**, 6 km N on D940; address 62930 Pas-de-Calais –

Atlantic, on beach, (21) 32.41.01: see text; fish dishes and spit roasts superb. New chef Jean-Claude Bailleul in best Atlantic tradition. Chausson de crabe (crab in pastry) is delicious; so are fish mousses and pâtés. 130F menu suggestion, and weekday menu étape at 100F changed monthly according to ingredients in season. Carte is formidable, expensive and tempting; rooms with wc and bath at 180-240F good value. Shut

February; Sunday evenings and Mondays in winter.

Centre, 78 rue Carnot, (21) 32.41.08: looks like old-style commercial hotel; locals use it; excellent value 48F menu. Straightforward cooking of good meat, excellent local fish. 100F Sunday lunch menu is very good. Rooms vary in comfort 80-150F.

At **Cap Gris Nez**, 14 km N, just off D940 –

La Sirène, (21) 94.84.09: my little white restaurant like a coastguard's station above this massive bay of sands and rocks, for which Channel swimmers aim, has grown into a big, busy restaurant with huge *viviers* for live lobsters and such; two sittings for Sunday lunch to feed 200. I am not surprised. Fish is quite excellent, meat very good, and the sea view attractive and sometimes *sauvage*. Sole, cooked in butter or stuffed, usually outstanding; tempting carte. Good value menu at 58F, recommended menu at 118F. Housewine 20F. Shut mid-November to Christmas Eve; Mondays except in July and August.

Montreuil-sur-Mer (address 62170 Pas-de-Calais) –

Château de Montreuil, (21) 81.53.04: see Chapter 8, luxury hotels.

Central (Chez Edouard), 7 rue de Change, (21) 06.10.33: old-style family hotel, unimpressive looks but comfortable, very friendly, good value meals. A touch of old France. Bedrooms mostly have cabinet de toilette (shower, basin,

no wc). The famous Edouard, an Englishman, departed to Côte d'Azur but cooking still good. Super moules espagnoles, cassolette de St Jacques (scallops) and fresh fish. Rooms vary in price and comfort – look before you hire. Menu 50F, 70F; wines 40-200F; rooms 78-200F. Shut Mondays; restaurant Saturday lunch, Sunday evenings.

Darnetal, 1 pl. Darnetal, (21) 06.04.87: for seventeen years I have homed on Robert Bureau's warm, happy, eccentric little restaurant and still I meet there the mayor, garage owner, shopkeepers, tennis club and respected senior citizens; sign of good value in France. Good old French dishes – try duck in Beaujolais, civet of hare, coq au vin, kidneys in wine and a lovely creamed scallop mousse. A good-humoured bistro. Menu 50F, 80F, 100F. Housewine (good Côte du Rhone) 48F. Shut Tuesdays.

Mimpy's, 46 pl. de Gaulle, (21) 06.08.65: on market square, snack or full meal good value; meals at any time; menu 50F, good carte choice; wines reasonable; fifty bottled beers from all countries – Chinese to Guinness. Shut December, Wednesdays except in summer.

At **La Madelaine-sous-Montreuil**, 3 km beside river Canche –

La Grenouillère, (21) 06.07.22: see Chapter 8, luxury hotels.

Vieux Logis, (21) 06.10.92: rustic inn with good straightforward cooking; menus change daily; we had good croûte of seafood with armoricaine sauce and estouffade of beef – stewed in a sealed pot with red wine, herbs and shallots. Menu 50F, 84F; patron's wine 16F, others 20-35F. Shut Mondays in winter.

At **Attin**, 5 km W on N39 –

Bon Accueil, (21) 06.04.21: Jacques Delvoye's village inn has grown into bigger, posher restaurant; instead of the Irish stew his wife Denise used to offer me the cooking is 'a compromise between traditional and Nouvelle Cuisine'. But still excellent value, menu or carte. Try stuffed mushrooms; scallops with leaks. Menu 47F; housewine 29F. Shut Sunday evenings; Mondays.

Near **St Josse**, 8 km E on D139 –

Auberge du Moulinel, (21) 94.79.03: young enthusiastic couple run attractive village inn; grills over wood fire, good ficelle picarde (pancake with creamy stuffing), sole from nearby coast. Menu 49F, 75F. Shut Wednesdays, Thursdays.

Calais (address 62100 Pas-de-Calais) –

Hotels
Meurice, 5 rue Ed. Roche, (21) 34.57.03: most comfortable in Calais; modern but historic lineage; your bedroom could be modern or Empire. In 1772 Augustin Meurice, Calais postmaster and stage coach owner, started Meurice inn in Calais to serve London–Paris passengers. He built up a string of inns, ending with the Meurice in Paris. Rooms 145F-185F. (Meurice in Paris will cost you around 1000F.)

Restaurant Diligence, (21) 96.60.48: in same building, different management; varying reports, but recommended to me locally for fresh fish; menu 55F, carte gastronomique. Shut Wednesdays in winter.

Sauvage, 46 rue Royale, (21) 34.60.05: very comfortable; good-value restaurant used locally for business entertaining, reasonable prices, good service. Menu 46F, 90F; housewine 25F; rooms 83-170F.

George V, next door, (21) 34.40.29: under same management, one star less; own restaurant.

Bellevue, 23 pl. d'Armes, (21) 34.53.75: very useful for bed and breakfast; fair comfort, rooms vary; rooms with breakfast 64-179F.

Restaurants
Le Channel, 3 bd Résistance, (21) 34.42.30: a winner with the British since it opened; open kitchen promotes customer confidence; service efficient; food straightforward and reliable; very good choice on four-course 56F menu; 120F menu includes outstanding confit d'oie (preserved goose) and several beef dishes; 36F weekday menu usually crudités, pork chop, cheese or pâtisserie, ¼ wine, or beer or mineral water, service included. Housewine 32F; all good value, especially fish. Shut Tuesdays; Sunday evenings in winter.

Touquet's, 57 rue Royale, (21)

34.64.18: bewildering; excellent value for families looking for cheap meals all the family will like; noisy, chaotic hell for shy gastronomes. 35F menu with free wine remarkable value, 65F menu pretty good; but the 150F menu – late at night perhaps, when the noise subsides. Casino – roulette, boule, blackjack – opens 8 p.m. to 3 a.m. Shut Mondays.

Coq d'Or, 31 pl. d'Armes, (21) 34.79.05: old favourite, went sadly wrong, now right back in favour. Old French dishes well cooked, mostly grilled; traditional sauces – hollandaise, armoricaine, bearnaise; coq au vin to lobster thermidor. Remarkable value 36F menu can fill restaurant with Britons running out of francs. I found five-course 77F menu even better value. 39F housewine (genuine Burgundy). Menu 36-140F. Shut Wednesdays.

At **Blériot Plage**, 2 km S on D940; beach from which Blériot took off for first cross-Channel flight in 1909 –

Des Dunes, (21) 34.54.30: pleasant little inn long since become a flashy modern concrete box, but good cooking pulls in the knowledgeable of Calais; fine shellfish; sole in champagne, rillettes of salmon. Menu 57F, 95F, 145F; wine 34F; rooms 77-112F. Shut Sundays evenings, Mondays.

At **Sangatte**, 9 km on D940; you can see the entrance to the Channel tunnel of 1877, abandoned; also big clifftop memorial to Dover Patrol, small

British minesweepers which swept the Channel in First World War –

Le Relais, 919 Rte Nationale, (21) 85.05.51: much underrated country- seaside restaurant with simple rooms; good value; nice coq au vin and fish. Menu 52F, 85F; housewine 28F; rooms 64F; half-board 100F. Shut Sunday evenings, Mondays except June, July, August.

At **Escalles**, 13 km on D940 (address 62179 Wissant, Pas-de-Calais) –

L'Escale, (21) 85.25.09: graffiti outside boosting this modern Logis kept me out for a while. More endearing to young families and teenagers than slow ancients like me but offers outstanding value. Choice of four menus and two seafood platters – one with a half lobster; menus 41-68F; housewine 28F; rooms 65-105F; bargain half-board three nights or more 95-115F each per night, so possible for short breaks. Close to beach famous for fossils and to Cap Blanc Nez. Shut September 19 to March 1 but restaurant open Sundays.

At **Guines**, 10 km on D127 S; address 62340 Pas de Calais –

Lion d'Or, 7 pl. Maréchal-Foch, (21) 35.20.51: super surprise to find, in old simple bar-restaurant looking like First World War relic, such good food at bargain prices, especially 40F menu with fair choice. Logis. Menu 35F, 40F, 75F; good housewine 35F. Rooms 50-80F. Two nights half-board from 220F for two people.

At **Ardres**, 17 km on N43 (address 62610 Pas-de-Calais) –

Grand Hôtel Clément, 91 Esplanade Mar.-Leclerc: the Coulen family have been here since 1917, I have known it since early 1950s, and I know Paul Coulen is a *great* chef. But I cannot ignore recent disappointments of friends and readers, the last being Barbara, my wife. Prices somewhat overinflated. As it is one of my favourite inns, I hope the hiccups soon go. Charming atmosphere, friendly service, Relais du Silence, pleasant bedrooms, nice garden for aperitifs. Menu 120-230F; Bordeaux housewine 35F; rooms 120-190F. Shut mid-January to mid-February.

Le Relais, (21) 35.42.00: pleasant rustic-style Logis overlooking green; family cooking of old-style dishes; nothing fancy to disturb delicate British stomachs. Fair value. Menu 55-150F; rooms 120-190F. Shut January.

La Chaumière, 67 ave Rouville, (21) 35.41.24: comfortable, clean bed-and-breakfast hotel, nice garden; rooms 82-159F; breakfast 17F; bargains off-season.

La Frégate, Lac d'Ardres, (21) 35.40.16: good-weather lunch spot for families, alongside lake off road to Brêmes. Pedalos and boats for hire. Menu 42F; wine 40F.

At **Brêmes les Ardres**, 1 km on D231 from Ardres –

Bonne Auberge, (21) 35.41.09: real country inn run by nice people; I find it very good value, so do the French who drive miles to it and nearly all my readers. Try trout braised in Chablis, ficelle picarde, interesting duck with pears, tarte tatin (upside-down apple pie). Menu 47F, 63F, 104F; wine 32F; rooms 67-84F; half-pension (two nights) 100F each per night; weekends one night, two main meals, breakfast 180F each. Shut Sunday evenings, Mondays in winter.

At **Lumbres**, 46 km from Boulogne on N42 (address 62380 Pas-de-Calais) –

Moulin de Mombreux, (21) 39.62.44: see Chapter 10, Stopovers.

Au Trou Normand, 18 Route Nationale, (21) 39.63.65: simple country inn; country dishes; trout, guinea fowl cooked in beer, local chickens (try fricassé – sauté, then lightly stewed in cream), home-made pâtés, soups, pâtisserie. Menu 60F, 90F; housewine 20F; simple rooms 60F. Shut Sunday evenings, Mondays.

At **Cléty**, 6 km past Lumbres on D192 –

Truite d'Argent, (21) 38.80.57: recommended to me for good-value cheap meals. Menu 30F, 45F, 60F; housewine 23F; rooms 55F; half-board 65F. Shut Tuesdays.

At **St Omer**, 40 km SE Calais N43 (address 62500 Pas-de-Calais) –

Comte de Luxembourg, 32 rue Comte-de-Luxembourg, (21) 38.10.09: old-style solid looking hotel near centre; recommended by locals and French visitors, especially for good-value meals; try trout. Menu 38F, 65F; wine 25F; rooms 65-130F. Shut Sunday evenings, Monday lunch.

Le Cygne, 8 rue Caventon, (21) 98.20.52: outstanding; elegant; 58F menu (four courses) splendid value; good fish and duck dishes; housewine 24F. Shut Tuesdays, Saturday lunch.

Truye Qui File, 8 rue Bleuets, (21) 38.41.34: nicely furnished in 1890s style, comfortable, very quiet; traditional cooking with good meat dishes; 65F menu generally acclaimed for value; some locals think 120F menu overpriced. Elegantly presented, good service; delicious râble de lièvre poivrade (saddle of hare in peppered marinade sauce). Excellent wine list (from 40F), strong in Bordeaux. Shut Sunday evenings, Mondays.

Dunkerque (address 59140 Nord) –

Richelieu, pl. Gare, (28) 66.52.13: outstanding station buffet; Flemish cooking; brasserie menu 40F; restaurant 76-120F; shut Saturdays, Sunday evenings.

Victoire, 35 ave des Bains, (28) 66.56.45: Philippe Levebre lures Flemish gastronomes; try fish soup, sole stuffed with crab, grapefruit sorbet with geneva gin (trou flamande?); menu 105-160F. Shut Saturday lunch, Sundays, part August.

At **Malo-les-Bains** (address 59240 Dunkerque) –

Hirondelle, 46 ave Faidherbe, (28) 63.17.65: interesting cooking; own smoked lamb and fish; excellent wines; very good value; menu 35F (not Sundays), 60F, 85F (Sundays); shut Sunday evenings, Mondays; part September. Rooms 61-130F.

Au Bon Coin, 49 ave Kléber, (28) 69.12.63: superb fish; choose trout, crayfish, lobsters from two viviers; weekday menus 45F and 100F (with as many oysters as you like!); carte weekends.

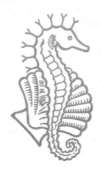

2 Dieppe, Le Havre

Dieppe is my delight. Since I first called it 'Instant France' thirty years ago, that has become a cliché , but it remains true. And it has been for 200 years.

Boats ran regularly from Brighton in the 18th century, and during the French Revolution three Brighton masters of the Channel Packet Service – John Chapman and Samuel Barton father and son – ran a regular service for escaping aristocrats! The Newhaven Packet was running a daily service by the 1850s. Yet this convenient crossing to quite the nicest of the Channel ports has sometimes been so neglected by Britons that there has been talk of closing the route. Not in my lifetime, I hope.

Dieppe is all French and grossly underestimated by British mileage-collectors who hurry south.

Step off the boat on to quai Henry IV and you are immediately in the heart of Normandy, with fishwives selling miniature mussels, langouste, brill, shiny sole, John Dory, pink and brown shrimps and mullet in the little quayside market, while the fishermen drink the salt out of their throats in the harbour cafés alongside Arcades de la Poissonnerie and visitors sit in and outside little restaurants consuming mountains of mussels and shrimps and lapping litres of wine at prices which would be a giveaway in Paris, Cannes or even Orleans.

Dieppe is a stronghold of good cheap meals. In small streets behind the promenade are more little cafés where you can eat as well for under £5 as anywhere else I know.

The long beach from the castle to the harbour has a big open-air swimming pool and is flanked by a promenade with wide grass lawns where everyone in Dieppe with a dog seems to exercise it before breakfast. It gives the resort a spacious, wide-open look. The casino has good entertainment throughout the year. But the joy of Dieppe for me is Grande Rue, most of it now for pedestrians only, with seats for weary window shoppers. Individualistic shops are scattered higgledy-piggledy, with a fashion boutique and a silversmith separated by an old-time grocer, with trestle tables laden with chickens, cheese, butter and pâtés which have never seen a freezer.

The Saturday morning market is splendid. The street is packed with stalls offering farm-fresh food, huge barrels of butter, great dishes of farm-made pâté, sausages in scores of shapes and sizes, jumbo-size cheeses and big bowls of cream, alongside mounds of local vegetables and, at one end, barrows of fish, sometimes one whole barrow filled with little oysters at bargain prices.

Once I filled an old wartime parachute bag with tiny slim sticks of asparagus bought here for 10p a pound, and took them home to make gallons of real asparagus soup.

'What have we got in there, sir?' asked a suspicious customs officer.

'Asparagus', I said.

He gave me one of those 'we've-got-one-here' looks. 'All right, open up!'

I did. 'My God, it *is* asparagus. You realise that you should really have an import licence for that lot, don't you?'

In Dieppe the market spreads into side streets and knowledgeable locals make for a road parallel to Grande Rue, rue St Jean. Here smaller farmers sell their produce, often from a basket, prices are lower, and you can buy superb herbs and some of the best butter I have ever tasted.

Two sedate family hotels I have known for years both have views of the sea and right down the promenade. They are L'Univers*, where the great chef Jean Tilquin does the cooking, and the Windsor*, sympathetically run by Claude Lambert and with good sea views from the first-floor dining room. Both serve meals typical of this part of Normandy. You will get

*See page 42 for details.

dishes like sole à la dieppoise (cooked in white wine, with mussels, mushrooms, crayfish and thick cream added), mussels in sauce normande of cream and wine, many dishes à la normande – with cream, cider and calvados, the spirit of cider. Also a splendid Norman apple tart, made with whole skinned apples.

I think it patronising for a visiting Englishman to congratulate a French chef unless he asks you if you enjoyed the cuisine, but I did break my rule once after a meal which was exceptional even by Windsor hotel standards. From the kitchen, dressed in full chef's regalia including tall hat, came the hotel director Claude Lambert. His chef had fallen off his motorcycle and was being repaired in hospital, so he had cooked. He was, he explained simply, a trained chef of some experience. But I wondered how many directors of computerised modern hotels could take over the kitchen successfully.

At the end of Grande Rue is Café de Tribuneaux – an 18th-century inn, dark inside, often chaotic, as waiters, trying to answer calls from several directions at once, weave through tables around which people stand talking to the people sitting down. It has the atmosphere of Impressionism and the 1880s in modern dress. And rightly so, for when they were not meeting in the studio of the painter Jacques Emilie Blanche, Renoir, Monet, Walter Sickert, the ageing Pissaro and James Whistler were drifting in and out of the Tribuneaux in the '80s. In the '90s you could see in there the thin figure of Aubrey Beardsley, near to death, Henry Harland, editor of *The Yellow Book* for which Beardsley drew and which was believed then to be so outrageous, and the greatest *Yellow Book* contributor of all, Oscar Wilde, dying in Dieppe in poverty and exile, but still with enough genius to write the magnificent *Ballad of Reading Gaol*. Tribuneaux has been the centre for young people's wit, arguments, plans, laughter and sorrow for more then 200 years – and still is.

Dieppe always attracted painters. Sickert moved in with a local fishwife, Richard Bonnington the watercolourist and Turner painted coast and seascapes, Sisley, the underrated Impressionist, gutted fish here when too poor to buy canvasses, Braque lived nearby and Picasso visited him

An English colony almost took over Dieppe society around 1900. Lord and Lady Cecil, with a villa in Puys, were the centre, but there was one British visitor they avoided. That was the Prince of Wales, the future Edward VII. In Villa Olga, near the west cliff, lived the Duchesse de Caracciola, who had left her Neapolitan husband at the church door, having married him to escape from her parents. She had lived in England and had become a close friend of the Prince. He was 'godfather' to her daughter Olga and visited them incognito in Dieppe. Olga had a seat in Westminster Abbey for Edward VII's coronation, married a baron and later became a

photographer for *Vogue*.

The British imported sea-bathing from Brighton, tea, kippers, Scotch and Indian-Empire-style snobbery, treating all but very important Dieppoises as 'natives'. Among them was the beautiful and stately Lady Blanche Hozier, who loved gambling so much that she queued with her sandwiches for the casino to open. One of her three children, Clementine, became the wife of Winston Churchill and floored General de Gaulle with her fluent French.

Where rue St Jean meets place Nationale is St Jacques church, much rebuilt since the 12th century. Almost anything old in Dieppe is connected with Jean Ango, a 16th-century privateer who became governor of Dieppe. Ango was a Norman Drake, hero in France, pirate to the English but especially the Portuguese. Hardly surprising, for he captured more than 300 Portuguese merchant ships. Then he retired to a palace of wood he built in Dieppe and a country mansion at nearby Varangeville. His town palace was destroyed by British bombardment in 1694. A frieze from it is above the church's sacristy door; it shows a file of Brazilian Indians, recalling the voyages of Dieppe's explorers. Ango is buried in the church, in a chapel he built. Once he lent a fortune to Louis XIV. He died poor and forgotten. I bet that the Sun King never paid him back.

The castle on the cliff which dominates Dieppe was built in the 15th century around old fortifications. In summer you can walk to it from square du Canada at the end of the seafront. At any time you can enter over the drawbridge on rue de Chastes, running inland from square du Canada.

The castle museum has models of ships and navigation equipment and maps dating back to the 16th century, many paintings, and superb carvings in ivory. The art was developed in the 16th and 17th centuries, when tusks were landed from India and Africa. Most carvers were Protestants and fled to Britain and Holland after rights of religious freedom were revoked in France. But two direct descendants still work at the art. The museum closes on Tuesdays except midsummer.

Below the castle in square du Canada is a monument to Dieppe New World explorers of the 16th to 18th centuries, and a plaque to the Canadians and Britons killed in the 1942 Dieppe raid on Nazi defences when the Canadians lost 1000 killed, 600 wounded and 1779 taken prisoner from a force of 5000. The RAF lost 113 air crew. Churchill called it a 'reconnaissance in depth'. Most historians agree that the experience gained saved tens of thousands of lives in the 1944 Normandy invasion. Some still call it a costly mistake. The one success was by Lord Lovat's Scouts, who landed at nearby Sainte Marguerite, achieved all their objectives and got back.

At Château Miromesnil, 6 km away, Guy de Maupassant spent his early years. On the edge of the splendid park is a statue to him. You can visit park, gardens and house from May 1 to October 15.

Ango Manor is more interesting. In patterned brickwork, steep-roofed buildings surround a huge courtyard with a dovecote, almost like a ranch. Jean Ango built it in 1532. It is open afternoons from April 1 to November 10.

It is just off D75 to Varangeville. Here, too, near Pourville, is a museum of Second World War armour including tanks. On the clifftop at Varangeville is a 12th-century church saved recently from slipping down the cliff and now being restored. In it is a superb coloured window by Braque, original Cubist, who was buried in the churchyard in 1963 with a grave designed in his style by pupils. Another Braque window is in the nearby chapel of St Dominique.

Monet's painting of Varangeville church is in the Barber Institute, Birmingham. He lived in Varangeville when too poor to afford canvases. Parc des Moustiers (open Easter to November 1) is a garden of superb shrubs at its best in May and June, around a house built by Sir Edwin Lutyens. A tiny clifftop road takes you to Ste Marguerite with a 12th-century church illuminated by modern coloured windows by Max Ingrand. Beyond, tiny resorts are tucked between cliffs. Veules les Roses, once a port, is small and pretty, with charming hinterland. St Valéry en Caux has a long harbour used by fishing and pleasure boats, and clifftops with monuments to the French and our 51st Highland Division who fought a rearguard here in 1940. Yvetôt has a circular modern church with magnificent windows by Ingrand.

Fécamp, further south, wedged

between steep cliffs, is a cod fishing port and resort – an odd mixture which works. Fécamp monks gave us benedictine, which is still made here. You can visit the distillery and museum but it closes weekends from October 1 to Easter. Etretat is framed in cliffs, too, eroded into architectural shapes. Its beach is of smooth pebbles, its atmosphere elegant French; it has a casino and famous golf course. Honfleur, across the Seine estuary from Le Havre, is one of my favourite places. I shall write about it later.

Le Havre owes a debt to Auguste Perret, Le Corbusier's teacher and the man who persuaded some town planners and architects that reinforced concrete is as good to look at as brick or stone. It was planned, after terrible war destruction, on a grid-iron system, with concrete, glass and steel girders. You either like it or you hate it. For me, it is sombre, with no intimacy, and totally lacks the untidy warmth of older French towns. But it has certain advantages. The arcades are useful for window-shopping in wet or cold weather; Perret's huge church of St Joseph, like a set for a *Dr Who* episode or a rocket on a landing pad, makes a convenient landmark to avoid getting lost in the concrete jungle; and the Malraux Fine Arts Museum, in metal and glass with huge windows towards the sea, is ideal for showing paintings in almost any light. The Malraux has many treasures – pictures by slightly lesser known but highly important 19th- and 20th-century

artists such as Gericault, Michel, J. B. Corot and Fantin-Latour, seventy paintings by Raoul Dufy and 200 by Boudin, son of a Honfleur river pilot who brought together young painters to give birth to Impressionism. I wonder who inspired the Le Havre local council to send this self-taught printer's apprentice to Paris to study. When he came back, he persuaded a 15-year-old boy bent on being a caricaturist to try landscape painting. The boy was Claude Monet. Dufy was born in Le Havre. A decorator and painter, he was an Impressionist until he went to Paris and met the Fauves. He painted the people of the coast rather than the landscapes.

Avenue Foch, designed to be a modern Champs-Elysées, has shops as smart and expensive as in Paris. A new cultural centre in place Gambetta has concert halls, a theatre and conference centre under flattish igloos.

Le Havre is, of course, a big commercial centre rather than a tourist centre, and the second biggest port in France next to Marseilles, which is why the signposts from the ferry quay lead you as fast as possible out of town.

The original port was planned by Francis I in 1517 and called Franciscopolis. Any town with a name like that was courting disaster from the gods, and it came – from a freak tide to shifting salt marshes which collapsed its walls. An Italian refugee engineer, Bellarmato, showed the French how to build on tidal mud. Perhaps he came from Venice.

When I saw Le Havre in 1946, I

could not believe it. We arrived on the first postwar 'cruise' by Sealink on the old *Falaise*, up the Seine to Rouen. As we stepped ashore in the docks, there was total desolation. I had seen bombed German and British cities, but this port had even lost the very road surfaces, burned up by flame-throwers. The only bar open within sight was in a cellar with no building above. An old lady and a teenage girl ran it. In his replanning Perret certainly did not have to worry about preserving the old.

Bitterly the French claimed that their left-wing resistance had liberated the town and had told the Americans so before their bombing and attack began. Stopping a war machine is harder than starting it up.

Although we prefer Dieppe, for anyone who can get to Southampton easily Le Havre is a good springboard for reaching the Seine at pleasant places like Caudebec, for the charming coast and hinterland below Harfleur, for still-delightful Deauville and above all for Calvados, that splendid area of Normandy below the landing beaches, the lush, pretty country of the Suisse Normande and the Orne. Here everything seems rich – the pastures, the old manor houses, the farms with beautiful horses and above all the food; land of the really rich Norman cooking with cream, cider and calvados. Read Chapter 11 for some places to hide away there.

Hotels and Restaurants

Dieppe (postal address 76200 Seine-Maritime)

Hotels
Windsor, 18 bd Verdun (seafront), (35) 84.12.23: see also page 38; try scallop pâté, super tarte normande with whole apples, cream gateaux with calvados. Quietly comfortable; not for the jolly and hearty. Pricier menus better value. Menu 66F.50, 83F.50, 110F; housewine 36F; rooms 78-189F; half-board (two nights) 116-178F each per night. Shut mid-November to mid-December.

L'Univers, 10 bd Verdun, (35) 84.12.55: see also page 38; fine rich old Norman cooking; not for Nouvelle fanatics. Beautiful seafood platter worth every franc. Menu 98F.50, carte 120-150F; rooms 170-300F. Shut early December to mid-January.

Restaurants
The best place to find good cheap meals is no longer quai Henry IV (opposite Sealink boats) but past the fish market on arcade de la Poissonerie, where old-style bar-restaurants still have menus from 30F. Exception is:

Du Port, 99 quai Henry IV, (35) 84.36.64: still used by many of my local friends, most of whom have abandonned La Petite Auberge (round corner in rue de la Rade) since tourists discovered it. Try blanquette of sole, turbot terrine with langoustine sauce. Menu

55F, 85F; housewine 30F; shut Thursdays.

La Marine, 1 arcade Poissonnerie, (35) 84.17.54: younger locals use excellent-value modern restaurant. Young Marcel Blin is enthusiastic chef-patron. Try matelote (local fish and shellfish), fish soup, sole or turbot dieppoise, creamed mussels, estouffade (beef in red wine and herbs), mirliton (apple and almond tart). Good service; wine from 30F; menu 40F.50, 58F (good value), 83F, 130F. Shut Tuesday evenings, Wednesdays.

Moderne, 21 arcade Poissonerie, (35) 84.12.33: two storeys, modern décor; very ambitious menu and dishes; Britons pour in; local friends suggest concentration on fewer dishes. Good value. Norman cooking, lots of cream and cider, good use of local fish. Menu 45F (not Sundays), 70F, 100F; housewine 26F; Muscadet 43F. Shut Tuesday evenings, Wednesdays.

Marmite Dieppoise, 8 rue St Jean, (35) 84.24.86: for value, still one of the best fish restaurants in North France. Deliberately simple looking; willing service; Jean-Pierre Toussat is not only a fine chef – he knows fish and the right fishermen to buy it from. Marmite dieppoise is Norman soup-stew of fish and shellfish, with cream. He cooks it superbly. I am not too fond of choucroute du pêcheur – sauerkraut with fish – but chicken in cider is excellent. Superb 120F gastronomic dinner; good-value 42F and 68F menus (not served Friday, Saturday evenings).

Red housewine 18F, Gros Plant sur lie 38F.

Normandy, 16 rue Duquesne, (35) 84.27.16: times change – little 'rustic' Norman-style restaurant once had nine menus separately priced, with huge choice on each. Now only two and à la carte meals. Dishes more sophisticated – excellent sole normande is stuffed with fish mousseline (fish puréed and beaten with egg whites and cream) in thick lobster sauce, marmite du pêcheur (fish soup-stew), apple sorbet in calvados to settle your stomach. Menu 45F, 61F.50; wines from 25F. Tables close, bustling service, candlelight in winter; good value. Shut Sunday evenings, Mondays.

Belle Epoque et La Criée, 3 rue Guillaume-Terrisen (between two bridges, across harbour from ferry terminal), (35) 82.16.17: new smart spot of Dieppe. Belle Epoque is 1930-style; *Criée* bistro-style. Specialities mostly fish, also aiguillette of duck in cassis, ham in cider. Reasonable prices. Menu 75F, 90F, 120F. Shut Sundays.

At **Pourville**, 4 km SW on D75 (address 76550 Offranville, Seine-Maritime) –

Trou Normand, (35) 85.11.45: Johnny Vaillant, chef-patron, proving worthy successor to popular J-J. Baton in this little beach resort; many drive out from Dieppe even in winter. Happy rustic décor, friendly. Cheap and good value. Menu 47F.50, 69F; housewine 17F. Shut Sunday evenings, Mondays.

At **Varangeville** (8 km on D75; address 76119 Seine-Maritime) –

La Terrasse, Vasterival (3 km), (35) 85.12.54: attractive, comfortable, lovely country position high above sea with views; very reasonable prices. Menu 47F, 84F; housewine 20F; rooms 54-150F; half-board two nights 102-134F each. Open March 15 to October 31.

At **Ste Marguerite-sur-Mer**, 3 km on D75 –

Sapins, (35) 85.11.45: Denis Grout, patron, known to British guests over years, joined by son Denis Grout, chef. Simple, cheap, friendly, nice garden. Super veal Vallée d'Auge (in wine, cream, cider). Menu 50F; wine 34F; rooms 76F. In nice village with wooded background but steep walk from sea. Shut December, January.

At **Martin Eglise** (6 km SE on D1, where pleasant Forêt d'Arques begins; address 76370 Neuville-lès-Dieppe, Seine-Maritime) –

Auberge du Clos Normand, 22 rue Henry IV, (35) 82.71.01: Michelin pointed us here several years ago, but it seemed overpriced and we were put off by snobbish British customers, not to mention the managerial classes of Dieppe. My friend Victor Wear, traveller and restaurant owner, called it 'strictly Henley/Ascot/Pimms job', which clashed with very rustic beamed old Norman cottage, red and white gingham tablecloths, curtains and even lampshades. But the garden was superb for summer's day eating. We were unfair. Prices are high, décor a bit overdone, it does lure snobby Britons, but food is excellent and worth the price (around 150-200F for a meal, à la carte only). Patron-chef Regis Hauchecorne courageously cooks open plan at the end of the dining room, and delightful smells of pastry, garlic and cooking meet you. His tarte aux moules, with light fluffy cheese topping, is a joy, his turbot in estragon cream sauce delightful. Garden to the river is charming. Wines begin at 50F; rooms in a converted barn vary in comfort and price, 80-150F, but are not dear. Sleepers must dine first. Hotel shut November to March; restaurant Monday evenings, Tuesdays; mid-December to mid-March.

At **Arques la Bataille**, 8 km on D1, tiny industrial town, historic castle ruins on edge of forest (address 76880 Seine-Maritime) –

Manoir d'Archelles, (35) 85.50.16: recommended constantly by friends; I have not yet been inside. A 16th-century fortified manor, looking as formidable as a prison, with squat guard towers. But it is a Logis de France, sworn to treat you as a family friend and all is good cheer within, it seems. Prices won't frighten you: 43F weekday menu, four others 57-135F; housewine 30F. Rooms 80-150F; half-board three nights 110-130F each per night. Shut Sunday evenings, Mondays.

Le Havre (address 76600 Seine-Maritime)

Hotels

I would not stay in Le Havre itself. Villequier, Caudebec, Pont Audemer, Honfleur are all so near. To be right by the Townsend ferry terminal, try:

Les Vikings, 25 quai Southampton, (35) 42.51.67: comfortable, cheap; cheap fair meals. Menu 40-65F; rooms 60-100F. Closed Sundays.

Charolais, 134 cours de la République, (35) 25.29.34: comfortable rustic-style hotel within easy reach station, docks. Rooms 85-120F. Breakfast 15F.

At **Ste Adresse**, posher suburb of Le Havre on cape with sea views (address 76310 Le Havre) –

Des Phares, 29 rue Gén.-de-Gaulle, (35) 46.31.86: fine fin-de-siècle French house with modern annexe; friendly, helpful, English spoken. Bath or shower, wc to all rooms; some very spacious; rooms 113-120F. Three good restaurants nearby.

Restaurants

Quick cheap meals on quai Southampton, where Townsend boats leave.

Monaco, 16 rue Paris, (35) 42.21.01: convenient for dock and long recommended, but now some readers talk of unfriendly attitude and overpricing; others praise it skywards. The truth is the cooking is excellent, choice large, and for that you must pay. Try duck in Bouzy wine, kidneys in calvados, Norman apple soufflé, lobster Neuberg; oysters usually splendid. Menu 70-180F; some rooms

85-185F. Shut late February, early September; Mondays.

La Chaumette, 17 rue Racine, (35) 43.66.80: amid Le Havre's concrete and glass, a thatched roof and fake beams hide genuinely good cooking by Christine Frechet. Small, and has become popular, so book. Readers who got in were delighted. Now our local favourite. Fresh ingredients according to market and season freshly cooked, so you can't hurry. Menu 78F, carte around 150F. Shut Saturdays, Sundays, late August.

Petite Auberge, 32 rue Ste Adresse, (35) 46.27.32: locals being edged out by Britons; good value; try sole in mushrooms and wine, poulet Vallée d'Auge. Menu 62F (not Saturday evenings), 90F; shut August, early February; Sunday evenings, Mondays.

L'Huitrière, 4 rue Paris, (35) 21.48.48: fish only and superb; try turbot, stuffed oysters, moules soubise (mussels in onion purée, after Prince de Soubise, friend of Louis XV); good seafood platter. Menu 60F, 105F; wine Gros Plant 50F. Shut Sundays, Mondays.

Guillaume Tell, pl. Hôtel de Ville, (35) 42.90.96: large; grill and 'gastronomic' range; original built in 1855 for a Swiss by Russian prisoners of Crimean War. Bombed 1944; new one looks better within than without. Great fun; meeting place of townsfolk. Specialities fricassée de canard Henry IV (it seems Henry IV liked artichokes – duck cooked in cream), lobster quenelles, veal Vallée d'Auge; good pâtisserie.

Menu 55F, 75F. Housewine 26F. Shut Sundays.

At **Ste Adresse** (see above) –

Yves Page, 7 pl. Clemenceau, (35) 46.06.09: Superb sea views over harbour from balcony and big picture window; live lobster tank; inevitably, excellent fish, especially sole with wild mushrooms, and renowned dessert table. Menu 80-98F; wine from 54F; shut Sunday evenings, Mondays; mid-August to early September.

Beauséjour, 3 pl. Clemenceau, (35) 46.19.69: attractively renovated; air conditioned; same panoramic views; live oyster tank; good fish dishes. Menu 75-160F (worth the price); wines 48-800F.

3 CHERBOURG, ST MALO, ROSCOFF

Cherbourg is a strange little port. After visiting it over thirty-eight years I can still neither quite understand it nor like it. The French themselves have neglected it for whole centuries and seem to be doing the same now. But some Britons love it, especially yachtsmen.

With so many more pleasant places within a very short drive, I would not stay overnight if I could drive on. For it is the gateway to the Cotentin peninsula which, thought unimpressive at a glance, has many treasures hidden down the narrow lanes of its *bocages* – its farmlands networked with thick hedges – and on its changing coastline of rugged cliffs, sand beaches, muddy estuaries and huddled fishing hamlets.

Just a few kilometres from Cherbourg on the wild north coast are spectacular spots like the wild and rocky Cap de la Hague to the west. Here at **Goury** is one of the most vital lifeboat stations in Europe. It has saved hundreds of experienced fishermen and amateur, sometimes foolhardy, yachtsmen from the wicked Alderney race. At **Nez de Jobourg**, just to the south, you can walk the last mile for a grandiose view of the racing sea

and fatal rocks. From the tip you can see the Channel Isles of Alderney, Sark, Guernsey and Jersey. In a little bay to the north is **Port Racine**, said to be the smallest port in France, and cosily attractive, and towards Cherbourg at **Gruchy** is the house where the painter Millet was born in 1814. He was the son of a peasant and few have painted country scenes so authentically. Later he lived in Jersey but Cherbourg calls its main museum and art gallery after him and devotes a whole room to his paintings, drawings, and documents and photographs.

When Vauban, the great military engineer, fortified Cherbourg more than 300 years ago, he called it 'Tomorrow's Channel Inn'. It was nearly a century later that work actually began on the breakwater to turn it into a big port, and it was another seventy-seven years before the cones stuffed with rubble and mortar sunk to make a base accumulated sufficient strength to be used for that purpose.

Then Cherbourg declined again, until in 1933 a deep water channel was dredged to take the big transatlantic liners. That was in the fashionable days of the great transatlantic boats, and the main sight to see in Cherbourg was the rich and famous coming and going aboard the great boats like *Ile de France, Queen Mary* and *Queen Elizabeth* down at the docks.

The Germans sunk blockships in the harbour when they were driven out by the Americans in 1944, but Royal Navy divers cleared them in days, the Pluto prefabricated oil-line was installed to pump oil from the Isle of Wight, and so many Allied supply ships came in that for a year Cherbourg carried more traffic than New York. Now the ornate transatlantic terminal is being partly demolished, the main traffic is in car ferries from Britain, and the importance of Cherbourg to France is as a yard for building and operating submarines.

Eastward from Cherbourg is a lovely area for an overnight stay or a few days beside the sea. Along the Corniche road to Barfleur are fine sea views, though not perhaps so magnificent as the Michelin green guide to Normandy suggests. It is worth visiting the park of the elegant Renaissance *Château de Tourlaville* just inland from Bretteville, with exotic plants, little lakes, and groves of big, old trees. The house, closed to the public, was the scene 300 years ago of a love story fit for grand opera. A sister and her young brother, Marguerite and Julien de Ravelet, had an incestuous love affair. The scandalised family married off Marguerite to a boorish man thirty years her senior, but she and her brother fled to Paris. They were finally caught and arrested. A few days later she gave birth to a son.

But they were executed for incest and adultery. She was twenty, he only seventeen.

Barfleur is a sleepy little fishing port except during some fine days in high summer when boats from Fécamp and Brighton sail in and weekend sailors join the fishermen at the bars and in the cafés.

Barfleur claims to have built the ship which carried William the Conqueror to England. Certainly it was a favourite cross-Channel port in the Middle Ages for royals and their courtiers. In 1120, the *White Ship* sailed for England carrying the son and heir of Henry I of England and many of the court. It went down and drowned all but one of them off the reef at Quilleboeuf.

You can drive to the lighthouse at **Gatteville**, 4 km away – 56 m of granite built in 1828 and still one of the most important. Gatteville, the inland village, is attractive and rich in flowers.

Saint Vaast La Hougue southward is an even better place than Barfleur for a short holiday. But more on that in Chapter 4, on seaside hideouts.

For years after Sealink ended its St Malo service, Cherbourg was the entry port for Britons making for Brittany. Now that Brittany Ferries has firmly established its St Malo service, this has become the main entry for Brittany and a rival to Le Havre for people making for Calvados, the attractive stretch of Normandy from the wartime invasion beaches to the pretty Suisse Normande hills and the rich pastures and rivers of l'Orne.

St Malo is a fascinating port.

Walking through the inner walled town, Intra-Muros, around sunset or after, especially out of season when visitors are few, evokes for me a real feeling of living in its turbulent past. I feel that round the next corner will come a French pikeman of the watch or a cutlass-wielding corsair, seeking the blood of an English intruder. The bark of a dog can make me shudder at the thought of the pack of wild Chiens de Guet, the ferocious mastiffs which for 500 years were turned out at night to guard the approaches to the town and recalled at dawn by a trumpet blast. They were English mastiffs, but it was mostly the blood of the English that they were after.

St Malo was the scourge of the English from the 15th century until the Napoleonic Wars. Despite its smart little shops, its many cafés and restaurants excellent for fish, it seems to have changed little since we called it the Pirate's Nest, and as I drink wine in the little Porte St Pierre or Chiens du Guet restaurants*, huddled under the ramparts at St Peter's Gate, I can imagine the bloodthirsty old corsairs carousing at the other tables to celebrate another successful 'course' against the hated English. Yet it is nearly all new – rebuilt to the finest detail after destruction in 1944 when the Americans tried to liberate it from the Nazis.

Technically, few of St Malo's pirates were actually called 'pirates'. They were 'corsairs', licensed by the King of France as

*See page 56.

Drake and Hawkins were licensed by Queen Elizabeth I. They were supposed to obey set rules and attack only enemy ships or those taking goods to the enemy; they were supposed to capture ships and crews and take them into port, where they and their cargoes were sold. A tenth of the price would go to the King, and of the rest, two thirds would go to the *amateurs* (ships' owners), while one third only would be divided between captain and crew. Thus there was little incentive to bring a ship back, and the corsairs would loot it, sink ship and crew and sell the loot in another port for gold. Furthermore it was academic to their victims whether they had their throats slit by a 'licensed' corsair or a pirate. Still in the end the *amateurs* got rich and built fine houses whereas the corsairs mostly died violently or in poverty.

The two most notorious corsairs were very different. René Duguay-Trouin, son of an aristocrat turned shipowner, was educated for the priesthood but preferred wine, gambling and women to chastity and prayer. He maintained his aristocratic courtesy even towards prisoners. When in 1711 he captured Rio de Janiero from the Portuguese to release its French prisoners, he stopped his men pillaging the town and executed eighteen of them for looting a church – remarkable. He was a corsair captain from 1692 to 1712 and in twenty years sank or captured 85 English ships, including ten Royal Navy boats and 100 ships of other countries. The English took him prisoner but oddly he was allowed to wander around Plymouth (possibly because he was an aristocrat), so he persuaded the French wife of an English merchant to get him a boat to escape. When he died in 1736, he was Lieutenant-General of the French Navy, and for 300 years warships have been named after him. We captured one at Trafalgar, renamed it *Implacable* and it was a Royal Navy training ship until it sank off Portsmouth in 1949. I believe that the current ship called *Duguay-Trouin* is a frigate carrying guided missiles.

Duguay-Trouin was a gallant dandy. Robert Surcouf, corsair in the Napoleonic Wars, was a courageous thug. He, too, was trained for the priesthood, but escaped from religious college to sea. The Royal Navy captured more than a thousand of Napoleon's corsair ships. But never Surcouf. He started as a slave trader, then corsair preying on the armed merchantmen of the East India Company in the Indian Ocean, using the French isles of Mauritius and Réunion as a base. With only eighteen men, he captured one merchant ship with 26 guns and 150 crew. He retired from the sea to become a shipowner and backer of corsairs and slave-traders.

St Malo's own greatest sailor was Jacques Cartier. In 1534 he sailed to look for gold in Newfoundland, discovered instead the mouth of the St Lawrence river, which he thought was in Asia, took possession of the land in the name of the King of France and called it Canada, which he thought was the Huron Indian name for the area but which really meant 'village'.

You can find interesting records of these sailors of St Malo in the castle keep museum inside the old walled town. Here too is an enlightening show of photographs of the devastation of 1944 before the rebuilding.

Leave your car outside the walls on Esplanade St Vincent and enter the walled town through St Vincent Gate beside the castle. A staircase to the right leads to the 12th-century ramparts which survived the Second World War. As you walk along the ramparts you get interesting glimpses down the town's narrow streets and superb sea views, especially at high tide. You can see the mouth of the Rance river, where the waves have been harnessed for hydro-electric power, the big beach at Dinard, and several small isles, including **Grand Bé.** You can walk to this at low tide. It takes about forty-five minutes.

On the isle is a plain unnamed stone topped by a great cross – the tomb of François-René de Châteaubriand. He asked to be buried here. He was born at St Malo in 1768 but lived later with his parents at the Château at Combourg, further south. His father, a vicomte, was a disagreeable, bad-tempered man who alternated between lengthy silence and loud rage, and young Châteaubriand lived a lonely life, much of it in his bedroom in a turret. He had a brilliant life later as writer, politician, ambassador (including to England, where he was also in exile for seven years) and traveller. His burial place fits an introspective man whose themes of sadness and loneliness still affect French literature.

Châteaubriand steak was invented by his chef, Montmireil. It is a middle fillet, grilled in butter, with sauce of wine, shallot, tarragon and lemon. Some chefs now serve it with béarnais sauce.

The St Malo ramparts end near St Thomas' Gate, which opens on to a beach adjoining the enormous Paramé beach and 3 km promenade. Inside the gate is an aquarium and Quic-en-Groigne, a tower built by Duchess Anne, last ruler of a Free Brittany. King Charles VIII of France married her to get hold of Brittany. Even so he failed, but her daughter married the future Francis I, and their son ruled Brittany and France. Many Bretons, like many Welsh, are still fighting for independence. And for agricultural causes. I drove the last few miles to the Brittany ferry recently on a squelchy, skiddy cushion of onions, dumped from lorries and trailers by irate farmers protesting at low prices. St Malo citizens were frenziedly scooping them into boxes for their larders.

The road over the River Rance tidal-power barrage has made the neat, attractive family beach resort of **Dinard** almost into a St Malo suburb. I shall mention Dinard in Chapter 7, on family holiday resorts, but the tidal-power dam is well worth the short drive. The river estuary is closed by a 750 m (800 yd) long dam with a road over it, and the flow and ebb tides are used to make electricity. The reservoir made by the dam is 22 sq km (8 sq miles) in size, and

ships pass through the dam by a huge lock. The power station is in a 390 m (400 yd) tunnel and has twenty-four generators of 1000 kilowatts each, producing 550 million kilowatts a year. It is just the sort of scheme suggested for the river Severn, to ensure our energy future and to get many of our industries moving again. You can have a tour of the power station; panels explain the workings, and from the dam platform you get fine views over the estuary to St Malo and Dinard.

Dinan is the place to make for, by boat down the river from St Malo or by road. The trouble with the boat trip is that you get anything from fifteen minutes to eight hours in Dinan, according to the tide, before returning. However, even eight hours is not enough for this delightful, interesting and beautiful little medieval town. I would stay overnight or go by car alongside the river, returning along the other bank to St Malo or Dinard.

The route I suggest is to take the N137 from Dinard, turn right on the D5 to La Passagère, back to the N137, right on the D117 to St Suliac, where a half-mile walk past an old mill to the point of Mont Garrot gives you lovely views. Take the D7 right to Ville-ès-Nonais and make a short detour to Port St Jean bridge for more lovely river views. Join the D29 to Pleudihen, La Vicomte, the N176 to Lanvallay, then the D2 under cross-river viaduct to Dinan (41 km from St Malo).

Dinan's old houses and narrow streets are almost entirely enclosed in medieval walls. It stands 200 feet above the river Rance, which can now be crossed by a viaduct. It is a delightful place to wander, browse and eat, but best in spring and autumn – before French school holidays begin in the first week in July or after them. The window boxes of the old houses are often bright with flowers, especially in rue Jerzual, where painters, weavers and potters live. From here rue Petit Fort leads down to the old bridge across the Rance and the delightful little port where I sit at Restaurant des Terraces* drinking Muscadet and awaiting the splendid fish. You can sit there even in winter, for then the terrace is enclosed in glass and heated.

Above, you get good river views from Jardin Anglais. In the church alongside is buried the heart of Bertrand du Guescelin, a local lad who became a legend for valour in France, but is regarded as a traitor by most Bretons because he led French troops against them.

He and his brother Oliver were defending Dinan in 1359 against the Duke of Lancaster when Oliver was taken prisoner by an English knight, Sir Thomas of Canterbury, during a truce – a breach of chivalry. Bertrand challenged Canterbury to single combat, with Lancaster presiding. Guescelin won, Canterbury was discharged from the English army (presumably for losing), the English withdrew; one way of settling a battle. Guescelin was captured three times by the English, who liked him and let him live freely at court. But

*See page 57.

the Bretons point out that he got started by stealing his mother's jewels to set up his own little army. He became Constable of France.

The du Guescelin family owned the 11th-century castle at **Combourg**, 13 km from Dinan, where the Châteaubriand family lived later. Châteaubriand the writer's father slept in Tour de Chat (Cat Tower), haunted by a former owner who had a wooden leg and a faithful cat. Sometimes only the leg and cat appeared, seemingly looking for their owner. The cat's skeleton was found under the stairs later and some swear that the wooden leg clomps around looking for it. Combourg is a simple old town beside a little lake, and I find it a pleasant little hideaway. The Château hotel is friendly and attractive, and there are several small, good value restaurants.

Mont St Michel, known as Le Merveille or First Site in France, is

52 km from St Malo, eastwards, on the Brittany Normandy border. But you see it best across the water from the north, coming down the Granville road, rising spectacularly out of the sea at high tide. To a pyramid rock clings a fortified town with ramparts and a monastery, capped by a 900-year-old abbey church with a slender spire and a gilded statue of St Michael brandishing his sword. You reach it by a long causeway cutting across water or mud flats with fatal quicksands, according to the state of the tide. You leave your car at the base of the rock and walk steeply uphill along a street of medieval houses of granite or half-timbering, turned mostly into souvenir shops and restaurants with inflationary prices. With many more steep steps inside the abbey, you need to be fit for a complete visit. The abbey was founded more than 1000 years ago and has had a changing history. Pilgrims included our Edward the Confessor, who gave St Michael's Mount off Penzance to the monks. In the Hundred Years' War, an English garrison on neighbouring Mont Tombelaine did a nice trade by selling safe-passes to pilgrims. After the French Revolution it became a prison in which the inmates made straw hats. Now it is a national monument with one monk living there to say mass daily at 12.15.

It is spectacular and interesting, but for me Rocamadour in the Dordogne and St Malo are more so.

Take the coast road east from St

Malo round the Pointe de Grouin for 23 km and you reach **Cancale**, not pretty but probably the best place for oysters in France. You find lobsters, clams and mussels, too, but above all, oysters. Bred at sea, farmed in pounds down by muddy sands, they are sold in hundreds of thousands to wholesalers, in boxes to retailers, in dozens to travellers from quayside stalls and in fiercely competitive restaurants lining the quay. I arrived innocently once to find the oyster festival at its zenith, and two restaurateurs recognised me. Mountains of shellfish appeared and there was no way of avoiding a single oyster. At midnight I escaped. For the first time I was the worse for food, not wine. Luckily I was driving a motor-caravan. Round the corner, I drove into a field, pulled the curtains and went to bed. Next morning I made coffee, then drove away.

Better to stay the night at Pointe du Grouin hotel, where the sea views are splendid and Yves Simon's cooking is better. So are his shellfish.

The Plymouth–Roscoff ferry, useful not only to West Country people but West Midlanders and the Welsh, has opened up West Brittany quite dramatically for shorter holidays. A rather grey little town, Roscoff has enough attraction to lure Britons who intended to sweep through it to stay there a while. Vegetables – especially onions – are loaded here for Britain. Not a happy place for the Scottish Stuarts: in 1548 five-year-old Mary Queen of Scots

landed here for her engagement to the future disastrous Francis II of France and 'Bonnie' Prince Charlie landed here after being routed by the English at Culloden.

Morlaix, 28 km south, is where I would stay. Its streets of fine old buildings slope down the sides of a valley to a charming estuary port packed usually with bright yachts and cruisers. A huge railway viaduct joins the hillsides. Once it was a corsairs' hideout, used by Jean Bart, Cornic and Duguay-Trouin. One of them, John of Coetanlem, attacked Bristol in 1522. So eighty English ships sailed to Morlaix and the sailors ransacked it, including wine cellars. Morlaix citizens were away at a festival. Returning, they found Bristolian drunks lying in woods and in streets around town. They massacred many of them.

Hotels and Restaurants

Cherbourg (address 50100 Manche)
With so many good places very near (Bricquebec, Barfleur, Valognes), I would not stay in Cherbourg. Michelin does not recommend one restaurant. If you have to eat there, a convenient, reliable restaurant is:

La Vauban, quai Caligny, (33) 53.12.29: two-faced restaurant with 'snack' with 50F meal – recommended if only for help-yourself hors d'oeuvres with a good choice of pâtés and charcuterie; and à la carte restaurant, with Norman specialities – ham in cider, boudin brochet, civet of lobster, scallops in cider, various crêpes flambés in calvados (apple spirit); marvellous seafood platter would make a meal. Full meal costs 150-200F, cooking very good, service heavily criticised by readers; wines dear. Shut Fridays; February.

Café de Paris, 40 quai Caligny, (33) 53.10.05: famous for its enormous plateaux de fruits de mer; dreary room, but fine fish. Menu 45F, 65F. Shut mid-December to mid-January; Mondays; Sunday evenings in winter.

At **Fermanville**, 14 km E on D116, attractive coast road –

Neptune, (33) 54.28.00: remarkable value; good cooking over charcoal and in old bakers' oven; menus start at 26F, three courses with choice; my 50F Sunday lunch worth almost double. Also wide choice of crêpes. Separate bar; disco some nights.

At **Maupertus**, Anse du Brick, 11 km E on D116 –

Maison Rouge, (33) 54.33.50: six tries to eat here have found it totally booked – by refugees from Cherbourg. Next time I phone before climbing the stairs. Friends say 60F menu is great value; another at 120F. Famous for lobster. Seafood platter for two includes half lobster 200F. Good sea views. Shut Mondays.

At **Barfleur**, 27 km E by D116, nicer than D901 (address 50760 Manche) –

Phare, (33) 54.02.07: old hotel, old-style cooking; good fish but I had tired mussels. Menu 79-140F; old-fashioned bedroom at 160F rather cramped, but own shower, wc. Rooms 68-160F. Shut Sunday evenings; Mondays out of season; November 1 to February 5 except Christmas, New Year.

Moderne, (33) 54.00.16: 500 m from beach, port; 1920s style, traditional Norman cooking; raie sauce normande, lotte (monkfish) normande, veal Vallée d'Auge (cream, cider, calvados), seafood platter with lobster or not; food praised by readers for value; two called bedrooms 'scruffy'. Menu 45F (weekday), 60F, 90F, 120F; wine from 25F. Exhibition in dining room of paintings of this coast. Rooms 65-200F. Two nights, two breakfasts, four meals 298F each (good value).

At **St Vaast-la-Hougue**, 30 km E by D120, D56, D1 (address 50550 Manche) –

France et Fuchsias, rue Maréchal-Foch, (33) 54.42.26: see Chapter 4, on seaside hideaways.

At **Quettehou**, 2 km on D1 from St Vaast –

La Chaumière, (33) 54.19.94: reliable restaurant with wood grill; St Vaast oysters. Medium prices.

Bricquebec (address 50260 Manche), interesting old town with 14th-century castle remains; huge interesting market on Mondays. Trappist monastery – Abbaye Notre-Dame de Grasse – 3 km on

D121. Men and women may visit 3.30 p.m. except Sundays –

Vieux Château Hôtel, (33) 52.24.49: a real favourite with us and readers. Hubert Hardy's little hotel in part of the old castle, inside the castle close, is delightful. Lovely old rooms, excellent cooking means restaurant is often full. Mainly straightforward cooking, with some imaginative dishes. Try veal kidneys in cider, moules au champagne; beautiful fish. Bedrooms vary in size. Queen Victoria slept here after opening Cherbourg–Caen railway. Superb value. Pleasant, friendly atmosphere. Menu 38F, 65F, 90F; wines from 23F; rooms 100-136F; half-board 100-136F each. Shut January.

St Malo (address 35400 Ille et Vilaine)

Hotels
Elizabeth, 2 rue Cordiers, (99) 56.24.98: beautiful little luxury hotel without restaurant in 16th-century house in old town; bedsitter suites furnished in period style, with own entrance hall, separate bathroom and wc. Rooms 230-300F.

Central, 6 Grande Rue, (99) 40.87.70: big comfortable hotel-restaurant in heart of walled town. Marvellously fresh fish. Change of chef has altered nothing – not even old coffee-house décor. Seafood platter at 85F excellent value; good fish soup, moules marinières and fillet of St Pierre (John Dory – tasty, ugly, spiny fish we don't eat much). Carte only,

minimum about 100F; housewine 25F; rooms 165-300F.

Hôtel Porte St Pierre, 2 pl. Guet, (99) 40.91.27: readers of my other books on France love it – so do I. Little old-style hotel under sea walls; warm bright décor; warm welcome; simple clean bedrooms. Fresh fish from St Malo quay and Breton lamb, all good value. Menu 42-100F; housewines 18F, 22F. Rooms 80-160F; half-board 130-150F each. Shut Tuesdays; November 15 to January 28.

Chiens du Guet, 4 pl. Guet, (99) 40.87.29: next door to Porte St Pierre; pleasant; solid wood, comfortable beds; my two meals there were good value; lovely fish, of course. Menu 42-75F; housewine 17F; rooms 67-107F; half-board 163F each.

At **Paramé**, outside walls –

Rochebonne, 15 bd Châteaubriand, 35400 St Malo, (99) 56.01.72: handsome, white end-of-century hotel; dishes include Alsatian sauerkrauts (choucroutes); comfortable rooms. Menu 43-80F; rooms 100-200F; half-board 150F each per night.

At **Saint-Servan**, 5 km on D301; quiet resort at mouth of Rance river; beaches on sea and river; big swimming pool in Anse des Sablons (address 35400 St Malo) –

Le Valmarin, 7 rue Jean XXIII, (99) 81.94.76: expensive, lovely bed-and-breakfast hotel in 18th-century house; delightful furnishings; peaceful garden;

rooms 270-340F. Shut February.

Bar Le Cancalais, 1 quai Solidor, (99) 81.73.77: good seafood platter 90F.

At **St Suliac**, 13 km on N137, D117; attractive village on river Rance with fine views (address 35430 Ille et Vilaine) –

La Grève, (99) 58.40.35: overlooks river; excellent 65F menu with good choice. First-course choice offered me was smoked fillet of goose, six oysters, asparagus, prawn salad or smoked salmon; main course sole meunière, barbue (brill), steak or lamb chops; then strawberries and cream, strawberry tart or good cheeseboard. The gastronomic menu at 135F includes lobster armoricaine. Remarkable value from patron-chef Yves Doré. Three bedrooms, overlooking river, 65-75F.

At **Pleudihen**, 20 km on N137, D29; known for cider and Doux Eveques apples; tidal mill on side road to Mordreuc, attractive riverside village –

L'Abri des Flots, Mordreuc-Pleudihen, (96) 83.20.43: last time I had help-yourself home-made vegetable soup, ham crêpe, pork chop in rosemary, jacket potato, French beans, cheese and dessert. The meal cost 24F, with a litre of red wine. Inflation has struck. The meal now costs 30F, and the wine another 10F, still one of the best bargains in France. Rooms 60F. Shut September.

Dinan (address 22100 Côte du Nord)

Restaurant des Terrasses, le Port, (96) 39.09.60: see text. Try fish terrine, asparagus with pineapple mousse, best end of lamb in orange sauce; twelve oysters 48F; super seafood platter for two 190F; most attractive position. Menu 55-210F; wine from 33F. Shut Wednesdays; Thursday evening.

Chez la Mère Pourcel, 3 pl. des Merciers (96) 39.03.80: something of a legend, partly because of magnificent 15th-century house; retains friendly fast service, and good food in nice surroundings; highest quality ingredients. Try gratin de langouste armoricaine, veal escalope normand and raw sardine marinated in herbs and cider vinegar. Rather pricey. Menu 90-170F; housewine 38F. No bedrooms.

Avaugour, 1 pl. Champs Clos, (96) 39.07.49: old house in wonderful position, with garden seemingly suspended above ramparts and castle lawns, tables outside front looking across place du Guesclin. Georges Quinton makes imaginative and sometimes unusual dishes from the best buys in the market. Bone marrow in flaky pastry with caper sauce is much better than it sounds, so are hot curried oysters. Good old-fashioned pot-au-feu excellent. Well-chosen wine list. Menu 70-190F; rooms pricey 200-300F; half-board minimum three nights 240F each per night.

Le Marguerite, 29 pl. du Guesclin, (96) 39.47.65: nice position with balconies overlooking main square; mostly big rooms; old style, comfortable; unusual but nice fish dishes. Menu 45F, 63F, 98F; housewine 24F; rooms 70-190F; half-board 110-165F each per night.

Pélican, 3 rue Haute-Voile, (96) 39.47.05: I found it over twenty years ago when very short of francs and could not believe the portions, choice and number of courses I got for my money; nothing has changed except that you now meet other Britons; incredible value. Five menus 36-60F; housewine 15F, réserve 20F.

Cancale, 14 km E of St Malo

(address 35260 Ille et Vilaine). Row of restaurants along port and quai Gambetta. I pick one open to street, if warm enough, to carry away fishy smells. You get what you pay for – bigger and better oysters, mussels, clams cost more. Lobster sold usually by weight.

Phare, at port, (99) 89.60.24: picked this last time for crab on 68F.50 menu – there was no crab; but huge bowl of excellent, filling fish soup, oysters, mussels and skate (raie) all good; menu 68-150F; wines good, Muscadet 45F; shut Wednesdays mid-February to mid-March.

Continental, at port, (99) 89.60.16: good for lobster; try homard à l'armoricaine (with that super tangy sauce – pricey, of course). Menu 80-155F; shut Mondays; rooms 80-270F.

Hôtel La Pointe de Grouin (4 km N), (99) 89.60.55: see also page 54. Delightful; wonderful sea views; elegant dining room; one of our favourites in Brittany. Yves Simon cooks very well. Menu 73F, 100F; housewine 28F; rooms 91-195F; half-board 205F.

De Bricourt, 1 rue du Guesclin, (99) 89.64.76: one that got away. I am told that this is the best restaurant for many miles, but have not tried it. In upper town, good, it seems, not just for fish but for lamb from Mont St Michel salt marsh (pré-salé) and duck cooked in perry (pear cider). Menu 75F, 135F; shut Tuesday evenings, Wednesdays; December, January, February.

At **Port-Mer**, tiny beach hidden

between Cancale and Pointe de
Grouin –

La Godille, (99) 89.65.65: tiny bar-
restaurant with good seafood;
woodfire grill; copious helpings
(five lamb chops!); menu 45F.80,
70F.

At **Pontorson**, good place to eat
or sleep to avoid Mont St Michel
crowds and prices; 9 km S Mont St
Michel on N176 (address 50170
Manche) –

Chalet, pl. Gare, (33) 60.00.16: Logis,
reasonable; good value; salt-marsh
lamb excellent; menu 39-90F;
housewine 21F.50; rooms 65-143F.
Shut November 1 to April 1.

Bretagne, rue Couesnon, (33)
60.10.55: delightful 14th-century
house well renovated; sympathetic
décor, furnishings; menu 50-100F;
rooms 74-159F. Shut Mondays;
open February 1 to November 1.

At **Brée**, 9 km S Mont St Michel
N176, D80 –

Sillon de Bretagne, (33) 60.13.04:
simple, friendly, rustic, old
Norman house, nice garden, very
good traditional Norman cooking
and shellfish; menu 48-115F;
rooms 60-94F; shut Tuesdays low
season; part January, November.

Combourg – see also page 52. 29
km SE St Malo by D4, D795
(address 35270 Ille et Vilaine) –

Château, (99) 73.00.38: charming,
friendly couple, Marie-Thérèse and
Christian Pele, run comfortable,
excellent hotel with lovely garden;
try Châteaubriand steak with
old-style genuine Châteaubriand
sauce, lobster in Bourgeuil sauce,
stuffed amandes de mer (dog-
cockle, little shellfish), lamb ragoût
in cider; mussels in cream with
sweet peppers; good desserts.
Children's playground. Menu 50F,
80F (good value), 120F; rooms
(some family rooms for four)
61F.50-225F. Weekend breaks,
room with bath or shower, wc,
half-board three-nights 500F each,
two nights 350F each. Shut
December 17 to January 21.

Du Lac, (99) 73.05.65: pleasant
position beside little lake, castle
views other side. Cosy bedrooms.
Family, regional cooking by owner
Bertrand Hamon; try sole soufflé
au champagne. Menu 60F, 130F;
housewine 27F; rooms 65F, 83F,
166F; half-board 95-142F each. Shut
November.

Du Marché, (99) 73.05.52: Michel
Leroux's restaurant gives
remarkable value; much better
than it looks. Set menu at 32F (three
courses); plenty of choice in menu
at 36F.50; several dearer menus.

La Charrette, 1 pl. de l'Eglise, (99)
73.00.60: nice old restaurant
redecorated, with terrace added;
rustic, with open fireplace; good
fish, especially moules marinières
and patron's own lobster dishes;
also couscous, paella choucroute
(sauerkraut). Three-course menu
41F; good value four-course
including oysters, large helpings,
58F; special 75F menu. Shut
Wednesday evenings.

Dol de Bretagne, 24 km SE St
Malo by D4 (address 35120 Ille et
Vilaine) –

Old market town for rich agricultural area, reclaimed from sea which flooded it in 8th century; big market on Saturdays; 13th-century cathedral called St Samson's after the dragon-killing Welshman – not the strong man.

Logis de Bresche-Arthur, 36 bd Deminiac, (99) 48.01.44: pleasant Logis, family-run with enthusiasm, friendliness and imagination, which made us extra sad last time when a waitress accidentally dropped a tray and slightly spattered the clothes of a British couple. Despite profuse apologies by staff and patron, the British stormed out. Small wonder that Britons are not always popular abroad. Christian Faveau offers five menus between 43F.50 and 145F, plus a good children's menu for 33F, a *promotionelle* three-course menu at 37F with super home-made pizza from pizza oven, and a *dégustation* at 270F for two people, with an enormous seafood platter, strawberries and cream, a bottle of Gros Plant and coffee. Our five-course regional menu at 81F.50 was good value; smoked salmon served with real cream and chive sauce; fish course of bar (sea bass) cooked in foil with rosemary and algues; what's algues? A seaweed, which adds to the flavour but is hard to chew. Menu *comme chez soi* (home cooking) at 54F, very good value, had excellent choice and a delicious creamy poulet Vallée d'Auge flambé in calvados.

Housewine 20F; rooms (with shower or bath, wc) 160F; half-board 160F each per night. Shut November 2 to December 12.

Hotel Bretagne, 17 pl. Châteaubriand, (99) 48.02.03: lucky Dol to have two such hotels; Catherine Haelling-Morel is an accomplished cook; excellent value, low prices. Splendid 59F menu offers oysters, snails, langoustines and salmon; period furniture, open fires; menu 42-72F; housewine 18F; rooms 52-107F; shut end September to end October.

For **Roscoff**, at **Morlaix** 28 km on D769 (address 29120 Finistère). Old town on Dossen estuary; fine old buildings, especially in Grande Rue, where there is a market. Huge viaduct strides the river.

Europe, 1 rue d'Aiguillon, (96) 62.11.99: nicer inside than it looks from without. Young chef Patrick Jeffroy making his name in Brittany with a fine mixture of traditional, modern and creative dishes. Remarkable ravioli stuffed with calves' sweetbreads, mussels in saffron, boned wild rabbit in farm cider, tripe in cider with prunes; also good old beef in bordelaise sauce, and shrimps and prawns from the bay. Menu 80-160F; brasserie 48-100F; rooms 75-225F; worth driving from Roscoff. Shut December 15 to January 15.

4 Hideouts by the sea

Signposts point to **St Vaast la Hougue**, but locals call it St Va. It stands on the east coast of the Cotentin peninsula, a pleasant 30 km drive from Cherbourg. Still a working fishing village and small port, it has fortifications left from past wars and some still used, so in no sense is it only a picturesque holiday centre, dying out of season. At certain tides the water goes out so far that it leaves tracts of muddy sand and rocks. The beach is about a kilometre away.

The oyster beds in the bay produce some of the best oysters in Normandy and Brittany. And that was just what I fancied when I arrived there recently in mid-afternoon – oysters. I had not eaten all day, but I wanted to do justice later to Madame Brix's marvellous meals at the Hôtel de France et des Fuchsias*. Oysters were the answer.

At the end of the long quay was an 11th-century fishermen's chapel, flaking a bit but still a daymark for sailors. The bar alongside was half-filled with fishermen in their working blue denims and peaked caps, drinking among pictures of local football teams of the past. There were no

*See also page 70.

women. And there were no oysters.

The fishermen finally included me in their conversation, but I could not understand their accent, so I nodded wisely and they seemed satisfied. That is a bad habit of mine when I cannot understand. One day I shall mistime my nodding and get thumped.

It was spring and most of the craft alongside the quay were working boats. In summer there would be many pleasure boats and dinghies from the local sailing school. The bar at the other end was posher and the drinkers included young couples, older women and local lads. You could even get table service. On the walls were old photographs of 'St Va' with sailing boats, men in neat suits with watch chains across their waistcoats and women in voluminous dresses carrying umbrellas and holding the hands of boys in sailor suits. There were snacks at the bar – croques monsieur, ham rolls, toast. But no oysters.

It was now five o'clock. The shops were shut – even the fish shops. But a very old-style bar called Moderne was open, with a few old men drinking in it.

'Could I please have a snack?' I

asked the lady behind the bar.

'Certainly,' she said.

'Oysters, perhaps?'

'Six or a dozen?' she asked.

'A dozen, please – and a whole bottle of Muscadet.'

The oysters were superbly fresh. The bread was home-made. The butter was fresh farm butter of Normandy which never reaches an EEC mountain. The Muscadet was *sur lie* and fruity. The cost was £2.60.

The France et Fuchsias is a favourite of mine – old-fashioned France in décor and atmosphere, with reasonably modern plumbing. The fuchsias have climbed round balconies to the roof, turning the walls red when in glorious bloom. There is a delightful back garden, and flowers on most bedroom walls. But the main secret of the Brix hotel is the freshness of the food. Not only does the fish come from that port 200 metres away, but pork, veal and chickens, butter, milk and cream come direct from Pierre Brix's farm nearby. Braised pork from the farm is delicious, the rabbit in mustard sauce a lovely surprise, and veal kidneys a delight. There are five menus from 50F to a 137F gastronomic menu and a magnificent seafood platter includes oysters, a crab, langoustines, praires and half a lobster.

There is not much to do in St Vaast except watch the boats coming and going, but time seems to pass pleasantly between bottles of wine and super meals. It is a fine place to relax, eat well and perhaps take some gentle walking exercise.

Holidaymakers and weekenders are so sea- and coast-minded these days that it is difficult to find an uncrowded little seaside hideaway in countries like France and Spain. But there are some which miss the crowds providing you miss the French school holiday times. And even in high season there are places which the crowds miss. You are not likely to find one which inspires postcard photographers but you *will* find some with the atmosphere to inspire painters. One hotel of character can make an ordinary seaside village into a delightful haven. There are several of these along this Cotentin peninsula, reached easily from St Malo or Cherbourg.

St Jean-le-Thomas, at the bottom end of the Cherbourg peninsula, is attractive enough for a postcard, especially when the mimosa and the wisteria are in bloom. It has sands with good bathing and a view of Mont St Michel across sandbanks which so impressed General Eisenhower when he was Allied commander-in-chief that he mentioned it in his war memoirs.

I cannot remember when I first found André Gautier's Logis hotel here, Les Bains. Then it was used by a few knowledgeable British and French from inland towns. Now it is famous among French and British and he has added an annexe beside the sea 300 metres away to cope with midsummer visitors. He has added a heated swimming pool, too. But this friendly family-run hotel has changed little in atmosphere and good service, and M. Gautier's Norman cooking is a delight. Naturally, fish predominates – grilled lobster flambé in calvados with cream sauce, outstanding scallops and local sole, mussels in cider; but there are some fine meat dishes, too – local ham in cider, chicken in cider on a bed of cream. Alas, it shuts from October to mid-March, although this little corner is protected from north winds by wooded hills.

Carteret, too, has a mild climate. It is protected by a cape and washed by the Gulf Stream. It is a delightful little place – a bit disorganised, happy and very French, though long popular with Britons. With its twin, Barneville – virtually one place – it is one of those rare little resorts which appeal to the three generations, from small children to their grandparents. Carteret is still a fishing port and has more vitality, Barneville across the estuary is more prim and relaxed. Both have good beaches. There are three routes between the two – a road, a coastguard path round the headland, and at low tide a walk across the sands.

There is a strong tide, but bathing is good most of the time. A careful watch is kept on the beaches in season and if you obey the red flag signals you should come to no harm.

I love the harbour. Local fishing boats still land and sell their catch on the quay and little yachts sail in from Cherbourg, from Britain, and especially from the Channel Isles. From May to September ferry boats run from Jersey, taking sixty-five minutes, and Jersey people pop over for lunch and shopping. They come over especially for Barneville's Saturday market, where stalls sell beautiful butter from huge slabs brought straight from farms and local farm cheeses, fresh local fish and meat, and cider from Calvados. This, of course, is cider country. The nearest wine is Muscadet made mostly way down near Nantes. Most cider is matured for at least a year, so that it is strong, and the dry Normandy cider is so dry that it almost disappears in your throat. It is an acquired taste. Cidre bouché is sparkling and drunk a lot with crêpes, Breton and Norman pancakes.

My favourite along this coast was always **Coutainville**, simply because it is pure French fin-de-siècle. The pseudo-Gothic, ornate houses, some with turrets, lining the promenade always made me feel that starched, long-skirted nannies should be pushing overdressed children in high-wheeled prams, to the passing winks of moustached gentlemen in straw hats and striped blazers. I was there this last summer and little has changed. Plastic décor has only a small foothold. The bar tabac is from another decade, the major diversion is sitting on the big sand beach.

I have known it since the war. The old posh Grand Hôtel de la Plage alongside the sea is now the Neptune*, has no restaurant but is a good place to sleep. The old Hôtel de la Gare has long since

*See also page 71.

been Hôtel Hardy* because the railway has gone and the Hardy family have owned it for three generations. And Hôtel Hardy has put me in a dilemma known to every experienced travel writer.

When I first went there Madame Hardy presided at the old cash desk, arms folded on ample bosoms, her eyes surveying with true professionalism the pavement café, the bar, the dining room in solid oak and mahogany, and the kitchen where her son Emile, internationally known chef, did the cooking superbly. 'Il faut *aimer faire la cuisine*,' she told me. ('It is necessary to *love* cooking.')

Madame was a charming but formidable lady, and with one glance could persuade my little daughters to walk downstairs with decorum instead of tumbling or sliding down the banisters.

One of Emile's great dishes is a half-duck in orange sauce. Dr Johnson called duck 'a tedious fowl, sir – too much for one and not enough for two'. The Hardy ducks are none of your frozen plastic fowls. They have lived around a farmyard and *are* big enough for two. But Emile's lobster à l'armoricaine is his greatest dish. There is endless argument in France about whether this is the correct title, meaning that the dish originated in Brittany – the Armoricaine coast, or whether it should be 'à l'américaine', which is nothing to do with America but is a Provençal name. Anyway Emile's sauce is piquant, creamy and a delight.

*See also page 71.

Madame has, alas, gone. Emile cooks and runs the hotel. Over the years, dozens of people I sent to this hotel were delighted. Then the criticism started: offhand service, disorganisation, very ordinary meals and inflated prices. A famous British hotelier told me that the meals over a week were mediocre. It was no good going to check up personally. I am a friend of the family. So I sent another experienced travel writer as spy. He came back raving about the cooking, just as a British guidebook was talking of 'universal disappointment' and accusing Hardy of cashing in on its reputation. But the last word so far has been with the French Gault-Millau guide, tougher than Michelin in its judgements. It wrote of 'impeccable service – cuisine of Emile Hardy full of fresh ideas behind its classic greatness'. It seems that the Hôtel Hardy is out of a bad patch and back to normal. One dish nobody ever criticised to me was the splendid platter of seafood.

In a different world is **Montmartin sur Mer** just south of Coutainville. A tiny market town 3 km from several sand beaches and with some winding, secretive lanes inland, it has one pleasant hostelry, Du Bon Vieux Temps, where a nice meal need cost no more than 40F, served on a spotless white tablecloth, or you can pay 100F for a grand meal with lobster. A double room will cost around 70F. It is the local bar, tabac, café, centre for wedding receptions and celebrations, and is a Relais Routiers – with a 'casserole' for outstanding cooking.

Though the coast of Normandy is mostly very well known and hideaways are on the whole inland, there are still some little seaside places which, because they have no beach or major roads to them, do not lure crowds.

Mesnil-Val, a hamlet south of Le Tréport, above a tiny cove and 2 km north of Criel Plage, has not changed for thirty years except that the old auberge changed hands a few years back. La Vieille Ferme is an old favourite of mine. An auberge made from a 17th-century farm with a big, flowery garden, it has comfortable but not luxurious bedrooms which you reach by going outside from the bar and a fine old dining room. The cooking is now more ambitious and the prices relatively higher, but I still think it good value. The shellfish is excellent and the cooking still Norman, with sauces rich in cream. I had splendid sole normande (poached with a sauce of mussels, mushrooms, oysters, shrimps and cream), very nice tourteaux (large crab) and excellent poulet Vallée d'Auge – a free-range chicken jointed, partly fried, then cooked in its own juices, with sliced mushrooms, bay leaf and thyme, in a covered pan. Then it is flamed in calvados, the apple spirit, and the resulting juice is mixed with a cup of fresh cream to make the sauce. Some chefs use bacon and shallots in the pan. If you find one of these Norman meals becoming a little rich, do as the Normans do and take a *trou normand* in the middle of the meal – a glass of calvados. It works, although the new fashion is for an apple sorbet in a beaker of calvados. You can always ring the changes with a simpler, cheap meal at the little Relais on the roundabout at Criel Plage. It is good value.

A few kilometres south of Dieppe is one of the most charming tiny seaside towns in Normandy, **Veules-les-Roses.** Hidden between high wooded cliffs, it has one main street rich in flowers, a stream running through the town with the odd trout flashing past, a pebble beach, and in season a small casino, a little entertainment and a children's club. Off-season it sleeps. Alas, the hotel which I used has become a block of flats and I know no other, although there is a very good, very pricey restaurant, Les Galets, and there are hotels 8 km away at St Valéry en Caux.

This is the St Valéry where the 51st Highland Division made a last stand against the Nazis in 1940 while tens of thousands of their British colleagues slipped out of Dunkirk, and there is a memorial to them on a cliff at one side of the harbour. On the other end is a memorial to the French 2nd Cavalry. Though St Valéry was much destroyed in 1940, it has atmosphere and charm. A working fishing and coastal trade port and a refuge for yachtsmen, it has a deep working harbour where something is usually happening, and some of the old town has survived across the drawbridge. It is a good base for exploring several little seaside villages, such as Veulettes, quiet, attractive, in a gap in the cliffs, and the Durdent Valley inland.

Le Crotoy is only just 'on sea'. One way, it faces into the river

Somme estuary. So it is a bathing
resort, yachting centre and one of
France's most important suppliers
of shellfish – cockles, prawns,
praires, and also eels. The great
attraction is Chez Mado, restaurant
of the La Baie hotel where Mado
Poncelet, smiling, bejewelled and
always busy between the dining
room and the kitchen, presides
over the cooking of her own special
dishes such as moules façon Mado,
sole Mado, turbot façon Mado, as

well as a splendid fish soup and
more general dishes like grilled
lobster and apple tart.

It is fashionable among some
travel writers to decry restaurants
as soon as they become popular,
especially when the British
discover them. Chez Mado has
been popular with French and
British for years, and I would never
decry it. I would go a long way to
eat there.

One guidebook writer compared

Honfleur unfavourably with St Tropez last year. What an odd comparison! St Trop, which I still love, is a beautiful, expensive, high-class whore. Honfleur is a working port which has grown so attractive that yachtsmen love her and artists have not been able to resist painting her since long before Impressionism was launched here. It is an industrial port, with surrounding industries, including metalwork and timber. Nor is it a quiet hideaway, but a superb spot to wander, explore or sit and watch. It was an important port 600 years ago. In the 16th and 17th centuries, it rivalled Dieppe for producing explorers and corsairs. One, de Gonneville, is said to have reached Australia in 1503. A century later Samuel de Champlain was sent to colonise Canada, and he founded Quebec in 1608. The first colonists were nearly all Normans and Percherons. The inner harbour (Vieux Bassin), built in 1668 for Louis XIV and enlarged next century, was replaced as the commercial dock a hundred years ago by another and is now a delightful scene, surrounded by tall, thin buildings, their ground level storeys mostly restaurants, bars, art galleries and antique shops. I can spend hours here watching yachtsmen fuss with their boats while I drink a bottle of wine and let the world go by. I arrived here with my young children many years ago to find the camp site almost flooded and the banks closed for a public holiday. We had no money, and credit cards did not exist. That evening we went to the restaurant on the corner by the Vieux Bassin and asked if we could pay for a meal with a personal cheque. 'Of course you can,' said the patron. 'You have an honest face.'

Though others, including the English painters Turner and Bonnington, had been struck by the effects of light and sea and had painted this coast, it was the son of an Honfleur pilot, Eugene Boudin (born here in 1824) who really began the fashion for painting seas and skyscapes and whose meetings with other painters to drink cider in a farmhouse inn led to the birth of Impressionism. He was the centre of the group who met at Ferme St Simeon. Monet, whom he had encouraged as a young man, Sisley, Pissaro, Cézanne, Corot gathered there at one time or another. Courbet painted the *Garden of Mère Toutain*, who owned the inn. Dufy was inspired by Honfleur. But Boudin himself was not really appreciated until he was old. The Honfleur museum in rue Albert Ier is called after him, and there are some of his paintings there, but better ones by Monet, Dufy, Jongkind and Courbet.

Poor Boudin, and certainly poor Sisley who was usually too broke both to eat and buy a canvas, could certainly not have afforded to eat at Ferme St Simeon today. It costs around 250F for a meal, wines start at 85F a bottle, and a room costs 600-900F. It is some years since anyone was rash enough to buy me a meal there, but I am told that the cuisine is better than ever. And the new chef, Pierre Arnaud, was trained by two of my absolute favourite cooks – the Troigos brothers at Roanne. The inn is certainly a beautiful example of 17th-century Norman rustic building and its manoir 300 metres away is even more grandly Norman. You will find it on the road to Trouville.

There are small restaurants behind quai St Etienne at the old harbour and more in the attractive cobbled square place Ste Cathérine where the market is held around the wooden church.

Rather fun to think that this church was built at great speed by local craftsmen to thank God for getting rid of the English! It was the end of the Hundred Years' War, in 1468. Honfleur was ruined and impoverished after English occupation, stonemasons were busy rebuilding all over France. So the local shipwrights built a 'temporary' church of timber from Touques forest. It is still there. I like the carved panels in the organ gallery with angels playing seventeen different instruments. Quite a group!

Beware – Parisians flock to Honfleur on weekends. So seek the beauty of Côte de Grâce hill, with panoramic views over the Seine estuary, a mariners' chapel and restaurants.

Among the coves, inlets, and rocky twists and turns of the Brittany coast are dozens of little fishing villages huddled together against winter weather and Atlantic waves, and although not all have even one simple inn, those which have are delightful places to hide yourself for a few days.

One of our favourite areas is the Corniche l'Armorique in the north, west of Trebeurden, with a road which follows a heavily indented, eccentric coast. At one end is a charming little village called **St Michel en Grève**, by the magnificent Lieue de Grève beach, which is 4 km long and 2 km (more than a mile) wide at low tide. Here trout streams run into the sea through little green valleys and the road follows the wooded coast to a huge rock 80 metres (262 ft) above the sand. St Michel has only 300 people, but it has the old hotel La Plage* where the meals are some of the best value we have had in recent travels. A four-course meal cost us 50F, five courses cost 80F. The fish course included a choice of oysters, moules marinières, scallops or sole; the main course included quail, duck in orange, turkey, guinea fowl or grilled steak.

The road leads to **Loquirec**, a super little fishing port and resort. It has good sands, good dinghy sailing and a delightful walled harbour, a charming church which once belonged to the Knights of Malta who held that island so magnificently against the Saracens of Suleiman the Magnificent. There is a walk round the point with lovely views of the Bretonne Corniche.

Further east along this rugged northern coast is a small resort, **Paimpol**, known to yachtsmen and to all who love oysters. Oyster farming has replaced cod-fishing in the very town about which Pierre Loti wrote *Icelandic Fisherman*. Loti used to stay in a 16th-century

*See also page 73.

house in place du Martray. It is still there. North of Paimpol, 6 km, is **Pointe de l'Arcouest**, with splendid views on the way down to its creek. It was recommended to me way back in the early 1950s by the writer Eric Whelpton, 'But you'll have to improve your French,' he said. 'No one speaks English.' Now it gets a small summer invasion of artists, writers and academics and its Hôtel Le Barbu has a swimming pool. There is a tiny lobster port, Loguivy de la Mer, nearby. From Arcouest you can get a boat to the island of Brehat, a refuge from motor-cars. They are banned. It is really two islands joined by a narrow tongue of land, and is only 3½ km (2 miles) long and half as wide. Its rocks are pinkish and look colourful against the changing colours of the sea. It has become quite popular in summer, but it has a mild winter climate and mimosa, oleander, myrtle and figs grow in the open. The island's fishermen were fishing the Newfoundland banks before Columbus 'discovered' America and locals say that one of their sea captains, Coatanlen, told Columbus about the New World eight years before he sailed to it and showed him the course used by the fishermen.

The south of Brittany has a gentler coast in most stretches, and, as Michelin says, La Forêt Fouesnant is a quiet village 'buried in greenery' at the head of a bay. It was very quiet indeed until a few years ago when Port-la-Forêt was built – a very pleasant marina for pleasure boats from which you can take a delightful trip up the Odet river or to the Glenan Isles, nine isles surrounded by reefs, three of them inhabited, the others bird sanctuaries where terns predominate. They are known best for their sailing and skin-diving schools.

The little beach at Forêt Fouesnant is rarely crowded because there is so much to see in the area. The tiny town of Fouesnant is 3½ km west among cherry and apple orchards and here the best Breton cider is made. Fouesnant is known for its particularly attractive traditional costumes and coiffes (women's head dresses), which are worn at festivals and at the Pardon of St Anne on the Sunday after July 26. 'Pardons' are traditional Breton festivals with religious hymn-singing, processions of people carrying candles, banners and statues of saints, church services for the forgiving of sins, followed by feasting, sports, dancing and often traditional Breton wrestling. These days one or two fresh sins may be committed by dawn.

Brittany has 7847 saints – enough to call upon to help fight any ill, tragedy or misfortune in people or animals. Mostly they were monks who led the Celtic immigration from Britain in the 5th century AD and founded settlements which were named after them.

St Yves, a medieval saint, is the most popular. He was a lawyer who is patron-saint of lawyers, and he wore a hair shirt and lived on bread and vegetable soup – just like members of our Bar I have met in the Wig and Pen Club in Fleet Street!

Much more colourful was St Sansom, a North Welshman educated at the Llantwit monastery in Glamorgan. He defeated a dragon by singing psalms to it, which made it roll itself into a ball and start eating its tail. Then he told it to drop dead and it did. He could do the same trick with witches and wizards.

Only 8 km from Forêt Fouesnant is **Concarneau**, third largest fishing port in France and with a walled town dating from before the time of William the Conqueror, regarded as impregnable by the 14th century, made even stronger by Vauban for Louis XIV in the 17th century. The remarkable thing is that Ville Close, as it is called, remains the same as it was 300 years ago, and despite its many souvenir shops, crêperies and restaurants, looks as if it lives in those days. The English under John de Montfort held it for thirty years, and it took three separate sieges by du Guescelin to get them out.

Huge fleets of trawlers can shelter within Concarneau's harbour and most mornings you can see them taking aboard their traditional blue nets before sailing. One of France's most colourful festivals is Concarneau's Fête des Filets Bleus (Feast of the Blue Nets) on the second from last weekend in August. Then you can hear the Breton bagpipes in full blast.

There is a golf course at Fouesnant, and in summer an air service from Gatwick to Quimper, 15 km away, so golf weekends are possible. And there is a sailing school at the marina.

On the Atlantic coast of Brittany, 4 km from the sardine, crayfish and lobster port of Douarnenez, steeped in history, and 4 km from the beaches, is a fine old farmhouse converted into an hotel – Auberge de Kerveoch. In attractive grounds, it still has its great old open fireplaces, is pleasantly furnished and has traditional meals based on local fish and farm produce. It is only 8 km from the superb little town of Locronon, with beautiful old granite houses and fine old square with a well in the middle. Once they made sailcloth here; now it is a ville d'art, with artisans working in glass and wood, and weaving wool, linen and silk. It is a charming place. Two kilometres from here is another favourite hideaway – Manoir de Moëllien. A fine old manor house of 1642 with a tower, it was restored from a ruin by Marie Anne Le Corre, and it is delightful. It is a Relais du Silence, and a Château Hôtel Indépendant and is exceptionally good value.

Hotels and Restaurants

St Vaast La Hougue – see also page 61; 30 km E Cherbourg; (address 50550 Manche) –

France et Fuchsias, rue Mar. Foch, (33) 54.42.26: see text. Delightful. Menu 50-137F; housewine 33F. Neat rooms 65-160F; half-board 160F each per night; weekends 700F for two (two nights bed and breakfast, two dinners, Sunday lunch). Shut January 10 to February 10; Mondays off-season.

Isigny-sur-Mer, 50 km S of Cherbourg on N13 (address 14230 Calvados). Mouth of river Vire, not quite *sur mer*; quay with little fishing boats, which bring in shellfish; sea-washed salt meadows produce fine lambs – pré-salé –

Commerce, 5 rue Emile-Demagny, (31) 22.01.44: cheap traditional Norman inn; locals use it. Menu 44-80F; housewine 12F; rooms (cabinet de toilette) 60F; half-board 95F each per night. Shut February.

Saint-Jean-le-Thomas – see also page 62. W coast Cotentin peninsula, 15 km S Granville, 83 km St Malo, 120 km Cherbourg; (address 50530 Sartilly, Manche) –

Des Bains, (33) 48.84.20: see text. Excellent; heated pool. 70F menu very good value. Menu 45-128F; housewine 28F; rooms vary a lot 68-170F. Shut winter October 10 to March 20.

La Plage, rue Gustave Bellai, (33) 48.84.17: nice atmosphere; shut only January and Fridays in summer. Mme Redon cooks well, big portions; try guinea fowl, local fish and lamb. Garden tables in summer. Menu 45F, 85F, 120F; housewine 16F; rooms 55-70F.

Barneville-Carteret – see also page 63; 36 km SW Cherbourg by D904 (address 50270 Manche) –

Marine, Carteret, (33) 54.83.31 or 53.83.31: old charming waterside inn, looking across harbour, extended, most bedrooms modernised and very comfortable.

Superb fish and shellfish from boats in harbour; lovely, very pricey lobster; sea views; summer terrace over water. Menu 60F, 92F.50, 140F; housewine 25F; rooms 65-197F; half-board (three nights minimum) 170-200F each per night.

Les Isles, Barneville, (33) 54.90.76: across road from beach; fine views, even to Channel Isles. Charles and Marie Duplaissy (poet and artist) have left; I have not been there since. Menu 60-120F; housewine 24F; rooms 95-215F. Shut mid-November to mid-January.

Coutainville, 77 km Cherbourg on W coast of Peninsula, 13 km Coutances on D44 (address 50230 Agon-Coutainville, Manche) –

Hardy, (33) 47.04.11: see text; menu 58F, 100F, 150F (with lobster); rooms 120-160F; shut October 15–30, January 4 to February 4; Mondays off-season.

Neptune, (33) 47.07.66: see text; rooms 153-210F. Open March 1 to October 30.

Montmartin sur Mer – see also page 64; not quite *sur mer* by 3 km, 78 km from Cherbourg, W coast, 10 km Coutances (address 50590 Manche) –

Bon Vieux Temps, (33) 47.54.44: see also page 64; very good value; menu 40F, 60F, 100F; rooms 60-72F. Always open.

Mesnil Val – see also page 65; 25 km up coast from Dieppe (address 76910 Criel sur Mer, Seine-

Maritime) –

Vieille Ferme, (35) 86.72.18: see also page 65; meals 80-200F; rooms 90-220F; restaurant shut January 3 to 31.

Le Crotoy – see also page 65 (N side of river Somme estuary, 55 km N Dieppe, 67 km S Boulogne; address 80550 Somme) –

La Baie (Chex Mado) (22) 27.81.22: see text; menu 80-120F; housewine 35F; rooms 80-95F; half-board (three nights min.) 110F each per night. Always open.

Favières, 3 km inland from Le Crotoy –

Clé des Champs, (22) 27.88.00: no rooms; rustic restaurant with log fire and warm welcome; good regional cooking; menu 53F, 74F, 105F; housewine 17F; shut Fridays low season.

Honfleur – see also page 67; across Seine estuary from Le Havre; (address 14600 Calvados) –

Cheval Blanc, quai des Passagers, (31) 89.13.49: pricey but delightful; redecorated, much refurnished; overlooks fishing and yacht harbours. Famous for fish. Menu 150F; rooms with breakfast 188-242F; restaurant shut Mondays.

Hostellerie Lechat, 3 pl. Ste Catherine, (31) 89.22.85: medium prices in high-priced town; they like you to dine in; menu 100F, 200F (gastronomic, wine included); rooms 100-200F; full board 200-300F; shut November 20 to December 20; restaurant shut Mondays.

Auberge du Vieux Clocher, 1 rue des Lingots, (31) 89.12.06: uninviting from outside, tiny, rather pricey, but superb cooking by Didier Romy; try pithiviers of salmon (in puff pastry), delicious feuilleté of seafood in winey cream sauce (more puff pastry); papiette (rolled fillets) of turbot au choux (more puff pastry); and his dessert pastries are absolutely delicious! Lovely beef and duck, too. Book – gourmets are discovering it. Menu 80F (four courses), 126F; housewine Touraine Gamay 50F. Shut Monday evenings, Tuesdays.

La Ferme Saint-Simeon, route A. Marais, (31) 89.23.61: see also page 67; wonderful place to celebrate a golden wedding or a big pools win; or you could sell a Cézanne! Years since I was there, but richer friends tell me it is still marvellous. Meals à la carte around 250F; wines from 85F; rooms 620-920F; shut January 2 to February 4.

At **Barneville le Bertran**, 5 km from Honfleur, just off D579, 10 km from Deauville –

Auberge de la Source, (31) 83.25.02: just inland but a superb spot for a short break; nice village, lovely countryside; country auberge in pleasant garden with trout pond; Lionel Legeay's menus naturally include much fish – trout, hot oysters, turbot, John Dory (St Pierre), but are well balanced. Menu 62F.50-90F; wines Gros Plant 32F; rooms 150-160F; half-board for two around 300F per night. Shut

January; Wednesdays.

St Jacut, 14 km from Dinard on Chevet Point; small fishing port and tiny resort just before Plage du Rougeret; real hideaway; fine views nearby (address 22750 Côte du Nord) –

Vieux Moulin, (96) 27.71.02: well known for seafood, including oysters, lobster; seafood platter (75F); menu 48F, 65F, 80F; rooms 89-155F; full board 161-214F. Open end March to October 1.

Le Terrier, (96) 27.71.46: pretty restaurant, attractive sheltered courtyard with tables; inevitably strong on fish; menu 43F, 63F; housewine 18F. No rooms. Shut Mondays to Thursdays in winter.

St Michel en Grève – see also page 68; 11 km SW Lannion on N coast (address 22300 Lannion). Charming little beach resort at end of superb Lieue de Grève beach (4 km long and 2 km wide at low tide); one of our favourite areas; trout streams run into sea –

La Plage, (96) 35.74.43: see text; superb value; old house alongside beach; terraces open and enclosed; menu 50F (four courses), 80F (five courses). Also good bar snacks. Rooms 80-140F. Full board 150-200F. Shut January 4 to end February.

On **Pointe de Locquirec**, on N coast in Lannion Bay, 22 km W of Lannion (address 29241 Locquirec-Armorique) –

Armorique, (98) 67.40.06: see also page 68; overlooking sands and harbour; charming creeper-clad hotel; known for shellfish, especially lobster armoricaine, and fish soup. Menu weekdays 44-88F; Sunday 88-130F; rooms 80-110F; shut September 25 to October 20.

Pointe de l'Arcouest – see also page 69; 6 km N of Paimpol on N coast, near Ploubazianec; opposite isle of Brehat (address 22620 Ploubazianec, Côte du Nord) –

Le Barbu, (96) 20.92.15: lovely position by beach in superb garden with pool; nicely furnished; good food; very pricey but worth it; menu 90F, 160F, 250F; housewine 35F; rooms (all with bath, wc, sea views) 235F; half-board 250F each per night. Gastronomic weekends 1400F for two people (two nights bed and breakfast, two gastronomic dinners).

Camaret – delightful resort and lobster port opposite Brest across bay in south Finistère; fair drive even from Roscoff (111 km) but worth it; small beach (address 29129 Finistère) –

France, (98) 27.93.06: on harbour quay; very fresh fish landed nearby, beautifully cooked; comfortable bedrooms in chestnut wood, with wc, shower or bath. Six menus 60-190F; housewine 1978 apellation controlée 27F; rooms 140-218F; 80F in annexe. Reduction on weekends on presentation of this book except in July, August. Half-board 155-195F each per night. Open March 1 to November 14.

Near **Douarnenez**, 4 km off D765

(address 29100 Douarnenez, Finistère) –

Auberge de Kervéoc'h, rte de Kervéoc'h, (98) 92.07.58: see also page 70; delightful converted farmhouse; try scallops in cider; menu 50-180F; housewine 22F; rooms 112-153F; half-board 166F.50 each per night. Shut November 15 to December 15.

Near **Plonévey-Porzay**, 3 km from Locronon (address 29127 Plomodiern, Finistère) –

Manoir de Moëllien, (98) 92.50.40: see also page 70; fine cooking of seasonal specialities; menu 54-144F; fine list 70 wines 33-300F; rooms 190F; half-board 200F each per night. Shut early January to March 15.

La Forêt Fouesnant – see also page 69; 16 km from Quimper airport – seasonal service to London (address 29133 Finistère) –

Manoir du Stang, (98) 56.97.37: see Chapter 8, luxury hotels.

La Baie, pl. de la Baie, (98) 56.97.35: old favourite opposite golf course, 1½ km from sea; Jean Yves Henaff speaks English, understands our oddities and appetites; superb gourmand meal with lobster 150F; other menus 59F, 98F; try coq au cidre; rooms 95-165F; half-board 114-150F each per night. Open April 1 to October.

5 Inland Hideouts from Calais to the Seine

For sheer one-upmanship, the dining room at the charming Auberge de la Durdent in the Normandy village of **Héricourt en Caux** takes the Grand Prix. Not content with having the pretty river Durdent, jumping with trout, running through the garden, cutting off the bedrooms from the house, it also has a little arm of the river running under the dining-room floor. Through a big glass panel you can watch beautiful plump trout flashing and jinking beneath your feet. Luckily the patronne covers the glass at dinner time. I should hate to see the reproachful looks of a proud fish as I filleted his cousin, baked in almonds.

This is a true old Norman inn in country where traditional black-and-white timbered farmhouses are as thick beside the fields as bungalows in Sussex, and the hamlets and little towns are too busy going about their agricultural business to notice tourists. Tucked away in the country, far from the main routes, 37 km from the sea at Fécamp, 38 km from Dieppe and 60 km north-east of Le Havre, it is served by little narrow roads and lanes on which we have quite happily got lost many times.

True, there are sometimes two or three GB cars outside the auberge, for it is on the list of three-night package holidays by Vacances Franco Brittaniques of Cheltenham, but French diners far outnumber British, and local regulars use the bar each night. Last time I was there, I had a long wine-drinking session with the butcher, a road repairer and the count from a nearby château.

Fortunately, the wooden bridge which you cross to reach the bedrooms has a handrail. One could be a bit unbalanced with food and wine. Meals are excellent value, and cream is not spared, whether on the trout, the hot stuffed eggs with tomato, garlic and herbs, or the strawberry tart. Madame Lebraq, a widow, seems to have unending energy and good humour. She serves early breakfast and is still serving behind the bar around midnight. I love her auberge. It is a place I tend to go back to when I should be finding somewhere new. And there is a nice Relais down the road where you meet more locals and can get a very cheap meal.

Bedrooms at the auberge are modern, bright, efficient and have showers and loos.

For shopping you can drive to **Yvetôt**, a cheerful market town rebuilt after 1940 destruction, which accounts for the spectacular modern circular concrete-and-glass church, with walls made of huge coloured glass windows by Max Ingrand – a joy to see. Yvetôt was a legendary 'kingdom' of old songs, because, from 1392 to the Revolution, it was an independent territory where the lord was called king.

The **Durdent valley** is green and lovely and there are old watermills dotted along the river. Normandy and the Pas-de-Calais are rich in valleys like this – almost luxuriant, little known to tourists. Frankly, I find them better places for hiding away for short holidays than staying by the sea. France is a country where it is better to stay inland and make sorties to the sea than the other way.

The valley of the **river Course** between Dèsvres and Montreuil on D127, which I mentioned in Chapter 1, remains almost deserted because there are few places to stay. I had a super little hideout here, Relais de la Course at Estrée, run superbly by a good chef, Pierre Morel and his family. Alas, he had a heart attack, and the inn was forlorn and deserted. Now it is open again, with cosy bedrooms, a fine dining room with lawns outside for summer, huge wood fires for winter, the river Canche running opposite and a four-course meal with three choices on each course for 60F. Meanwhile, we have stayed at Le Relais Equestre, a bed-and-breakfast Relais attached to riding stables.

Riding is not compulsory, and

young Madame Boudron is certainly not a horsey lady. Rooms are pleasantly furnished with old traditional furniture and most have french windows opening on to a garden. But don't expect to sleep late in the morning. Last time I was awakened about 7 a.m. by loud bangs and thumps, as if someone was demolishing a wall. I looked out to see an indignant horse peering from his box and systematically kicking the bottom door of his stall because someone had not taken him out to grass with his mates!

There is a good choice of places to eat around this valley. The cooking at the attractive Auberge d'Inxent is very good and the atmosphere pleasant and friendly. Regnis Lignier's restaurant by the watermill and old station at Beussent looks dull but his good meals at very reasonable prices make up for that. The Bon Accueil, just down the river at the tiny hamlet of Engondsent, looks like an unambitious bar-café but has a restaurant hidden behind, is slightly eccentric and gives incredibly good value. Lunch only is served – a huge meal costing 40F. Last time I had a beautiful trout as fish course and the main course was a large plateful of slices of beef, chicken and duck, with mountains of vegetables. A bottle of real Sancerre cost 35F.

Just in **Zerables** on the D127 Course valley road is a notice 'Auberge' pointing down a lane. In a farmyard you find café-restaurant Cocatrix-Grémont* – simple but

*See page 83.

with views over a little lake. Here the Grémont-Delame family serve four courses for 35F, five courses for 45F and either way it's a bargain.

Hesdin, a pleasant old town 23 km south-east of Montreuil, is a centre for exploring the Canche valley and the woods north with paths, carriage tracks and picnic tables, and to see the spot just off the D928 to the north where our history was changed. At **Azincourt**, which we call Agincourt, in 1415 Henry V and his exhausted English army, weak with sickness, defeated a French army more than twice its size, thanks mostly to the English longbowmen. A simple cross marks the historic spot in peaceful farmland.

Hesdin's market square, where a crowded and useful market is held weekly, is overlooked by a town hall which was once the palace of Marie of Hungary. She was sister of the Hapsburg Emperor Charles V, who ruled this area in the 16th century, as well as ruling the Austro-Hungarian Empire, Spain and the Netherlands. He built Hesdin as a fortified town to guard the river crossing. The palace ballroom is now a threatre. The Renaissance church is delightful inside but has an incongruous belfry from 1857. The old one was knocked down by French artillery when freeing Hesdin from Spanish rule.

The N39 road from Montreuil to Hesdin is a busy lorry route and not attractive. Take the small D113 north of the river – a pretty route through Beaurainville and skirting the forest. The Val de Canche next to Beaurainville's church is an unimpressive-looking inn, but André Decobert's meals are splendid value. If you like tiny river eels, try his local anguilles Val de Canche.

In Hesdin I stay at La Chope. It looks ordinary, its bedrooms are clean and simple, its atmosphere just right, and Madame Samper cooks lovingly in Flemish and Ardennes style.

On the way from Hesdin to Frévent – a disappointing place – there are some delightful Villages Fleuries beside the river just off the D340. At **Fillièvres**, opposite a pretty millpond bordered by flowers, is a watermill modernised into an auberge – called inevitably Auberge du Vieux Moulin, with good French family cooking, pleasant simple rooms and a bar where locals pop in and out for anything from a Pernod to a chocolate bar. The meals are excellent value, the trout outstanding even for this area. I love Madame Royon's real old-fashioned pot-au-feu.

Boubers-sur-Canche is a little livelier, and quite a proportion of the local men seem to spend part of their day in the friendly La Crémaillère bar-restaurant in the tree-shaded square. But they must work hard in their gardens, which are so ablaze with colour in season that it has been voted top of France's floral villages.

Drive through Frévent to Doullens, another dull place, turn left for 7 km along the N25 to **Pommera** and you will find a gem of a restaurant, La Faisanderie. It is in all the guidebooks so telephone, but its reputation is deserved.

Drivers heading southward down the dreaded N1 road or the D140 miss one of the most attractive valleys in northern France – the **Authie river valley**. You can reach it by taking the little D139 from Montreuil through Boisjean, or by turning off the N1 at Nampont.

Start along the Authie's north bank on the D119 to Maintenay, then take a little lane marked 'Vieux Moulin'. At a charming little bridge over the river beside a millpond with a big watermill is Vieux Moulin itself – once a restaurant, now just a bar and a wonderful place to sit by the water with a glass of wine and dream. I am greeted here as a regular, although I go only two or three times a year. But I have been going for thirty-eight years.

Across the bridge is a fortified farm. Climb the hill beside it and pick up the D192, then follow the river to the 12th-century **Abbaye de Valloires**, once a Cistercian abbey, reconstructed in the 1700s and now a children's home. The bodies of the French knights killed at the Battle of Crécy in 1346 were brought here. There are guided tours. Don't miss the magnificent choir stalls.

Just down the road at **Argoules** is the Auberge du Coq en Pâté, run by a friendly eccentric patronne, Mme Despret. She is a dynamic enthusiast, working, talking, running non-stop.

It is a typical North French auberge, with solid furniture, red-check tablecloths, décor of fishing nets, old lamps and miner's gear used by Madame's grandfather. An old mine telephone communicates with the bedrooms, which are in a garden annexe and very small. The menu costs around 40F for four courses of good country cooking. Weekend prices are a bargain.

Argoules was once known for Pierre Bony's Auberge du Gros Tilleul. Alas, he has died, and dozens of sad English people are waiting to see what will happen next to the auberge.

Most of us now make for **Saulchoy**, across the river, where in the square is a spruce, attractive little restaurant, Le Val d'Authie, run by an enthusiastic couple. Unusually for France, Madame, not her husband, does the cooking, and does it well. She offers a simple three-course menu based on the plat du jour for around 50F and a dearer ambitious menu. Her ficelle picarde – pancake stuffed with cream, cheese and ham – is excellent.

Clères is a delightful little town among little lanes with overgrown hedges among which you can easily get lost. It is in the triangle between the N29, N27 and N28, along a local road, D6, and it has a stream through its centre, a medieval castle 'modernised' last century and a fine old market hall. It also has a wildlife park around the castle where antelope, deer and wallabies wander free among storks and peacocks, and web-footed birds of types I never knew existed plod, flap and swim around the lake.

There is a fine museum of old cars, too, in the castle – not of Beaulieu standards but a delight to me. I once found the place surrounded by old giant Le Mans Bentleys, all with GB plates and nearly all in British racing green. The Bentley owners club was holding a rally.

But Clères is only 29 km from Rouen and from spring until winter it gets very crowded on weekends. Although it seats over 300 people, the local inn, Cheval Noir, where we used to stay, gets crowded too. No wonder, considering the excellent value of meals. Happily a new hotel has appeared, hidden among maze-like lanes to the south at **Mont Cauvaire**. It is in a magnificent 17th-century Louis XIV château called Rombosc. I almost wish that not many people will find it, but that would be unfair to the Levieux family who have taken such care to restore it, so I will tell you the secret – drive from Fontaine Le Bourg along the road to Clères and take the fourth turning on the left. 'Repos garanti et calme absolu,' the family promised me – 'guaranteed rest and absolute quiet'. That is about what you will get. It is open all the year.

Though the river Seine carries much more commerical traffic than the Thames, it is long enough to pass through long stretches of open country and small villages. When the great hotel-keeper Maurice Lalonde owned the Marine hotel at **Caudebec en Caux**, he had a terrace alongside the Seine where you could sit with an aperitif or a coffee and watch the whole river scene. Now he has moved to the nearby Domaine de Villequier (which I shall mention in Chapter 8 on châteaux hotels), the beautiful and useful suspension

bridge crosses the river at Caudebec, the Marine is not what it was and the riverside terrace is a car park. So we prefer little Villequier, 4 km westwards beside the river. Nothing happens there, except eating, drinking and watching the boats go by.

Caudebec was a lovely old town before the war but it was burned down in 1940. Luckily the church of Notre-Dame was saved. It is a wonderful example of flamboyant Gothic, built in the 14th century, and Henry IV called it 'the most beautiful chapel in my kingdom'. The eight-sided belfry, topped by a three-stage stone spire, is quite remarkable, and the interior of the church is graceful.

Caudebec's market is on Saturdays. It has been held since 1390 and is still a place to buy the wonderful vegetables and the butter, cheese and cream which the Caux farms produce in abundance.

Villequier has two simple inns alongside the river, both offering good cheap meals, and wooded slopes behind it. Victor Hugo used to holiday here until his daughter and her husband were killed in a boating accident.

St Wandrille's Abbey is 4 km east of Caudebec. It nestles among trees in a hamlet with a good restaurant, and its interesting history makes up for its mongrel architecture.

Wandrille was a count at the court of King Dagobert in the 7th century – wise, handsome and athletic. At his wedding, he and his bride decided that their love was so perfect that they should consecrate it to God. So, to the King's fury, she went straight into a convent and he became a monk. No doubt there are many married couples who wish they had had the same idea. He founded this abbey at Fontenelle in 649 AD and was still so saintly and fit that he was known as the 'athlete of God'. It was destroyed at various times through history until, in the last century, it was owned by an English peer, the Marquis of Stacpoole, who started restoration. After a brief spell as a Benedictine monastery it became a private house and Maurice Maeterlinck, the author of *Life of the Ant*, Nobel prizewinner for literature, lived there for a long time. The monks returned in 1931 and you can attend the services and hear the Gregorian chant. But women are not allowed in the cloisters.

Over the Brotonne bridge is the **Brotonne forest**, cool, peaceful, with small roads to drive around.

We returned with some trepidation last year to a little village on the Seine's rocky south bank just south of Rouen – **La Bouille**. We feared the very worst, for a motorway has been built within 3 km of it since we last saw it.

It has survived remarkably, despite the invasion of Rouen's citizens on fine weekends. It is a hamlet of half-timbered old Norman houses, three hotels and many restaurants packed with Rouennais on Sunday lunchtime. It is definitely the place to stay if you want to enjoy exploring what is left of old **Rouen** but not get too involved with its industries and very heavy traffic. Old Rouen is a joy, but is not, in my view, the place

to spend a weekend, when many of the locals are trying to get out of it. From La Bouille you can get a ferry boat to Rouen, so I would stay there.

Drive under the motorway and you climb into the pleasant beech forest of **Londe**. Overlooking the motorway to the river are the ruins of a castle which belonged to Robert le Diable (the Devil), father of William the Conqueror by a Falaise tanner's daughter, Arlette. In the Hundred Years' War, the French blew it up to stop the English taking it, and now its ruins are pleasure grounds for tourists.

La Bouille has gone up in the world since we knew it. The delightful Saint Pierre hotel, with its charming terrace beside the Seine, is now starred by Michelin, with menus at 100-160F, 90F for a housewine, and rooms around 200F. Mind you, the cooking of Patrice Kukurudz is excellent and the bedrooms attractive, so you can hardly complain. It is a lovely spot. And, as a local patron-chef put it to me: 'Bouille is a very agreeable little gastronomic centre.' His restaurant is called Les Gastronomes.

A place on the Seine highly recommended to me for a short break, and which certainly looks pleasant, is **Les Andelys**, 39 km past Rouen. It is perhaps the most beautiful spot on the Seine. The surviving ruins of Gaillard Castle on a cliff over the river still dominate the little town. Richard the Lionheart of England and Normandy built it in a year in 1196 to bar the route to Rouen from the French. Louis Phillippe of France dared not attack it when Richard was alive. But when the weaker King John reigned, he attacked and took it in a remarkable assault in which French soldiers got in through the latrines – the way we got out of Oflag XXIB in Poland during the Second World War. A Scottish king, David Bruce, lived here when he fled to France in 1334, and two French queens were imprisoned here for sleeping with boyfriends. In place St Sauveur is a plaque to Blanchard, first man to cross the Channel in a balloon and the inventor of the parachute.

The twin townlets of **Grand** and **Petit Andely** have several restaurants and hotels. Favourite of my friends is Jean-Claude Foucault's Chaine d'Or, with reasonably priced meals and eleven bedrooms overlooking the river.

Another attractive river valley is the **valley of the Risle**, especially inland from **Pont Audemer**, the first biggish town you reach after crossing the Seine by Tancarville bridge. I am still not certain why I and many friends have liked Pont Audemer so much for over forty years. Its old buildings which survived 1940 shelling are truly picturesque and the way the river breaks up into many streams to wander between them is attractive. But I think it is just the atmosphere of this quite busy little town going about its business as if the rest of the world was unimportant that appeals to me. And the choice of excellent, if expensive, restaurants. There is a splendid market right down the main street on Mondays and Fridays.

Driving down the Risle on the little D39 is very attractive. But it is well worth crossing the river to see **Bec Hellouin**, whose Benedictine abbey has links with England back to the Conquest in 1066. It was founded in 1034 by a knight who suddenly changed his armour for a monk's habit. Lanfranc, the great scholar-priest, joined the abbey, became adviser to William the Conqueror when William was warring in the district, and went to Rome to persuade the Pope to forgive William for having married his cousin Matilda – not too difficult, because the Pope had once been Lanfranc's pupil in Italy. William made Lanfranc Archbishop of Canterbury and virtual ruler of England when the King was away fighting. His successor at Canterbury was another Bec graduate, Anselm. You can visit the abbey mornings and afternoons except Tuesdays and during Sunday services. The Auberge de l'Abbaye serves true Norman dishes.

Nearby and linked to it in history is **Brionne**, another delightful market town suitable for an overnight stay or as a touring centre for a long weekend. It is built on islands where the Risle once more divides into channels.

There are two hotels further north with great atmosphere, excellent food and comfort. Bollezeele is not an exciting place but it is only 17 km from **St Omer**, which *is* interesting, and Bollezeele's Hostellerie Saint Louis is better than any St Omer hotel I have tried. It has been carefully and cleverly converted from an

18th-century manor house and its attached buildings, complete with spiky belltower. Patron-chef Phillippe Dubreucq cooks very well, with a Flemish accent, some bedrooms are smallish but all are comfortable, and the hotel and gardens are restful, as befits a Relais du Silence.

On the edge of North France's industrial belt, 18 km past St Omer on the N43, I was surprised some years ago to find a well-kept old market town called **Aire sur la Lys**, with many 18th-century houses round its market place and old beamed buildings carefully restored They are still restoring the flamboyant 15th-century Renaissance church of St Peter's in an area where most old buildings tend to get knocked down to make way for factories or office blocks.

I was more surprised still to find, hidden away behind trees, a splendid hostellerie called Les Trois Mousquetaires, in a beamed and gabled château of the last century. Furthermore, it was in a charming little park with a small lake, had pleasant bedrooms, and a chef-patron Marcel Venet who spit-roasts so well that this soon became my favourite roast-and-grill restaurant in France. M. Venet's son Philippe joined him later at the rotisserie and cookers, and their fame spread so fast that they are now in every guidebook. But apart from the fact that you have to book a bedroom ahead and may have to wait for a table if you turn up on the off-chance, it is as delightful as ever – and still excellent value.

Friends tell me that I should have kept quiet about it in the first place and just whispered its name to a chosen few. That is nonsense. A place as good as the Three Musketeers was bound to find fame. But please leave a table for me and for BBC TV *Holiday Programme* producer Tom Savage. It is his favourite, too.

Hotels and Restaurants

Héricourt en Caux – see also page 75; 38 km S Dieppe by N27, D14 right, 60 km NE Le Havre (address 76560 Doudeville, Seine-Maritime) –

Auberge de la Durdent, (35) 96.42.44: menu 44-88F; rooms 95F; half-board (min. three nights) 122F. Shut October 10 to 30, February 10 to 28.

Estrée – Valley of the Course, D127 (address 62170 Montreuil-sur-Mer) –

Relais de la Course, (21) 06.18.04: 60F menu (four courses) includes trout and salmon among starters, ham in port sauce, stuffed pancake among second courses, coq au vin, shoulder of lamb or two stuffed quail as main course; cheese or dessert; rooms 80-120F, 150F (four people). Always open.

Inxent – Valley of the Course on D127 Desvres–Montreuil (address 62170 Montreuil-sur-Mer) –

Relais Equestre, (21) 90.70.34: see also page 76; six rooms; horse riding; rooms 100F.

Eat at any of these below:

Auberge d'Inxent, (21) 06.86.52:
where the locals go; pretty old
cottage restaurant opposite old
church, near Relais Equestre; very
good Norman cooking; menu
60-110F; shut Monday evenings,
Tuesdays; mid-September to
mid-October.

Beussent – Valley of the Course;
just off D127 –

Hôtel Regis Lignier, (21) 90.71.65:
see also page 76; no longer lets
rooms; grills over wood fire; menu
41F.50-80F; housewine 27F. Shut
Wednesdays.

At **Engondsent**, over river, down
lane –

Bon Accueil, (21) 90.70.63: see also
page 76; incredible value; I took a
wholesale caterer who just didn't
believe it. Family service informal,
friendly, efficient. Lunch only;
book weekends. Meal 40F.

At **Zérables** on D127 –

Café-restaurant
Cocatrix-Grémont, (21) 90.73.39:
see page 76; view over lake; vies
with Bon Accueil for value;
splendid local trout in cream sauce.
Menu 35F (four courses), 45F (five
courses); housewine 19F.

Beaurainville – 12 km E Montreuil
on D53, Canche valley (address
62990 Pas-de-Calais) –

Val de Canche, (21) 90.32.22: see
also page 77; simple inn, well run,
good food; menu 42-95F;

housewine 22F; rooms 85-150F;
half-board (three nights min.) 140F
each per night.

Hesdin – 23 km SE Montreuil; see
also page 77 (address 62140
Pas-de-Calais) –

La Chope, 48 rue d'Arras, (21)
86.82.73: old favourite of ours;
menu 48-80F, plus fresh fish menu
75-115F; very good French
traditional and Flemish cooking;
rooms 89-120F; half-board (min.
two nights) 200F a night for two
people; gastronomic 265F a night
for two; weekends two nights with
full board, 695F for two people;
gastronomic weekend 850F for
two. Shut Fridays winter only.

Les Flandres, rue du Bras-d'Or, (21)
86.80.21: modernised Logis; spit-
roast and grilled meat and fish
speciality; good Canche trout;
menu 44F.50-120F; wine Côte de
Rhône 32F; rooms 68-190F. Shut
December 20 to January 15.

Trois Fontaines, 16 rue Abbeville,
(21) 86.81.65: modern,
comfortable, but lacks atmosphere
and I prefer to be in, not outside,
this charming town; nice garden,
quiet, good bourgeois cooking.
Menu 50-95F; rooms (bath, wc)
130-160F. Restaurant shut Sunday
evenings.

Fillièvres – see also page 77;
*Canche valley, 12 km SE Hesdin
D340, 35 km SE Montreuil (address
62770 Le Parcq, Pas-de-Calais) –

Vieux Moulin, (21) 04.83.42:
bargain meals with Seraphin
Royon's family cooking; superb
trout; menu 45-75F; housewine

24F; rooms 72-82F. Always open.

At **Boubers-sur-Canche** – see also page 77; 17 km SE Hesdin D340, useful restaurant if staying in Hesdin-Montreuil area –

La Cremaillère, (21) 04.20.03: try trout; coq au vin; menu 75-95F. Shut Tuesdays.

Pommera – from Hesdin, through Frévent to Doullens, then 6 km left along N25 –

La Faisanderie, (21) 48.20.76: restaurant only, but a meal here will make your weekend; see also page 77; converted farm with beams, small garden; superb cooking by Jean Pierre Dargent – ex Flavio, Le Touquet, with touch of Nouveau; try grilled oysters in shallot butter and fricassé of guinea fowl (pintadeau); menu weekdays 70F (bargain), 140F; Sunday 98F, 140F, 205F. Good pricier wines only; do telephone; go now before prices rise. Shut Sunday evenings, Mondays.

Argoules – see also page 78; on D192, south bank of Authie river 20 km S Montreuil (address 80120 Rue) –

Coq en Pâté, (22) 29.92.09: a bargain; menu (four courses) 40F; good wine 22F; rooms (small) 70F; half-board 95F each per night; weekend 120F each for dinner Saturday, bed, breakfast, Sunday lunch. Shut Fridays.

Saulchoy – N side of Authie river, opposite Argoules, on D119 –

Val d'Authie, (21) 90.30.20: see also page 78; restaurant useful if staying in Montreuil–Hesdin area; we are almost regulars; good value, open every day; small menu (entrée, dish of day, cheese or dessert) 47F; others 78F, 92F. Housewine 38F (good).

Clères – see also page 78; 29 km N Rouen (address 76690 Seine-Maritime) –

Château de Rombosc, (35) 34.68.72: real hideaway in Louis XIV 17th-century château; open all year; Norman cooking; à la carte only around 80F; rooms 160-200F.

Villequier – see also page 79; beside Seine, 49 km Le Havre, 75 km Dieppe (address 76490 Seine-Maritime) –

France, (35) 56.78.70: André and Christine Loisel's little inn overlooking the Seine is now deservedly very popular; good-value meals; menu 50F (four courses), five courses 72F, 90F; simple rooms (shower, wc) 95F; half-board 110F each per night; weekends Friday to Sunday (two nights bed and breakfast, two lunches, two dinners) 450F – a bargain. Shut Sunday evenings, Mondays.

Grand Sapin, (35) 56.78.73: makes me feel old – it's so long since I first sat in the tiny garden by the Seine tasting young Gerard Octau's delicious cooking, with lots of cream. Now he is patron, too, and his pintade smitane (guinea fowl with cream and mushrooms) is better than ever. Menu 40F (weekday), 65-103F; rooms 59-134F

– some sleeping four. Shut Wednesdays in winter; part November ; three weeks in February.

Caudebec en Caux – see also page 79; 3 km from Villequier (address 76490 Seine-Maritime) –

Manoir de Rétival, (35) 96.11.22: some years since I stayed in this spiky-towered 19th-century manor in a park overlooking the Seine valley but I have peeped in recently and it is a joy – tastefully furnished in antiques; garden well kept. Madame Collet now privides a little meal – pâté, grill, cheese, dessert and 32F housewine; if she had a restaurant I should be a habitué. Bedrooms 145-300F. Shut November 2 to March.

Normandie, (35) 96.25.11: we have had some remarkably good-value meals here; old-fashioned French inn cooking with very good service; overlooks river; 38F weekday menu exceptional value; others to 90F. Rooms 60-120F. Logis 'casserole' for outstanding regional cooking deserved. Shut Sunday evenings, Mondays.

La Bouille – see also page 80; S bank of Seine, N180, river bend SE Rouen, delightful little town (address 76530 Grand Couronne, Seine-Maritime) –

Saint Pierre, (35) 23.80.10: see text; Bernard Huet and Patrice Kukurudz have a star from Michelin, which has infuriated Nouvelle Cuisine fans, delighted traditionalists like me, and made their many British fans sad because prices have risen

and crowds arrived. The Gault guide has accused Patrice of such crimes as overcooking lamb. Good for Patrice. Who decreed that lamb should be as bloody red as beef? Or duck, for that matter? The great old French chefs did not think so. It's a Paris fashion. I back Michelin about this hotel with nice bedrooms. But wine prices are too high. Menu 100F, 160F; wines from 90F; shut All Saints holidays (last week October, first week November); school holidays in February; Tuesday evenings, Wednesdays in winter.

Two good restaurants are:

Les Gastronomes, (35) 23.80.72: Philippe Demoget offers several good Norman dishes, in well-chosen menus; try marmite du pêcheur, escalope of veal Vallée d'Auge and the apple tart flambée in calvados; live lobster tank; river views from first floor. Menus 74F.50, 125F, 175F; Muscadet 48F; Côtes du Rhône 50F. Shut Wednesday evenings, Thursdays.

Maison Blanche, quai Hector Malot, (35) 23.80.53: very attractive, overlooking Seine; old Norman décor, fine old Norman cooking in cider (duck, salmon); I love it. Menu 75F, 130F; wine 46F; shut Sunday evenings, Mondays.

Les Andelys – see also page 80; SE Rouen on N bank of Seine but more easily reached from S bank through Gaillon, near Paris–Rouen motorway; superb river views (address 27700 Eure) –

Chaine d'Or, pl. St Sauveur, (32) 54.00.31: big rooms. Menu lunch 49F, 85F, evening 55F, 85F;

housewine 35F; rooms 90-240F.
Shut Monday evenings, Tuesdays.

Paris, 10 ave République, (32)
54.00.33: friends think it good
value; historic old house; garden;
menu 41-75F; housewine 32F;
rooms 65-80F.

Normandie, 1 rue Grande,
Petit-Andely, (32) 54.10.52:
old-style hotel overlooking Seine,
below château; menu 50F
(weekday), 70F, 100F; housewine
27F; rooms 63-110F; shut
Wednesday evenings, Thursdays.

Pont Audemer – see also page 81;
48 km Le Havre, 18 km S Tancarville
bridge, 100 km Dieppe (address
27500 Eure) –

Auberge du Vieux Puits, 6 rue
Notre-Dame du Pré, (32) 41.01.48:
really is a delightful 17th-century
house, authentically furnished and
decorated and I loved it for years;
charming garden with well (*puits*).
Michelin star always well deserved
for delightful cooking of traditional
dishes offered here for years.
Jacques Foltz is doing his
damnedest to fight inflation (aren't
we all?) but his set menu is up to
180F (trout au champagne, duck
poached with sharp cherries,
sorbet with calvados, local cheese
and house tart with cream), and à la
carte four-course meal around
200F; plenty of inferior places
charge as much. No housewine,
but a nice '78 Cahors red (I love it)
costs 60F, a good Sancerre 75F.
Rooms 80-155F; you must 'dine in'.
Shut Monday evenings, Tuesdays;
first week July; December 20 to
January 20.

Hôtel de la Risle, 16 quai R.
Leblanc, (32) 41.14.57: this little
modern hotel is either very good or
has a highly organised lobby! I am
not the only writer to get many
letters from readers demanding
that I put it into my books. Fate has
kept me away from it so far. I think
it must be good, certainly not dear.
Menu 46-56F; rooms 50-90F; half-
board around 100F each per night.
Shut August 20 to September 10;
December 20 to January 10.

La Frégate, rue La Seule, (32)
41.12.03: restaurant only; not
cheap but excellent cooking. Menu
90F, 150F; wines 56-350F; shut
August; Sunday evenings,
Mondays.

Bollezeele – see also page 81; off
D928 N St Omer 17 km, 54 km Calais
(address 59470 Wormhout, Nord) –

Hostellerie St Louis, 47 rue l'Eglise,
(28) 68.81.83: charming 18th-
century manor house beautifully
modernised; log fires; Relais du
Silence; becoming popular despite
dull town; menu 90-160F;
housewine 40F; rooms 100-180F;
shut January 9 to mid-February.

Aire sur la Lys – see also page 82;
60 km Boulogne by D341, D157, 56
km by N43 (address 62120 Pas-de-
Calais) –

Trois Mousquetaires, Château de la
Redoute, (21) 39.01.11: good
choice, very reliable cooking;
menu 52-140F; housewine 20-25F;
rooms 60-165F. Weekends 320F
each (dinner, room with bath, wc,
breakfast; Sunday lunch). Shut
Sunday evenings; Mondays.

At **Wierre-Effroy**, tiny hamlet, 12 km NE Boulogne via Pittefoux or 18 km by N1 to Marquise, right on D238; 26 km Calais via Marquise (address 62250 Marquise, Pas-de-Calais) –

Ferme Auberge du Vert, (21) 92.82.10: unusual and appealing hideout; old farm in heart of country where M. et Mme Bernard seek the 'authentique' life. Health cooking of all natural ingredients of the farm or district: chicken, duck, guinea fowl, free-range eggs with orange centres from the feed of maize, home-made bread which you can help to make, cheese made on the farm. Bicycles and horses for hire. Rooms with shower, wc 150F; midday meal served only weekends 90-110F; wine 35F. In week, breakfast, afternoon brioche, cakes, cider, beer or apple juice, then supper of hot and cold dishes, freshly made soups, terrines of fish or fowl, home-made dessert, wine or beer. This half-board costs 330F a day for two. Shut February.

6 Inland Hideouts in Brittany, Lower Normandy and the Cherbourg Peninsular

Looking for the Verte Campagne country hotel among the little lanes with high banks and hedgerows south of Coutances you can understand how this area of Normandy's countryside changed the Allied invasion plans on the Cherbourg peninsula.

Highly mechanised American units simply could not get along the narrow lanes or over the banks, and the US Army had to take to its feet, like the Paras and the British Commandos. Overnight, they had to learn a new way of fighting.

Even when you have found Trelly, 13 km south of Coutances, you must still find little signs to the Verte Campagne through a maze of what are virtually tracks to the hamlet of **Chevalier** – there were not even road signs when we first went there.

Your reward for winning this hotel hunt is perfect peace in a low grey-stone farmhouse built in 1717, with roses climbing it, green verges and flower beds leading to meadow in front, and chickens clucking and pecking among the outbuildings. Among trees in the meadow those contented-looking Norman cows in cream, brown and black with brown rings round their eyes look at you fleetingly, then get on with the serious business of chewing grass. From a front bedroom I have spent tranquil minutes watching them in the mornings and evenings. I do prefer to be woken by a gentle, deep mooing than a strident teamaker or hearty presenter on BBC radio 4.

I should be very happy living at Verte Campagne. Stone walls, flagstone floors, heavy old beams, fine Norman furniture of solid wood which has withstood the ages, a décor of pretty plates, bottles and copper utensils which are still in use, plus a few pictures and huge old stone fireplaces in which log fires burn at the hint of chilly air, all combining to give it simple comfort and stability.

Some bedrooms are small, but all are cosy and feel lived-in. Madame Meredith, who owns and runs it, is the widow of a British naval officer, and she makes me feel that I am simply a welcome weekend guest in her charming country home. Madame and her assistant cook well in classic French style. Their cuisine reminds me of the better meals I have had in houses of French friends who care about food.

It is in a lovely, secretive area for walking, strolling and pottering, with beautiful wild flowers on those bocage (woodland) banks, especially springtime primroses in incredible profusion and a liberal sprinkling of cowslips. Shades of old England before chemical weedkillers. The sea at little Montmartin is only 12 km away, Granville 32 km, and Mont St Michel 55 km.

Hambye is 15 km east of Trelly and 17 km south-east of Coutances. Most people go to see its ruined abbey on a high hill above the little town. For me, the lure is lovely hilly countryside to be explored and two good places to stay – Auberge de l'Abbaye, which is spendid value, and Restaurant de l'Abbaye which has simple rooms and bargain meals of local farm food, rich in cream and butter.

It is isolated, but for shopping you can make for a lively little town 18 km away called **Villedieu-les-Poêles** – which means 'God's Town of the Frying Pans', because it was the first headquarters in the 12th century of the Knights of St John, predecessors of the St John Ambulance Brigade and then a most holy order devoted to looking after wounded Crusaders. For centuries since the town has made copper milk-churns and cooking pans. Music is broadcast in its main street in daytime, with a few breaks for commercials, and copper pans and souvenirs glint in the sun from shop windows. I have a super pan for making sauces from there – but make sure you pay the price and get one with a genuine thick and heavy copper bottom.

Avranches is a nice, lively little town with rather a lot of traffic, so I like to stay outside it. Mont St Michel is only 22 km away, and between them are two comfortable hotels. Hôtel des 13 Assiettes at Pontaubault is a motel with bedrooms in chalets in the grounds. The building is old, bedrooms comfortable, and it has a pleasant flowered terrace. It is a Logis and France Accueil hotel, so gives good service and welcome, and is excellent value.

Manoir Roche-Torin at Courtils, 9 km from Le Mont, is a spacious Relais du Silence retreat – 19th-century manor house in quiet grounds. Not cheap, but comfortable, and good honest cooking of grills, roasts and seafood. Silence is endangered only by English TV in the lounge.

Brittany is rich in inland hotels where you can hide from crowds, and they vary greatly from simple Relais to lovely converted manor houses and castles. I have listed a number of places, like Combourg and Dol, in Chapter 3, and others under châteaux hotels, Chapter 8.

Just 14 km past Combourg and 20 km from the cathedral city of Rennes, interesting but terribly crowded, is **Hédé**, a charming village on a hill with castle ruins and hanging gardens to houses, set between a canal and a pool. The country to the east, dotted with small lakes, canals, windmills and woods, is delightful and little known. On the main road, but hidden from noise, is the welcoming Hostellerie du Vieux Moulin – one of Barbara's favourites. It is friendly, reasonably priced, with excellent cooking.

My favourite is dearer but delightful. I was a founder-guest at

Manoir des Portes near Lamballe when it was being converted from a 15th-century farm a few years back and the entrance was more like a farmyard than hotel. It is still very rural, with a fish lake across the lane, farmhouse-style comfortable bedrooms and views of meadows and woods with a tiny church. The countryside is very attractive and Lamballe a typical old-style tiny market town of whitewashed houses. It is still a market for pigs and cattle, though the town is better known for horses. Its stud farm for Breton draught horses and old-style post horses has 150 stallions, and from August until February you can see them going out daily in tandem, pairs or fours, but they are mostly away at stud from mid-February to mid-July. However, even then there are still plenty of horses about – forty from the dressage school and dozens from the riding school. Fine old buildings include a romanesque church and 15th-century houses. The old executioners' house is now the tourist office.

Hôtel du Commerce at **Quintin**, a charming old town 19 km south-east of St Brieuc, seems strangely named. This stone country inn with beams and rich old oak panelling is far better suited to holidaymakers seeking quiet among superb surroundings than to commercial gentlemen. Our bedroom was delightfully furnished in blue and pink, and each is different. François Le Gaudu cooks excellently in Breton style and prices are very reasonable. Although, being in Brittany, the fish dishes are very good, coq au vin is the celebrated dish of the house.

Quintin's houses rise in terraces

from the river Gouet, an attractive stretch of water overlooked by the 17th-century terrace of the restored castle. The countryside around seems like a lost little world of pools, streams, hamlets and overgrown green lanes which make many parts of central Brittany such fine countryside for walking and horse riding. We once took a horse-drawn caravan round some of these lanes and met nothing but the occasional farm tractor.

In a different price group but one of the most delightful and prettiest country hotels in Brittany is Les Moulins du Duc at **Moëlan-sur-Mer**, which is certainly not *sur mer* any more. It is within about 8 km of Brittany's south coast, on the river Belon, 10 km south of Quimperlé. The hotel has cottages grouped round an old mill beside a little lake, with the river, streams, rapids and ponds. It is all old except for the plumbing and the very modern heated indoor swimming pool with a glass wall leading on to a terrace. The mill dates from the 16th century and was owned by the old Duchy of Brittany.

The area of Normandy which Britons usually call **Calvados**, but which also includes the **Pays d'Auge** south of Deauville and the oddly named **Suisse Normande** in l'Orne, as well as the area around Bayeux and Caen, south of the Calvados landing beaches of 1944, is another part of France where you can find delightful hideouts which people on the main roads miss completely. And this is especially true now that the motorway from Paris reaches as far as Caen. It is just about the most boring motorway in Europe, bypassing superb little places. What a dreary way to travel!

South of Bayeux and that motorway, the countryside of farms, hamlets and châteaux joined by tiny lanes and narrow roads is little known even to the French, although a number of châteaux have become attractive but expensive hotels recently.

One of our favourites is neither a château nor expensive – Hôtel des Biards at **Balleroy**, 16 km south-west of Bayeux. It is quite an ordinary russet-red building with extraordinarily cheap good meals, including a menu with three choices in each course for 32F.50 and dinner, bed and breakfast for 80F. And there is a castle at the end of the road – the magnificent Château de Balleroy, designed by the great François Mansart in 1626 when he was only twenty-eight, and with gardens designed by Le Nôtre, who made the gardens of Versailles. The village's only street was built as an avenue leading to the castle. Interior decorations are magnificent, especially the painted ceiling and royal portraits, including Louis XIV's mistress Madame de Montespan, painted by Mignard, in the grand salon. It is a château well worth visiting, with the added attraction for me of a balloon museum. Each June an international balloon meeting is held, made especially important in 1983 as anniversary of the Mongolfier brothers' first balloon flight in Paris in 1783.

Suisse Normande certainly has its rocks, gorges and escarpments, with the river Orne running through, but it must have been an advertising man who called it Norman Switzerland, for much of it is gentle hills and green secret valleys. Forget the name and enjoy some rugged and some soft green scenery, peaceful and away from crowds. Walkers, scramblers, fishermen and canoeists use Clécy as their centre for exploring and it is a beautiful spot for this purpose. The river sweeps around the little town at the bottom of steep slopes covered in trees and topped with rocks. There are pleasant walks and fine drives around here. And the Moulin du Vey is a charming old creeper-clad inn, with a garden terrace directly overlooking the river, tastefully decorated rooms and imaginative cooking with a strong Nouvelle Cuisine accent. A lovely place to stay, though a bit pricey.

At the southern end of Suisse Normande, but still on the Orne river, is a tiny pleasant market town popular with French open-air holidaymakers but where I have rarely seen a British car. **Putanges-Pont-Ecrépin** is an old town with a fine main square, a river bridge and a photogenic setting. It has made sure that its new buildings are in stone and in traditional style. One is the Hôtel du Lion Verd, which gives very good value.

From here, narrow roads will take you through the **Gorges de St Aubert** to some magnificent views, some of which mean walking the last stretch. The most spectacular, and the most 'alpine' in this misnamed district, is **Roche d'Oëtre**, a glorious beauty spot

looking down on the wriggling gorges of the river Rouvre cutting its way to the Orne.

Further south, up the Orne river, is the spa resort of **Bagnoles** and its pretty little neighbour **Tessé-la-Madeleine**, in the forest of Andaines.

The first time I saw Bagnoles I thought that I had slipped back to the mid-1930s, when resorts and town centres seemed smugly cleaned, brushed and painted, grass was trimmed, flower beds weedless, and boys had creases in their trousers. This orderly little spa, hidden among woods, hills, lush meadows and streams so rich in trout that fishing is a way of life, has a casino shining in a tended lake, cure baths in a wooded setting, and flowers all around.

The story of the discovery of the spa is similar to many more. Hugues de Tessé, not wanting to kill his old charger Rapide who had grown old and sick, let him loose in the forest. The horse returned frisky, with bright eyes and shining coat. So Hugues followed his hoofmarks, found the spring and pools, bathed in them and went frisky, too.

The Great Spring water flows at 11,000 gallons an hour at 80.6° Farenheit (27°C), has few minerals and much radioactivity. It is used for circulation troubles, phlebitis, to prevent varicose veins and cure obesity. Just what I need in fact.

In the clean main street, French couples wander slowly, meticulously studying menus and discussing their ailments. None of your British stoical nonsense for the French. They like to *enjoy* their maladies.

I like Bagnoles as a wanderer's centre. There are woodland walks to other pools and shaded drives through **Ecouves forest**, with picnic spots, paths and peace. Another little spa nearby, **La Ferté Macé**, is famous for tripe roasted on skewers, if you like tripe. I don't.

You will find deer and squirrels in the Andaines forest. Once, the sick seeking the cure had to brave wolves and brigands. But they had the pleasure of mixed bathing in the nude, though the poor had to use another pool.

Domfront is only 11 km away – a very different sort of hideaway. An old feudal town with a castle and ramparts which saw much bloody fighting, it spreads spectacularly along a rocky spur above a ravine cut by the river Varenne. The bellicose Bellême family built it in 1011, but William the Conqueror had it off them before he invaded England. Here England's Henry II learned from the papal nuncio that his penance for Thomas à Becket's death was to walk barefooted to Canterbury to be scourged by monks.

It was a Scot who had killed another Henry II (of France) who withstood the bloodiest seige of the castle. In 1559 Captain Montgomery of the Scots Guards, then fighting for the French against England, accidentally killed the French king in a jousting match, thus making Catherine de Medici a widow and robbing Diane de Poitiers of her lover. Montgomery also became converted to Calvinism. He then held Domfront castle with 150 men against a royalist army, but wounds, illness and starvation reduced his force to fifteen sick men and he surrendered. Catherine had him stripped of his honours and possessions and executed. Secretly she was probably delighted at her wayward husband's death, for she then ruled France for her young son and got her own back on Diane by turning her out of the gorgeous château of Chenonceaux in the Loire which she loved, and which is the most beautiful house I have ever seen.

Domfront castle once had twenty-four towers. A bridge over the old moat leads to public gardens where there are beautiful panoramic views from the terrace over the river.

If you are coming to this area through Le Havre and you have the slightest interest in horses, route yourself through **Haras du Pin** (or Pin au Haras), 12 km east of Argentan, about 24 km east of Putanges and 13 km from Ecouves forest. It is a national stud built around a house designed by Mansart in 1716 at the meeting place of three superb forest rides. There are more than 100 stallions there, including many from England and Ireland, plus Norman riding horses, French trotters and percherons. It is a wonderful sight to see strings of them going for morning exercise, and in the meadows you can often see mares and their very young foals.

There used to be a thatched Logis de France by the gates which was my favourite in France. However, it was gutted by fire and is now staff accommodation.

The Queen has been to the stud, and the Duke of Edinburgh has driven his carriage team in competition there. The big steeplechase is in October.

Up in the Pays d'Auge north of here, 20 km south-east of Lisieux, in one of the nicest valleys of this fine countryside, is a bright little town of character called **Orbec**. Very few Britons seem to know that it exists. Nor do they know of the river Orbiquet, which springs from the ground 5 km away.

Apart from the scenery, this is a good place to tuck yourself away for a few days for the splendid food. Chicken, duck and escalope of veal are all cooked in the Vallée d'Auge manner, with calvados, the apple spirit, apples and thick cream; sometimes with cider, too. Vegetables and fish can come to the table afloat with cream, and cider and calvados appear in many dishes. They add particularly to the flavour of pork, ham and soufflé. As in most of Normandy, there are splendid local cheeses, including one called Pavé Moyaux, named after a village. It is firm, spicy, in slabs with a yellow rind. Very nice.

The best calvados comes from this area. Bottles marked AC calvados Pays d'Auge are the best, with Apellation Réglementée calvados on the bottle indicating a lesser spirit. Age in the wood is marked with three stars (a year in the wood); vieux or réserve (two years); VO or vieille réserve (three years); VSOP (four years); extra, Napoléon or hors d'age (at least five years). I have seen hors d'age calvados claimed to be forty years

old selling for £60 a magnum.

The *trou normand* (swallowing a glass of 'calva' in the middle of a meal to aid digestion) is a great help with Pays d'Auge meals. You can ease the shock by pouring it over an apple or lemon sorbet; but straight liquor is quicker!

Hotels and Restaurants

Trelly – take D971 Coutances S to Quettreville (10 km), left on D35, left again to Trelly, follow signboards to hotel; or 74 km from St Malo, 90 km Cherbourg (address 50660 Quettreville, Manche) –

Verte Campagne, (33) 47.65.33: see also page 88; delightful; off tracks; found for me years ago by Douglas Barrington of Lygon Arms, Broadway, doyen of British hotel-keepers; now member of Châteaux Hôtels Indépendants; menu 70F, 95F; rooms 102-214F. Shut Mondays; November 15 to December 15.

Hambye – see also page 89; 17 km SE Coutances by D7, left on D27, D58, 81 km St Malo, 80 km Cherbourg (address 50650 Manche) –

Auberge de l'Abbaye, (33) 61.42.19: really good restaurant, fine value; comfortable, good service; grills over wood fire; menu 60-140F; wines from 45F; rooms 65-85F; shut Mondays.

Restaurant de l'Abbaye, (33) 61.42.21: with bedrooms; simple, cheap, good; much food fresh from own farm; terrace overlooks river; no menu, but you can have a good meal with trout in real cream sauce for around 45F or lobster (advance order) or seafood platter. Charcoal grill. Rooms 50F. Always open.

Pontaubault – see also page 89; 7 km S Avranches N176, 41 km St Malo (address 50300 Avranches) –

Des 13 Assiettes, Le Val Saint Père, (33) 58.14.03: the thirteen plates are thirteen dishes traditionally served at banquets; good value; menu 40F.50-124F; housewine 24F; rooms 68-108F; weekends – room with shower, wc, one night, breakfast, two meals 183F. Shut November 15 to March 15; Wednesdays in low season.

Courtils – see also page 89; 9 km Mont St Michel, 36 km St Malo (address 50220 Manche) –

Manoir Roche-Torin, (33) 58.96.55: Relais du Silence; near St Michel coast; good pré-salé local lamb; meals around 100F; housewines 37F.50; rooms 130F, 200F, 235F; half-board room price plus 70F per person. Open April 1 to November 1.

Hédé – attractive area, see also page 89; 47 km S St Malo N137, 22 km N Rennes (address 35630 Ille et Vilaine) –

Vieux Moulin, (99) 45.45.70: attractive hostellerie; extremely good value; already popular with *Encore Travellers' France* readers, so book; menu 55-90F; try mouclade (mussels in creamy

sauce with saffron, white wine); housewine 30F; rooms 100-150F; half-board 160F each in room with bath, wc. Shut mid-December to January 31.

Lamballe – see also page 90; 51 km SW St Malo, over Rance dam, then D168, D768, 15 km N coast Brittany (address 22400 Côte du Nord) –

Manoir des Portes, La Poterie, (96) 31.13.62: Relais du Silence; member Châteaux Hôtels Independants; fishing, riding; very good regional cooking, especially fish; shellfish from own viviers; menu 70F; wines from 40F; rooms 200F; half-board (three nights) 200F each per night. Shut first two weeks May, mid-September to mid-October; Thursdays, Sunday evenings except July, August.

Tour d'Argent, 2 rue Dr Lavergne, (96) 31.01.37: genuine small-town Relais with some bedrooms in nice modern annexe (500 m); Relais Routiers with 'casserole' for good cooking; no frills; excellent value. Menu 40-95F; housewine 20F, Muscadet 30F; rooms 75-150F; half-board 120-150F each per night. Fishing. Shut part June, part October; Saturdays except July, August.

Quintin – see also page 90; 19 km SW St Brieuc, 86 km St Malo, 110 km Roscoff (address 22800 Côte du Nord) –

Commerce, 2 rue Rochonen, (96) 74.94.67: little stone country hotel, beams, pretty bedrooms; smiling service, Breton cooking; try stuffed praires (clam), fish in old-fashioned tasty sauces; coq au vin; potée bretonne; nice desserts; menu 49-144F; housewine 18F; rooms 77-143F; shut Sunday evenings, Monday lunch; early September, late December.

Moëlan – see also page 91; D116 10 km S Quimperlé, 8 km from S coast of Brittany, 177 km St Malo, 158 km Roscoff (address 29116 Finistère) –

Les Moulins du Duc, (98) 96.60.73: has been called a 'paradise of peace and hospitality'. Certainly a delight. Gorgeous grounds with lake. Japanese chef combines old sauces with Nouvelle Cuisine, some mysteries of the East and his own inventions. A big success. A Relais de Campagne 'de grand confort' of the Châteaux-Hôtels de France. You will love it; your bank manager may not. Menu 130F, 218F; housewine is Beaujolais 48F; rooms 240-390F; apartments 485-510F; half-board for two 555-825F. Open late April to October 31.

At **Hermitage**, 2 km S Quimperlé on D49, 10 km NE Moëlan (see above) (address 29130 Quimperlé) –

Manoir de Kerroch, (98) 96.12.97: old manor in nice grounds; heated pool; bedroom views to forest and country; 8 km from sea; 880 m riding stables; lovely spot; modern restaurant has old-style cooking; superb fresh fish and shellfish; creamy sauces; menu 55-145F; rooms 150-190F; half-board 173-193F each per night. Shut mid-December to

mid-January; February school holidays.

Balleroy – see also page 91; 16 km SW Bayeux, Cherbourg 98 km, 125 km Le Havre, 157 km St Malo (address 14490 Calvados) –

Hôtel des Biards, 1 pl. du Marché, (31) 21.60.05: remarkable value; 48F five-course menu has three choices on every course. Menu 32F.50, 48F, 80F; rooms 48-105F; half-board (min. three nights) 80-85F. Shut all January, February.

Clécy – see also page 92; beautiful spot (address 14570 Calvados) –

Moulin du Vey, (31) 69.71.08: really beautiful house, well furnished, in lovely surroundings with nice views to the river; my friends disappointed in 88F menu, so must pay 150F or 215F; nothing but praise for bedrooms, service and ambience. Rooms 165-220F; half-board 250F each per day.

Putanges-Pont-Ecrépin – see also page 92; 17 km S Falaise on D909, 146 km Le Havre (address 61210 Orne) –

Lion Verd, (33) 35.01.86: menu 35-85F; housewine 17F.50; rooms 44-122F; half-board (4 nights min.) 61-88F each per night.

Bagnoles de l'Orne – see also page 92; 45km S Falaise, 79 km S Caen, 187 km from Le Havre, 135 km St Malo; being a spa, has many hotels of all sorts; tourist office at railway station useful (open March 1 to September 30: (33) 37.96.22) –

La Bruyère, at St Michel-des-Andaines (2 km N on

D908), (33) 37.22.26: old-style
village inn; Logis; known for local
dish – tripe on skewer cooked over
open fire; veal normand. Menu
51.50-95F; housewine 26F; rooms
102-167F; half-board (min. three
nights) 130F. Shut Mondays in
winter.

Domfront – see also page 93; 19
km W Bagnoles, 115 km St Malo,
175 km Le Havre (address 61700
Orne) –

France, 7 rue Mont St Michel, (33)
38.51.44: traditional French
auberge; remarkably good value;
gardens, tennis, sauna, private
fishing; fine old Norman
farmhouse cooking; salmon, sole
normande, chicken in cider,
escalope normande, mutton stew
with vegetables (haricot de
mouton), andouillette; menu
40-78F; housewine 18F; rooms
74-174F; half-board (min. three
nights) 91-128F each per night;
weekends Friday dinner to
Sunday lunch) 330-410F each. Shut
November 2 to December 9.

Poste, 15 rue Maréchal-Foch, (33)
38.51.00: Relais gastronomique;
modern Logis, pleasant
atmosphere; efficient; pure
Norman cooking with some of my
favourites: cailles (quail)
normande, poulet Vallée d'Auge,
veal chop in cider; menu 50-150F;
housewine 33F; rooms 64-155F;
half-board 135-175F each per night.
Bargain breaks for walkers, six days
half-board, one day full board;
includes walking excursions, such
as car to Bagnoles, walk back (15
km), walk to farmhouses to try local
dishes; a gastronomic Norman

meal: 1000-1300F each.

Orbec – see also page 94; good
hideout, in Auge valley, rue
Grande delightful, 20 km SE
Lisieux, 93 km Le Havre (address
14290 Calvados) –

France, 152 rue Grande, (31)
32.74.02: 18th-century coaching
post-house, well run by young
patron-chef Georges Corbet; good
local products (trout, cheese,
chicken); menu 52-120F; wine 26F;
good local farm cider; rooms 77-
267F; shut mid-December to mid-
January.

Caneton, rue Grande, (31)
32.73.32: Michelin-starred famous
restaurant made from two 17th-
century wood-framed houses;
duck *is* served! Menu has gone
up to 175F but worth it; carte
around 250F; fine old Norman
cooking which I love – lots of
cream, cider, calvados. Try Josef
Ruaux's jambonette (ham sausage)
in cider vinegar. Charming dining
room, wood fire in winter. Shut
October, February; Monday
evenings, Tuesdays. Book – it gets
full.

Breteuil-sur-Iton – delightful
area between Risle valley and the
Ouche country, 25 km SW Evreux,
86 km Brotonne bridge over Seine,
96 km Tancarville bridge (address
27160 Eure) –

Mail, 175 rue Neuve-de-Bénécourt,
(32) 32.81.54: absolutely charming
18th-century Norman auberge;
nice garden, old-beamed rooms;
good reputation for cuisine; super
crayfish in cream, tournedos

perigourdine, peach soufflé; menu
96-159F; good wines if pricey
(60-300F); rooms 175-300F;
half-board for two 420F per night;
Relais du Silence.

7 Lively and family RESORTS

Among **Le Touquet's** smart seasonal shops, pricey boutiques, antiques and branches of Paris stores is a chaotic women's clothes shop near the promenade called Griffmode. Every girl under fifty knows that this is the place for a bargain. And so do I. Not for me, I assure you. I buy for my daughters.

It is chaos. Girls feel clothes, grab clothes, try on clothes, hump them through the crowds to ask the opinion of their friends and then badger incredibly hard-worked assistants to let them pay. The noise makes an aviary sound like a snooker hall during a championship match.

My problem is size. All right, so Louise takes size thirty-six, but which thirty-six? American, French, Hong Kong, Taiwan, British or Pakistani? So I spy a girl who looks exactly Louise's size and without actually hand-testing I ask her most politely if the top, skirt or whatever would fit her. The odd one will blush and look away as if I am trying to rent her for a 70F sweatshirt. But most join in with polite enthusiasm. One or two have simply stripped off their own sweaters and tried on the one of my choice. I suppose I shall get arrested one day, but it works. I mean, my daughters get the right size sweaters.

Not for nothing, you see, is Le Touquet still called 'Paris Plage'. And, like Paris, it is a different town to different people.

For children it is miles of sands, dunes to climb, mussels and cockles for collection in the estuary, gentle karting on the promenade, pedalling four-wheel 'bikes' around town, and riding horses in the forest.

The rather rich and fashionable still stay at the Westminster, gamble in the casino and pick Paris fashions, but not originals, in the expensive boutiques.

For sportsmen it means sailing at the club, show jumping at the very pleasant hippodrome, playing tennis whatever the weather on international championship outdoor courts or indoor courts with natural light, and playing golf on an international course.

To most women it means shopping, window shopping, a choice between fairly private sunbathing in the dunes or very public sunbathing below the long promenade, eating pleasantly in little restaurants and perhaps dancing at a choice of nightspots from teenage-orientated discos to sophisticated nightclubs.

I think that Le Touquet is much

underrated. It is not so rich and polished as Deauville, nor so highly organised and groomed as La Baule, but it has a wider appeal than either.

It has inevitably changed quite a lot since millionaires like Sir Bernard Docker, colourful boss of Daimler cars, Noël Coward, and theatrical stars from Paris owned the pleasant and pricey villas in the delightful forest. Before they flew off in jets to the Caribbean, the Bright Young Things, sons and daughters of the rich, besported themselves in Le Touquet. In those days, fashion stayed in the forest and the Plage was for bourgeois Parisians. Now the twain have met.

Parisian and Belgian industrialists, stockbrokers and lawyers have taken over most of the forest villas, although their names recall their past ownership – Byways, Lone Pine, Anchorage. Whilst along the seafront, villas and little hotels which had become seedy and forlorn have been replaced by small blocks of flats which add nothing architecturally but have brought new life to Le Touquet, especially at weekends when families of Parisians arrive by car on Friday nights, disgorge caseloads of household equipment into the apartments, and almost immediately start to fill the shops, streets, cafés and restaurants.

It is not the discos, night clubs or restaurants which make Le Touquet so pleasantly lively; it is the people you are likely to meet. And, thank goodness, even Flavio's Michelin-starred restaurant is no longer a sort of British ex-patriates' club, with upper-middle-class Britons hailing one another loudly in 1930s pseudo-Oxford accents. Its new French customers are more 'serieux' about the excellent but very expensive meals.

One of the joys of Le Touquet is Serge Perard's fish shop in rue de Metz, where mountains of fresh oysters, mussels, shrimps, prawns and clams flatten before your eyes as eager customers buy them. It's a take-away, too, for beautifully cooked fish dishes, including a fish soup renowned all over France. Also a fish restaurant; Sunday lunchtime develops into a scene made for an Impressionist painter – or even a modern Breughel – as French families work their way happily and very noisily through huge bowls of fish soup and bouillabaisse du nord, lobsters in armoricaine sauce, sole and lotte (monkfish) in delicious sauces, langoustines and crayfish and yards of crisp fresh bread with litres of Blanc de Blancs, Muscadet or Anjou rosé, while waiters and waitresses literally run around to keep them supplied.

The fish is mostly landed over the Canche estuary at **Etaples**, a truly bustling little town with a chaotic main square which is fun. Shops are cheaper than in Le Touquet. The old Lion d'Argent inn, looking like a leftover from the First World War, when wounded tommies sent to recover in Etaples called it 'Eat apples', has improved enormously since young Christian and Francine Pierreuse took over. They haven't spoiled its atmosphere, and their meals are very good value.

Le Touquet stages a series of big events through much of the year –

sports championships, including horse racing and show jumping; exhibitions; concerts. Its golf course is excellent – so is the covered market. Although some of the pricier boutiques close for the winter, much remains open, especially on weekends.

Another golf centre which lures as many Britons as French is **Hardelot Plage**, 22 km to the north, which has also a magnificent beach, expensive villas and a forest with fine horse-rides.

Stella Plage, 7 km from Touquet, is a strange little family resort. Its outskirts have smart villas in tree-lined roads. Then the sand dunes come into town and it becomes a seasonal family beach resort. Its sand beach is huge. Many of its shops and cafés shut in winter.

I have almost too much experience of taking children to holiday resorts and I believe that one of the biggest fallacies among parents is that all children need is sun, sand and sea. Children of the TV age tire very quickly of the unproductive pastime of building sandcastles and knocking them down again. They think that adults are slightly demented to lie around sands getting hot, sticky and cooked. They like long sands for running, of course. But they like dunes for climbing, rock pools and rocks, harbours where fish are landed, action on go-karts or crazy golf. Stella Plage doesn't have all these – just dunes – but it is a short drive from Le Touquet and from **Bagatelle**. The latter is a big amusement park with a zoo at Merlimont on the D940, 6 km south. It has a great variety of attractions, including an old airliner for children to scramble around. It is open April to September, and Parisians drive 220 km each way to take their families there on weekends. Like all such amusement parks, the cost of trying various items can add up fast.

Stella Plage does have a commendable, rather nutty, hotel called Sables d'Or. I found it by mistake when all those I liked in Le Touquet were full. The stairs and corridor to our bedroom were a bit sandy from the dunes across the road. The bedroom was simple and the plumbing noisy. The dining room was fine, the service friendly and willing, and Yves Duquesnoy's cooking outstanding. Prices are most reasonable. Yves' cooking would go down very well in Le Touquet.

Deauville is more elegant, fashionable, snobbier and much pricier than Le Touquet, and I don't like it so much. But it is good, both in season, when the rich and famous are there for the Grand Prix horse race, and out of season, when some of the Top People's places are shut. Then no one with social aspirations would be seen dead there, and **Les Planches**, the boardwalk above the sands, may be empty except for a ravishing but shivering model having pictures taken in next year's swim suits. In fact few people buy expensive accommodation here nowadays to use it only six weeks of the year simply because fashion dictates. And those saviours of off-season tourism, conference delegates, come to redistribute their company's money liberally. We dropped in last November and had lunch in the open-air sunshine on Les Planches.

Yet from early July until the Grand Prix, Deauville particularly glitters. There are still balls and galas every night, the casino is full, branches of Paris' most expensive shops are open, and it is called the '21st Arrondissement of Paris'. But no longer is it empty the rest of the year. New apartment blocks have appeared among the ornate Second Empire and fin-de-siècle hotels and villas, there is a 'Port Grimaud'-type marina at the end of the promenade where boat owners can tie up outside their cottage doors.

The trick in Deauville in high season is to walk down Les Planches in dark glasses aping the nonchalance of Roger Moore or dignity of Loren and hope someone will wonder who you are. Then have your picture taken with a background of the brightly coloured beach tents to take home and impress the Joneses. Hundreds of others are doing the same, so why not you? Be seen in the Pompeian baths and the Soleil Bar trying not to look surprised when you see one of your heroes or heroines in the flesh, looking considerably older than in their pictures. Go to the races, hang around the yacht basin and drift around the casino tables with a preoccupied look, as if about to join the people losing fortunes at the table when the inspiration strikes you. Don't actually gamble, of course. Save your money for more certainly rewarding pastimes, like hiring a horse and galloping down the sands, or for a minor flutter at the races, where you can at least see your horse losing your money in style, and even see a fine spectacle if you never put your seat or your money on a horse.

Nothing is cheap in Deauville, though there are some less pricey hotels, like La Residence in avenue République, where a bedroom for two will cost about 100-200F. If you could get into Les Trois Canards, you are laughing. It is a Relais Routiers . . . in Deauville! But it has only six bedrooms, which I last saw ten years ago. It shuts Saturday and Sunday, and its meals cost 55F which is high for a Relais but a giveaway in this town.

If you have to spend 150-200F on a bedroom, I would stay 5 km inland at **Canapville**. Hostellerie de l'Aubergarde is a delightful old

Norman house in green country, with old beams, log fires, pleasant garden, and is known for its good Norman food.

Snobs look down on **Trouville**, across the river, as a middle-class Deauville. It is certainly cheaper. It has a fine sand beach, a fair night life, a casino and very large open-air swimming pool. And it, too, has Les Planches.

You see, Trouville came first. A fishing hamlet, it became a fashionable watering place when the man who owned Maxims in Paris built a casino there. But Trouville became greedy and put the casino rent up so high that the Maxims boss moved across the river to a village with a beach and one street. Fashionable Paris moved with him. That is called pricing yourself out of the market!

Just west of Deauville is **Houlgate**, a quiet but pleasant place with a huge beach and wide tree-lined avenues, which might suit families with very small children, and **Cabourg**, a largish, quite lively resort with a fine boulevard terraced over the huge beach of fine sand. A friend of mine once described Cabourg as having a quaint, toy-like look and I cannot put it more aptly. It was planned as a fashionable resort in the 1860s, with roads radiating in a half-circle from the beachside casino and Grand Hotel. Cabourg is for people who like their weekends to swing rather more gently. It is 'select'.

Marcel Proust wrote about Cabourg in his great work *A la Recherche du Temps Perdu* (*Memories of Times Past*) and called it 'Balbec' in the novel. The

Grand Hotel's restaurant is called Balbec and the boulevard above the sea is named after him. It was called Boulevard des Anglais in my youth. And at nearby Dives, a dreary spot now, the most famous coaching inn in Normandy, Hostellerie Guillaume le Conquérant, has become flats, boutiques and just a restaurant. Recherche du temps perdu . . .

The beaches of Calvados read like a 1944 war communiqué: Sword, Juno, Gold, Omaha, Utah. Here the British, Americans, Canadians and French landed on D-Day to invade Hitler's 'Fortress Europe'. Inevitably, each of the little seaside resorts along this coast was almost totally destroyed, and after the war the French had too many other rebuilding problems to plan their rebuilding imaginatively. The planning was geometric, so they are mostly rather dull places for sailors, beach loungers and sandcastle constructors and are not very photogenic.

Riva Bella is the most ambitious of these resorts, and **Ouistreham** alongside, once the port for Caen, 14 km along the river Orne, is now an international yachting centre. **Caen** has shops almost in the Parisian class, and many supermarkets. The old part of the town which survived the 1944 invasion is interesting and attractive.

Avenue Michel Cabieu which joins Ouistreham's port and town is named after a sergeant who drove out the English single-handed in 1762. Admiral Rodney had sent a raiding party ashore to burn the little port. They had taken two forts when Cabieu set out with musket and drum, firing one, beating the other and shouting orders to non-existent forces. The English left. Cabieu was promoted to General by Louis XV and given a pension. The Nazis could have used him in 1944.

Just down the river is Pegasus bridge over the river and a canal at **Bénouville**. The British knew that they must capture it if the D-Day invasion was to succeed. So at 11.45 p.m. on June 5, 1944, the night before D-Day, British airborne troops landed, took the bridge and town hall, and held them for twenty-four hours until the Highland Division, who landed on Sword beach that morning, arrived, complete with piper. The airborne boys sensibly set up HQ in the pub, which claims to have been the first house in France to be liberated and now has a restaurant. Here at Bénouville is Manoir de Hastings, the only two-star Michelin restaurant in North France, pricey and worth every centime.

Granville, at the south end of the Cotentin peninsula's Atlantic coast, is a survivor from the days of French fishing off the Newfoundland banks, back in the 16th century. Fishing died, but Granville became a fashionable family resort last century and has survived into the jet age with the help of commercial port traffic. You would not think of it as a family resort. Its quiet streets are steep, the beach at the bottom of granite cliffs is narrow. But children love it because of its busy port and its drawbridge leading to ramparts; a fifteen-minute walk along a cliff path takes you to an enormous beach at **Donville**, and Granville's beach has a wonderful bonus for children. The tide goes out at least a kilometre and leaves a lovely world of seaweed and rock pools with prawns, shrimps and tiny silvery lancons. Beyond are firm sands over which you can walk to these vast sands at Donville. At spring equinox, Granville's tide goes out 14 km.

For adults there are a casino and good seafood restaurants. From the port you can get a boat taking an hour to Chaussey Isles – fifty-two little isles, with another 365 uncovered at low tide. One, **La Grande Île**, is inhabited by 100 people who live by lobster fishing. A fort there, built in 1558, was turned into a house by Louis Renault, founder of the car company long since nationalised. I am not surprised that he built a fortress home in view of the tragic kidnapping of his son.

The coast road to Avranches, 33 km south, is a charming drive. Only 3½ km along is **St Pair**, a tiny family resort with miles of firm sand.

A string of little seaside resorts follow: **Jullouville**, rather exclusive, with fine sands and villas among pines, **Bouillon**, **Carolles-Plage**, **Carolles Bourg**, then **St Jean-le-Thomas**, the delightful little place mentioned earlier.

I have a soft spot for **Avranches**. Various people there who have not known me have helped me out of trouble, such as the café owner who, when I had forgotten that it was a national holiday and that all banks were closed, changed me a personal cheque for £50 though he had never seen me before in his life. Luckily I noticed before I reached the boat that he had given me £500 in francs by mistake and I went back to return it.

It is a nice, bustling little town, which luckily missed much destruction in 1944 because the Americans took it quickly before shellfire or the Nazis could totally destroy it, as they did St Lô and others. From here General 'Blood and Guts' Patton and his newly formed Third Army launched, on August 1, 1944, their first attack against the Nazis, which took them right across Europe. The Patton memorial here, in soil brought from the US, reads: 'Making the Avranches breakthrough in the roar of its tanks, while marching towards victory and the liberation of France, the glorious American Army of General Patton passed over this crossroads.'

The British and Commonwealth memorial at Bayeux is more succinct: 'We whom William conquered have freed the land of the Conqueror.' It is in Latin, so was probably written by a Wykehamist.

Dinard, reached from St Malo by a road on the tidal dam, across the estuary, is still one of my favourite places in France, although it is certainly not typically French, is not in beautiful scenery, does not have historic interest and is not a brilliant gastronomic centre. I plead guilty to nostalgia because it was one of the first

places in France I ever saw. That was true of decades of British boys. Dinard was their first view of 'abroad' and they stuttered their first words of French on the sands to French girls who already spoke much more English. Meanwhile Mother learned to like wine with meals and Dad discovered that although Pastis tasted like lung tonic, it had a more interesting effect. But I also like Dinard because it is beautifully kept, quite pretty, friendly and fun.

It was not French in the first place. The Americans colonised and developed it in the 1850s, then the British took over. Artists, writers, retired people, non-working 'gentlemen' with smallish incomes could live here cheaper and better than in the Home Counties, but they never became even slightly French.

Dinard grew into an international resort, rather fashionable and gay – in its original meaning – with a thriving casino and a winter as well as summer season. Then families moved in, until package air tours took them to Lloret and Torremolinos.

Now the Brittany Ferries sail to St Malo and the road bridge over the Rance dam, saving many miles' motoring, have given it a renewed popularity. Deserved, I believe. It is lively in season. It has pools and rocks as well as a huge sand beach, and beaches face three ways, which means that you can avoid the wind. The golf course is good, and there are lovely water and road trips up and down the Rance river. So it is still a very good place to introduce children to France.

Trébeurden, on Brittany's north coast, is another of my favourites and a good place to take older children but not the very young, for it has steep slopes to the beach and sea. It overlooks a bay littered with islands, and prevailing westerlies give good sailing even for the fairly inexperienced. There are several good beaches, two divided by a rocky peninsula, Le Caster, which is joined to the mainland by a thread of sand.

Beg Meil in south Brittany used to be a wonderfully quiet and lonely little hideout. That was before camp sites appeared throughout the area. Now, its pine-shaded, big sand beach lures hundreds each day in high season and fine weekends, and cars are a curse; parked among the trees and along the roads, they spoil the ambience. But the beach is quiet enough early morning and in the evenings, and most day-visitors do not seem to find the little port with its lobster boats. It is still a good place for families who don't want entertaining. And it still has one of my favourite Logis de France, Hôtel

Thalamot, where the cooking has actually improved over the years.

I have had enormous fun in **La Baule**. It is good for anyone between five and seventy-five. It is well scrubbed and painted, has 5 km of fine sand, backed by 1000 acres of maritime pines, and, as it faces south, it can get warm. Technically it is in Brittany, but likes to think of itself as a seaside extension of Paris and reminds me in atmosphere of Cannes, but a little cheaper. The atmosphere is chic, the scene colourful in summer. It has a well-known casino, some really expensive luxury hotels, is an international centre for show jumping, riding, yachting from the new marina, and it stages many festivals, but is a family resort as well.

There are many small hotels, smart villas and gardens, and plenty of night life. I found a night club in an old Sunderland flying boat parked ashore. Though La Baule is crowded in midsummer, there is still room on the vast sands. It is lively in spring and autumn.

It has those beach clubs where children are persuaded to do exercises and gymnastics under commands from sergeant-like PE instructors and believe that they are on holiday, not back at school, so that their parents, who pay for the privilege, can snore in peace or drink too many aperitifs before lunch. Most British children, I'm happy to say, sturdily revolt against this semi-military treatment on holiday.

Just across the river is the former fishing port of **La Pouliguen**, a delight when not overcrowded in midsummer. **Pornichet**, round the bay, is a little resort where Paris journalists used to meet last century. The real fishing port is **Le Croissic**, where boats bring in sardines and shellfish. Its quays are flanked by 17th-century houses and the scene is most animated in autumn and winter, when the prawn fishers arrive. You have to get up early to see the fish sold in the Poissonnerie. The main sales are from 3 a.m. to 7 a.m. A lesser sale takes place at 3 p.m.

Past Pornichet, on the coast road to St Nazaire, is a little resort called **St Marc**, which you might recognise even if you have never been there. Here M. Hulot had his holiday. It has not changed much, and the Hôtel de la Plage is still there. But it doesn't look the same without Jacques Tati.

Hotels and Restaurants

Hardelot Plage – see also page 00; golf (address 62152 Pas-de-Calais) –

Pré Catalan, (21) 32.70.03: pleasant hotel, nice flower gardens; book early – British golfers pack it except in July, August; menu 40-72F; housewine 25F; rooms 62-74F; full board 128F each per night. Bargain. Open April 1 to September 30.

Le Touquet – see also page 99; golf (address 62520 Pas-de-Calais) –

Côte d'Opale, 99 bd Dr J. Pouget, (21) 05.08.11: on the front; fine flowered terrace; smoothly run; very good food, traditional

cooking; priority given to diners-in; menu 88F to gastronomic 248F with wine; rooms 120-250F; open mid-March to mid-November.

Caddy, 130 rue de Metz, (21) 05.11.32: very useful; clean, efficient service, cheap by Le Touquet standards; open all year except January. Locals use restaurant; near market. Menu 55-70F; rooms 85-155F; restaurant shut Mondays except July, August.

Chaumière, rue St Jean, (21) 05.12.11: renovated; much improved, if dearer; small but useful; meals 50F to around 100F; restaurant shut Tuesdays in winter; rooms 125-150F.

Restaurant Pérard, 67 rue de Metz, (21) 05.13.33: see also page 100; fish only and only superb fish; menu 58-76F; wines 22-135F. No rooms.

Les Deux Moineaux, 12 rue St Jean, (21) 05.09.67: good choice, reliable bourgeoise cuisine; menu 80F; shut Tuesdays. No rooms.

Etaples – see also page 100; across Canche estuary from Le Touquet (address 62630 Pas-de-Calais) –

Lion d'Argent, pl. Gén.-de-Gaulle, (21) 94.60.99: Christian Pierreuse cooks well enough to make his menus a bargain. Try succulent crêpe stuffed with seafood, turbot Vallée d'Auge. Menu 38F.50, 52F.50, 87.F50; housewine 25F. Shut Tuesdays. Rooms 72-91F; weekends: one night dinner, bed and breakfast 230F for two.

Stella Plage – see also page 101 (address 62780 Pas-de-Calais) –

Sables d'Or, 1184 ave Concorde, (21) 94.75.22: meals are wonderful value; mussels, sole, both excellent; menu 47-146F; rooms 85-178F; half-board 119-178F each per night. Shut December, January.

Berck Plage – not my favourite but some families love it; 12 km S of Touquet; 12 km beach of fine sand; unsophisticated but lively; establishments for treating bone conditions, especially in children (address 62600 Pas-de-Calais) –

Auberge du Bois, 149 ave Quettier, (21) 09.03.43: menu 48-155F; plat du jour 25F; good value, useful; shut Wednesdays, off-season.

Trou Normand, 31 ave Francis-Tattegrain, (21) 09.12.13: modern; 100 m from beach; reliable cooking; reasonable prices; menu 52F, 70F, 125F; rooms 72-156F.

Deauville – see also page 102; check your bank account before going (address 14800 Calvados) –

Trois Canards, 11b rue Victor Hugo, (31) 88.30.68: book for this bargain Relais Routiers where locals eat; menu 50F, 55F. Six rooms 53-64F; shut Saturdays, Sundays, mid-December to early January.

Nid d'Eté, 121 ave République, (31) 88.36.67: recommended to me for value, reasonable meal prices, good cooking; menu 50-130F; rooms 120-280F.

At **Canapville**, 5 km S on N834 –

Hostellerie de l'Aubergarde, (31) 64.15.63: see also page 102; my very first choice around here; menu 52-135F; housewine 29F; shut November 15 to February 1.

At **Touquis**, 2 km Trouville–Deauville, just off N834 –

Aux Landiers, (31) 88.00.39: restaurant only; good value; menu 80F; carte around 150F. Shut Mondays, Tuesdays, Wednesdays off-season.

Ouistreham-Riva Bella – see also page 103 (address 14150 Calvados) –

Le Chalet, 74 ave de la Mer, (31) 97.13.06: good bed-and-breakfast hotel; April Chevron, patron's wife, is from Bristol; all rooms have bath, wc. Rooms 140F; shut November to Easter.

Normandie, 71 ave Michel Cabieu, (31) 97.19.57: one of four Logis de France here; 'casserole' for good regional Norman cooking; willing service; menu 47-160F; rooms 80F; shut November 1 to 20; March 1 to 15; Tuesday evenings, Wednesdays.

Granville – see also page 104; west coast of Cotentin peninsula; 104 km Cherbourg, 93 km St Malo (address 50400 Manche) –

Normandy-Chaumière, 20 rue Paul Poirier, (33) 50.01.71: much-respected British restaurateur told me that Jean Pierre Dugue is one of the most imaginative chefs he has found in Normandy – ideas without trying to be too clever with fruit, and vinegars. Certainly his menus are excellent value, especially if you like seafood and cheese; menu 60F, 78F, 125F; housewine 32F; rooms 65-120F; shut Wednesdays.

Dinard – see also page 105; 12 km St Malo (address 35800 Ille-et-Vilaine) –

Altaïr, 18 bd Féart, (99) 46.13.58: Patrick Lemenager's good cooking well known to Britons; in the kitchens since he was fourteen and follows a family tradition, known for his *feuilletage* – pastry made of paper-thin leaves – mussel and artichoke flan. Fine old Norman furnishings and fireplaces; 100 m from beach. Menu 46-154F; housewine 17F; rooms 80-167F; half-board: off-season 75-112F each per night; high season 83-143F. Shut mid-December to mid-January.

Des Dunes, 5 rue Clemenceau, (99) 45.13.58: opposite casino and beach; comfortable and pleasant meals; old favourite; some signs of pressure on last visit; good seafood; wood-fired grill; menu 66-106F; rooms 74-245F (family room); shut November, December, January, except Christmas and New Year; restaurant shut Mondays low season.

Roche-Corneille, rue Clemenceau, (99) 46.14.47: by beach and casino; pretty flower garden; comfortable rooms; excellent cooking with a touch of Nouvelle Cuisine (sole à l'orange, duck breasts in peach sauce, John Dory in fresh mint – I

hate mint with fish but Barbara loves it); menu 80-100F; rooms 100-265F; hotel shut mid-October to end March.

Trébeurden – see also page 106; north Brittany on Bay of Lannion, 9 km NW Lannion, 74 km Roscoff, 160 km St Malo (address 22560 Côte-du-Nord) –

Manoir de Lan-Kerellac, (96) 23.50.09: beautiful hotel, very beautifully furnished, lovely position; expensive rooms, but not surprising; menu 100F (lunch), 115F, 165F; wines from 65F; rooms 300-420F; half-board 300-360F each with menu à la carte; weekends: room, breakfast, lunch, gastronomic dinner 900F for two people. Shut October 15 to March 15.

Hôtel Ti Al Lannec, allée de Mezo Guen, (96) 23.57.26: my old favourite; manor on clifftop with grounds to sea (rough path for the fit); terrace and dining room with fine views of sea and islands. Relais du Silence, best products of local farms, markets and fishing boats; menu 100-170F; rooms (all with bath, wc) 160-260F; open March 15 to November 30.

Ker an Nod, rue Pors Terman, (96) 23.50.21: nice hotel by beach; superb fish and shellfish, light modern sauces; half-board preferred; menu 70-130F; rooms 95-190F; half-board 125-190F each per night. Open Easter to November.

Beg-Meil – see also page 106; 6 km S Fouesnant on south Brittany coast, 25 km S Quimper, 125 km Roscoff, 240 km St Malo (address 29170 Fouesnant) –

Thalamot, (98) 94.97.38: see text; delightful Logis, 30 m from beach; try rougets (red mullet) in cream sauce, sea trout; menu 58-128F; housewine 30F; rooms 91-162F; half-board seasonal prices 133-210F; open April 1 to October 15.

La Baule – see also page 106; most sports, land and sea, 'best beach in Europe', still fashionable; 205 km St Malo (address 44500 Loire-Atlantique). As in most big resorts, hotels prefer full board in high season, but ask. Hotel information from: Office de Tourisme, 8 pl. Victoire, (40) 24.34.44 –

Castel Marie Louise, 1 ave Andrieu, (40) 60.20.60: superb hotel, elegantly and superbly furnished; in a park with flowers, heated seawater pool, 24 clay tennis courts, some covered; also has a new 18-hole golf course; expensive, but no more than some international chain 'shoebox' hotels. Menu 130F; carte 200-250F; recognised to be one of France's very best hotel restaurants; chef Henri Reverdy, formerly with Alain Chapel, 'makes dishes as if composing music'. Even smokes his own salmon superbly, and he isn't even Scottish. Light touch and imagination added to traditional cooking; beautiful rooms 300-700F (apartments); half-board for two 660-1050F; golf or tennis breaks (min. three days) full board 380F each per day. Shut February.

La Palmeraie, 7 allée des Cormorans, (40) 60.24.41: amid flowers and palms, 100 m from beach; rooms renovated, all with wc, bath or shower; charming, quiet, prizewinning hotel. Menu 72F; housewine 25F; rooms 175-185F; half-board (low season only) 163-183F each; full board 182-219F good value. Open April 1 to September 30.

L'Espadon, 6th floor, Residence du Golfe, Plage Benoit, (40) 60.05.63: magnificent position high above beach, superb views; restaurant with a few apartments; Daniel Cova is a fine young chef with a delicate touch; prices reasonable for food and position. Menu 72F (weekdays), 125F, 225F; try cassolette de belons aux épinards (oysters with spinach) and superb fricassé of lobster – or just shoulder of lamb with thyme; wine, gros plant, 46F; apartments 220F (low season) to 680F. Shut November, December, January.

8 Luxury hotels and Gourmet meals

Christian Germain's Château de Montreuil hotel, beside the top ramparts at **Montreuil sur Mer**, and Roland Gauthier's Auberge de la Grenouillère, below the ramparts at **La Madelaine-sous-Montreuil**, 3 km down the road, have one thing in common – they serve such good meals that I would travel from England just to eat at either of them.

Christian and his English wife Lindsay came in 1982 from the Waterside Inn at Bray in Berkshire, a restaurant owned by the Roux brothers, who also have Britain's only three-star Michelin restaurant, the Gavroche. Roland Gauthier came several years ago from just 3 km up the road. He was chef at Château de Montreuil. After he left the Château hotel it became run down. It has already run up again under Christian's control and deserves at least one of its Michelin stars back.

It is not an old château; it was built at the beginning of this century. But it is delightful, elegant, beautifully groomed and has a fine garden, and Lindsay has worked wonders refurnishing and decorating the bedrooms, leaving a few old touches like plaster parrots around a door. Christian has gutted, redesigned and re-equipped the kitchens.

He is the one chef I have met who has really been able to take some of the best of Nouvelle Cuisine and blend it into classical cooking. His magret de canard, a dish which makes me say, 'Oh dear – raw duck breasts again!' in fanatical Nouvelle Cuisine restaurants, has converted me to this dish. But he comes from this part of France, and is certainly not afraid to use butter, cream, cider and lots of wine. I know just how much he does use in some dishes, and how much butter goes into his superb, rich breakfast croissants. But this is another story, to be saved for another chapter. His own favourite is loup de mer en croute – stuffed sea-bass baked in a flaky crust. Christian Germain is one of the best young chefs in France. With the ramparts and narrow streets of Montreuil to explore, lovely lush valleys of the Course, Canche and Autine, and happy Le Touquet 13 km away, Château de Montreuil is one of my top choices for a short holiday. Not cheap, of course – you can't buy a cheap Rolls-Royce – but it is good value.

La Grenouillère – the Froggery – is in a narrow lane beside the river Canche: a simple old white farmhouse converted into an auberge many years ago. I have forgotten how many years it is since I first went there to taste the Flemish cooking of the lady owner of those days: heavy, satisfying meals with large portions and magnificent vegetables. I have never thought much of cuisses de grenouilles, frogs' legs. They usually feel like superannuated rabbit and taste only of garlic, herbs and butter of their sauce. But they were very good at the Froggery. Now, Roland Gauthier's are even better, and not even spoiled by the old wall-paintings of two frogs dining, overindulging and finally bursting – a shocking warning to obese gluttons like myself.

Trout from the Canche passing by the terrace are fresh and succulent, crayfish are as good, vegetables very good, upside-down apple pie, tarte tatin, is highly praised and Roland's marquise au chocolat (a sort of heavenly chocolate sponge with cream and fruit) is praised even higher, though I doubt if it could be better than Christian's. His wine list includes 1914 Burgundy, 1920 Bordeaux, and 50F wines people like me can afford.

There are just two rooms for two people and one family room for four.

Château de Montreuil is one of the Relais et Châteaux Hôtels. Most of these are in historic manor houses or châteaux and they really are very good. But there are only two north of the Seine, a few in the rest of Normandy. Brittany is better off. There is a newer organisation called Châteaux Hôtels Indépendants et Hostelleries d'Atmosphère. Many more of these are spread over the whole area we are covering and they too are in fine old buildings. Then there are Relais du Silence, which can be in anything from a castle to a superb old inn. They promise 'calme, tranquillité, repos'.

They are all dearer than the usual family-run Logis de France, but if you can treat yourself to a few days in one of them, you will always remember it. Not just the food and décor but the whole atmosphere is different from a normal hotel. Prices are still reasonable compared with those in other countries or in big cities, if you keep away from the French midsummer madness of sixteen million families taking to the road at once. Château de Montreuil, for instance, offers off-season *forfait* (package deal) weekends of two nights bed and breakfast and two dinners for two people for 1200F – just over £50 for each of you. Not bad for château living and gourmet food.

Even if travelling from the south or across France, we like to leave enough money and time for a really good last supper or lunch, and we would rather stint on other meals or other things than miss one gastronomic meal. I like to *start* my trips with a good meal, too. I like to take a deep breath and savour the smells of France – pastis, wine, freshly baked bread and cooking. Petrol and diesel smells will never overcome them.

If you are coming across from Strasbourg, or especially from

Belgium, there is a useful stopping place well known in the First and Second World Wars called **Mont Cassell**. It stands on a hill surveying the Flanders plain, 29 km from Dunkirk and 49 km from Calais. It was the French commander-in-chief's HQ in 1914-15 and in 1940 was defended step by step through the streets against a division of Nazi tanks by the British retreating to Dunkirk. Two thousand British were killed there. It has an enormous market square where you will find a splendid Relais Gastronomique, Le Sauvage, in an old house. In summer you eat in a dining room with panoramic views, in winter in a rustic-style Flemish dining room with open fires. Patron-chef Walter Decaester believes in Flemish regional dishes, in fresh ingredients from the market, and

bakes his own bread – a rarity these days. Try his excellent soupe de tourteaux au genièvre et cidre (crab soup-stew in Geneva gin and cider). He has 600 wines on his list.

If you are driving north of Paris near Beauvais, towards Rouen, make for **Gisors**, with its 11th-century castle and 12th-century church. 5 km north at **Bazincourt** on the Epte river is Château de la Rapée, another Relais du Silence, in a house which looks as if the architect was in two minds about Norman feudal with turrets or Gothic. It is called 'Anglo-Norman' style. The relais is charmingly furnished, mostly with old Norman pieces, and the Bergeron family's love of Norman folklore extends to many of the dishes, which include Rouen duckling, river eels (anguilles) in dry cider, and delicious douillon (local pears in pastry). There is a big sun lounge with country views, and bedrooms are pleasantly comfortable and spacious.

Southward on the Seine, 9 km from Mantes at **Rollebois**, is an hotel in a 'folly' château built for Leopold II of Belgium's house parties, with the most glorious river views. Château de la Corniche is a superb place to stay and a good place to eat. Even its heated swimming pool has views over the river. And it has the added bonus for me of Giverney, 12 km away, where the Impressionist Claude Monet lived and created his lovely water garden. Remember his painting of the lilies? The new young chef, Philippe Prévost, cooks some unusual dishes, like salmon trout with fresh figs. He has a big future.

When my go-anywhere, do-anything Rover was at last having a full service, I borrowed a turbo BMW 635 coupé, a deceptively staid-looking car with a top speed of 142 mph and a computer to tell me anything except the weather forecast.

Horses for courses, I thought, so planned to take this swift aristocrat for a swift run round some aristocratic châteaux hotels. We crossed to France after lunch, so broke our rule about wandering gently, and hurried down the coast to an hotel at **Eu** recommended by friends, Pavillon Joinville, a Relais du Silence.

Eu is a drowsy town, known for a vast castle beloved by King Louis Philippe and Queen Victoria and a collegiate church dedicated to the Virgin and a 12th-century saint called Laurence O'Toole, who was slightly Irish! The Pavillon, a fine old manor house used by Louis Philippe's son, the Duke of Joinville, as a hunting lodge, stands among farmland high above traffic on the road to Le Tréport, the fishing port and resort for Parisians.

At 7.30 p.m. we got a lovely old room with bathroom and breakfast foyer, and we cracked a bottle of Muscadet in the old lounge bar to congratulate ourselves for falling on our feet again.

Came 8.45 p.m. and the 'calm, tranquillity and repose' were complete. No one was moving except the girl behind the bar. No sign of activity from kitchen or dining room.

Were we the only guests? we asked. No, the hotel was full. The others were out. Then when was dinner served? She was aghast. Had no one told us? Dinner was *sur commande.*

We had not lunched. Around 9 p.m. the owner M. Eloy came back from a meeting. Full of smiles and sympathy, he rustled up a 'small supper' – superb home-made vegetable soup, his own delicious chicken pâté, a large omelette with mixed salad, local cheeses and crisp bread. Another bottle of Muscadet, a bottle of his pleasant red housewine, and two smooth old calvados and we were off to bed. The others, it seems, came back at midnight. Behind our thick oak door, we did not hear them mount the old manor-house stairs.

We woke to the sound of horses going from the stable into the meadow beyond the terrace and the garden. After breakfast M. Eloy showed us his new restaurant being made from stables alongside the swimming pool. It will be open from spring 1984. But it had shown us how necessary it is to read guidebooks carefully.

To stay at Pavillon Joinville, at the time of writing, costs 230-300F for bed and breakfast *for two people*. For such a delightful touch of old France, with atmosphere and friendliness, £10 to £13 each is certainly not excessive. We have paid that for some very mediocre hotels in other countries.

We have known Hostellerie les Champs at Gacé, on the N138 north of Alençon, for years. It is just undergoing a complete redecoration and alterations, including a new dining room, and is shut until March 1, 1984, because Christian Tironneau thinks that guests should not be messed around by painters and decorators. It is set back from the main road, in a nice park-like garden, has a swimming pool and fine old furniture. It has always had a friendly atmosphere and good cooking, with prices low for a Châteaux Hôtels Indépendants member, so I should guess that it is going to be a very good place to stay.

Bayeux is one of the best little towns in Normandy and the Lion d'Or one of my very favourite hotel-restaurants. Bayeux is lively, sometimes too crowded in the tourist season, and the traffic can be chaotic because of narrow streets and stupid drivers. Yet, because of the little shops, bars and hotels, it stays entirely Norman French.

The tourists come to see the tapestry and the cathedral, but I think Bayeux worth a few days even without them. And we had to go without the tapestry last year. It was away being cleaned.

It shows, of course, the story of the argument between Harold and William about the English crown, and William's successful invasion of England in 1066. It was commissioned by the warlike Bishop of Bayeux and Count of Kent, Odon of Conteville, from the famous Saxon embroiderers in England. There are fifty-six scenes and you can tell the English by their moustaches, the Normans by their shaven necks. The tapestry is 70 m (231 ft) long, 50 cm (19½ in) deep. It has been ill-treated many times. Napoleon took it to Paris to persuade others how easy it would be to invade England. It is in a former bishop's palace, with a plaque at the gate paying tribute to the Northumberlands, who freed Bayeux in 1944. In the 18th century a story was spread that the tapestry was woven by William's wife Mathilde. In France it is still called 'the Queen's tapestry'.

Bayeux cathedral, in Norman Gothic, has bits from several centuries from 1077 to the 1800s. I love the interior, with its funny grotesque carvings on arches between the columns, impressive tall windows and 13th-century vaulting, and a superb romanesque nave.

The Lion d'Or is an old coaching inn and a Relais du Silence. It is set right back from the road and traffic in a big courtyard and really is

quiet. It is magnificently run, furnished in fine old wood like an old Norman inn should be, has splendid service and wonderful food. The 67F menu is a bargain, the 150F menu is a joy. I could do without the Scottish plaid in the warm and cosy bar. But patron Edouard Jouvin-Bessière has a right to be proud of his gem of a hotel. No wonder the British war correspondents chose it as their HQ after the Normandy invasion.

There are several châteaux and manor houses south of Bayeux in the Calvados which have become hotels. They are mostly hidden away from the world among tiny lanes and those which I have seen still need some shaking down. But they have great potential.

One which has made it to the Relais et Châteaux accolade is Château d'Audrieu. It has an interesting history. It is gorgeous – a white house with grey roof round three sides of a carriage courtyard, a monument to the elegance of Louis XV's France. I have seen it, but not yet stayed. But I have reports of professionals who have stayed in almost as many châteaux hotels as we have. Its main rooms and most of its bedrooms are superbly furnished. The cuisine is praised, the service efficient. But two friends think that the bedrooms in particular are over-priced *by French standards*.

The present château was built in the early 1700s, but the lands belonged originally to the first Lord of Percy. He was William the Conqueror's chef, and is said to have felled Saxons at the Battle of Hastings with his colander spoon, for which William made him a baron. (I am surprised that he was not called 'Baron de Boeuf'.) He prospered in England and founded what was later to become one of the most powerful families in Britain, the Percys, Dukes of Northumberland.

Now for the great eating house of Normandy. Manoir d'Hastings at **Bénouville**, near the Pegasus bridge, really deserves its two Michelin stars. We don't always agree with Michelin, but here we certainly do. You will get superbly cooked, imaginative dishes, well displayed, immaculately served amid beautiful furniture in a charming stone priory of the 17th century, set in gardens and greenery. The ordinary menu at 110F is splendid value. The 270F gastronomic meal is a true feast. The 255F *dégustation* meal, with seven courses chosen by chef-patron Claude Scaviner according to what is fresh and best in the markets, is a great experience. It would be useless to try to describe his dishes; you must taste them. But they are all superb, even the simplest – ham in cider, cold tomato soup with basil, and lobster from the nearby coast cooked in dry cider, Norman tart with apples and almonds. He has some lovely starters, like breasts of chicken, duck and pigeon on a bed of shredded carrot, lettuce and cucumber. His mussel soup made with a lobster stock is delightful. His housewine is a Brouilly (a superior Beaujolais) at 65F. Alas, he has no bedrooms – but I would find one fairly near after one of his meals.

Our old favourite Château de la Salle at **Montpinchon**, 13 km south-west of Coutances on the Cotentin peninsula, has brought many letters from delighted readers of *Travellers' France*. It is an excellent choice for a short holiday right in the country, or an overnight with a really good meal before the Cherbourg boat. An L-shaped old manor where the Bishops of Coutances used to live, it has pretty gardens with a lovely beech wood behind and walks down to the little river Soulle. Its furnishings are a pleasure to be with, though bedroom sizes do vary, so it is worth asking for a bigger one for your 320F or more. The cooking is very good indeed and presentation imaginative. I love the duck in Chinon red wine. Duck is not a delicate fowl and should not be treated with delicate sauces. The patisseries are excellent. No choosing from a trolley. You get small portions of five different and excellent confections, dotted with the fruit in season, such as strawberries or raspberries.

Brittany is particularly well off for hotels made from fine old houses or châteaux, and I have mentioned some in other chapters, such as Manoir des Portes at Lamballe and Moulins des Ducs at Moëlan.

Louis XIII appreciated the cooking of the famous Breton chef Vanat at what is therefore called Le Relais du Roy in **Guingamp**, a convenient centre for the beaches of north Brittany. (Louis also appreciated some of the local duchesses.) It is a fine old building with Renaissance doorway, furnished with taste and comfort, and with good service. The meals are good value. The current chef is called Vattan: a near miss.

For anyone coming up from south-west France to St Malo or Cherbourg or wanting to explore the historic, interesting but crowded city of Rennes, **Questembert** is a good place to stop. It has fine old houses, an old covered market and a history which the French tend to ignore, as they do most battles which went against them, but the Bretons take pride in. Here, when the Normans invaded in 888AD, Alain-le-Grand (splendid name) defeated them and united Brittany.

Here, too, is a Relais and Châteaux hotel called Hôtel de Bretagne, with great comfort, pleasant and slightly eccentric furnishings, and a brilliant chef-patron, Georges Paineau. His drooping moustache makes him look like a Hollywood caricature of a French policeman, but his passion for cooking is intense. His wife is a smiling lady. His dishes follow the seasons and the market. That is the best way to cook. Not cheap, of course, but not very dear and excellent value.

Another further north is Château de Coatguelen, at **Pléhédel**, 8 km from Paimpol, not far from the resort of Perros Guirec. It is an 1850 turreted château in a lovely park with its own nine-hole golf course, riding stables, forest walks and rides, fishing lake, swimming pool and tennis. Except in July and August or midwinter when it is shut, the hotel offers five-day golf and riding holidays, and also cookery courses. There are gastronomic weekends of two nights' bed and breakfast and two gastronomic meals with wine, for 800F.

This is certainly a good place to eat. The chef, Louis Le Roy, was known as Le Roi Louis (King Louis) at La Porte de France at Lannion. He has some superb dishes, especially duckling roast in honey and vinegar – a sort of sweet-and-sour duck – and salmon in chives with red mullet in red peppers and cream sauce. Most French, especially Parisians, do underestimate Breton cooking.

In south Brittany, Château de

Locguénolé at **Hennebont**, by the Blavet river, is really luxurious, with genuine antique furniture and superb grand siècle tapestries (a weakness of mine). It is in a delightful park of lawns and woodland going down to the river, has lovely river views and a swimming pool. There is good fishing, beaches 9 km away and a disco-cabaret 1 km down the road. There are also charming luxury bedrooms in a fine old cottage two minutes away.

As well as classic dishes, chef Michel Gaudin offers some unusual creations, like a cold lobster soup served with a fondu of mixed vegetables and ravioli stuffed with torteau (large crab) flavoured slightly with curry. Delicious. I liked, too, the fried langoustine tails served with diced fresh tomato.

Belle Ile, 15 km off Quiberon on the south Brittany coast, is a strangely lush rock, growing wheat and fine trees. It was fortified for centuries against the English who took it twice. In the 18th century many French Canadians settled here, refusing to stay in Canada under British rule.

It has a modern 'castle': Castel Clara, which looks like a handsome hospital, but is a luxurious hotel, with heated swimming pool and tennis courts. It is in a lovely position, with wild, natural grounds to the sea, and its spacious bedrooms have balconies with sea views. The young chef, Yves Perou, who came from Moulins des Ducs at Moëlan (see Chapter 6), cooks fish traditionally and well. Rooms are pricey, meals better value.

One of my favourite luxury hotels in France, in one of my favourite areas of Brittany, **La Forêt Fouesnant**, is the Manoir du Stang, in a 400-year-old manor house with defence turrets. It was one of the first great old houses or castles in France to become an hotel. I shall never forget going there not long after the war, when most Continental hotels were still recovering and luxury was found mostly on the Côte d'Azur and in Paris. The effect on me of this peaceful old house hidden down a private drive in a valley, with its two big fishing lakes, delightful formal old-French gardens, beautifully tended grounds and kitchen garden, and woodlands down to the shore, was quite overpowering. The furnishings, too, were a joy.

It is even better now, and must be a near-perfect place to hide right away in utter comfort. For such pleasures, it is not dear, either. It offers demi-pension only, and they really like you to stay three nights. No hardship. Yet you can eat without staying. The sole soufflé au homard is absolutely delicious.

When I was travel consultant to the *Wish You Were Here* TV programme, I asked if we could film it from the terrace at aperitif time, before lunch.

The staff member I spoke to was sympathetic.

'We shall start aperitifs at ten o'clock, sir, and we shall ask as special guests a few couples whom we know well. After all, we should not like to show on television ladies and gentlemen sitting together here if it might embarrass them in any way.' Funny he should mention it. A little later I saw a very well known English lady with a young man who was neither her husband nor her son.

I pretended that I thought she was French.

Alas, the Manoir is open to the public only from May 1 to September 30. In off-season it is taken over for *seminaires*.

Hotels and Restaurants

Montreuil sur Mer – see also page 111; 38 km Boulogne, 72 km Calais (address 62170 Pas-de-Calais) –

Château de Montreuil, (21) 81.53.04: now one of our favourite hotels; see also Chapter 9 on its special deals; menu 95F, 150F; housewine 40F; rooms 250-600F; weekends (off-season) for two: two nights, two breakfasts, two dinners each 1200F; shut January, early February.

La Grenouillère, La Madelaine-sous-Montreuil (address 62170 Montreuil-sur-Mer), (21) 06.07.22: see also page 111; carte only around 200F; housewine 50F, others include 1920 Bordeaux, 1914 Burgundy; rooms 100F for two, 150F for four; shut February; Wednesdays low season.

Mont Cassel – see also page 113; 60 km NE Calais on D953, 74 km NE Boulogne (address 59670 Nord) –

Le Sauvage, Grand'Place, (28) 42.40.88: good for a last gastronomic meal; no rooms but will book you into another hotel; menu 94F, 169F, or try Walter Decaestecker's suggestions of the day; housewine 35F; 600 other wines; panoramic views over Flanders; shut Wednesdays, Sunday evenings.

Bazincourt-sur-Epte – near Gisors, 32 km SW Beauvais, 90 km Dieppe, 50 km Rouen, 138 km Le Havre, 143 km Boulogne (address 27140 Eure) –

Château de la Rapée, (32) 55.11.61: lovely big bedrooms; menu 102F, 123F; housewine 48F; rooms 200-320F; shut January 15 to March 1; Tuesday evenings, Wednesdays in winter.

Rolleboise – see also page 114; 3 km from A13 Paris–Rouen motorway, Rouen 70 km, Dieppe 131 km, Le Havre 158 km, Paris 69

km, Boulogne 249 km (address
78270 Bonnières sur Seine,
Yvelines) –

Château de la Corniche, (30)
93.21.24: see text; remarkable
views over Seine; try sea trout
normande, duck breast in pancake
(ficelle); menu 180F, 250F; wines
44-1000F a bottle; rooms 280-350F;
suite 650F; weekends: one night
bed, breakfast, one main meal
400-450f each. Shut January (three
weeks), March (one week); Sunday
evenings, Mondays in winter.

Between **Eu** and **Tréport**, 30 km N
Dieppe on coast, on D1995–

Pavillon Joinville, rte de Tréport
(address 76260 Eu, Seine-
Maritime), (35) 86.24.03: see text;
menu grill 70F; carte; rooms
(bathroom, wc) 210-300F;
swimming pool, tennis; always
open.

Gacé – 42 km SW Bernay on N138,
124 km Le Havre, 217 km St Malo
(address 61230 Orne) –

Hostellerie les Champs, (33)
35.51.45: in park, swimming pool;
set back from main road; menu
80F, 110F, 150F; also new well-
chosen carte; try soupe de poisson
dieppoise; rooms 82-192F; shut
January 15 to February 15.

Bayeux – see also page 115; 10 km
S of Arromanches (Normandy
landing beach), 92 km Cherbourg
(address 14400 Calvados) –

Lion d'Or, (31) 92.06.90: delicious
meals; imaginative Norman classic
cooking; menu 67F, 90F, 98F, 150F;
good cider 22F; big wine list;

rooms 130-200F; half-board
168-265F each per night; shut
December 20 to January 20.

Château du Molay, 4 km N Bayeux
on D5, rte d'Isigny, at Molay-Littry
(address 14330 Calvados), (31)
22.90.82: handsome house in fine
grounds with tennis, swimming
pool, snooker, sauna, big bar;
obviously aimed at Parisians and
those on small conferences; I have
not stayed; varying reports on
food, but a French girl told me that
her huge bedroom in pink from
carpet to ceiling made her feel
'deliciously like a highly paid
courtesan'. I wonder if she
behaved like it. Menu 100-145F;
housewine 60F (Chablis, claret);
rooms 250-460F; weekends (two
nights bed, breakfast, two main
meals 460F per person.

Audrieu – 17 km W Caen by N13,
D94, Le Havre 125 km, Cherbourg
103 km (address 14250 Tilly-sur-
Seules, Calvados) –

Château d'Audrieu, (31) 80.21.52:
menu 100-250F; chef's daily
suggestions well worth following;
housewine 40F, 150F others; rooms
358-576F; half-board (min. three
nights) 389-571F each per day. Shut
December 1 to February 15.

Caen – 120 km Cherbourg, 108 km Le Havre; interesting town, good shopping centre, but, as with Rouen, I prefer to stay outside and visit it; some old parts survived 1944 fighting; modern part pleasant; city of grass, trees and, alas, traffic. Good restaurant is:

Les Echevins, 36 rue Ecuyère (address 14300 Caen), (31) 86.37.44: charming restaurant in old part, near Abbaye aux Hommes; candles, music, woodfire, shiny silver, crystal – classical 'intimate' décor; brilliant chef Patrick Regnier, previously at Benoit in Paris, l'Oasis at Napoule and Tour d'Argent, pleases Nouvelle fans with modern dishes, and me and most others with lovely classic sauces rich in wine or spirits; I would give him a Michelin star of his own. Menu 95-137F; wines 66-400F. Shut mid-May to mid-June; Sundays, Monday lunch.

Bénouville – 10 km NE Caen near Ouistreham (address 14970 Calvados) –

Manoir d'Hastings, (31) 93.30.89: see also page 117; as good as everyone says it is; menu 110-270F; wines from 68F (Brouilly); no rooms; shut first two weeks February; Sunday evenings; Mondays low season.

Montpinchon – 13 km SW Coutances by D7, D27, Cotentin peninsula, 112 km St Malo, 88 km Cherbourg (address 50210 Cérisy-la-Salle, Manche) –

Château de la Salle, (33) 46.95.19: see text; excellent; menu 100-165F;

wines from 48F; rooms 320-375F; half-board 576F for two people per day. Shut November 1 to end of March.

Brittany

Guingamp – 28 km W St Brieuc, 28 km S Paimpol, 104 km St Malo (address 22200 Côte du Nord) –

Relais du Roy, 42 pl. du Centre, (96) 46.76.63: see text; menu 68F, 120F, 180F; wines from 50F; rooms 180-280F (some take three); half-board 550F for two per night.

Questembert – 22 km inland from coast at La Roche–Bernard by D174, on D775 between Vannes and Redon, about 180 km St Malo (address 56230 Morbihan) –

Bretagne, 11 rue St Michel, (97) 26.11.12: see also page 118; Georges Paineau is one of the great chefs of France, and the answer to those Frenchman who decry cooking in Brittany; menu 140-170F; rooms 295F. Shut Sunday evenings, Mondays.

Pléhédel – 8 km on D7 S of Paimpol near N coast, only 7 km from coast at Bréhec, 36 km St Brieuc on D7, D6, 111 km St Malo (address 22290 Lanvollon, Côte du Nord) –

Château de Coatguelen, (96) 22.31.24: see also page 118; golf, riding, tennis, fishing lake and rivers; wooded park; five days' full board holidays, cookery lessons 2250F; golf, half-board 1150F; riding, half-board 1350F (none July, August); superb cooking;

pâtisseries delicious; menu 120-250F; rooms 220-370F. Shut December, January, February.

Hennebont – rather close to the port of Lorient but hotel in lovely open-country position beside river Blavet, 197 km St Malo (address 56700 Morbihan) –

Château de Locguénolé, rte de Port Louis, (97) 76.29.04: see also page 119; mouthwatering dishes, you won't know which to choose; two-star Michelin cuisine in delightful, peaceful surroundings; rooms inevitably pricey, but *so* good. Menu 158-238F; wines from 49F; rooms, July 1 to September 15, 351-478F, apartments 575-710F; other months, 270-453F, apartments 486-561F; half-board 321-437F; weekends one night bed, breakfast, two main meals 1100F for two people. Shut November 15 to March 1.

Belle-Ile – see also page 119; isle off Quiberon in Morbihan on S coast, 45 minutes by boat, then 9 km across isle to hotel at Port Goulphar (nearest village called Bangor!), Quiberon about 210 km from St Malo (address 56360 Moribihan) –

Castel Clara, (97) 31.84.21: most comfortable; Relais et Châteaux hotel; tennis, pool, children's playroom; menu 100-160F; wines, Muscadet 53F; rooms 500F; half-board 400F each per night. Shut mid-October to mid-March.

La Forêt-Fouesnant – see also Chapter 4; lovely country, especially good for sailors, 18 km SE Quimper (address 29933 Finistère) –

Manoir du Stang, (98) 56.87.37: see page 119; truly delightful; menu 140F; half-board (min. three nights) 570-670F for two people per night; full board 650-750F for two people per night. Open May 1 to September 25; all year for groups.

9 Inclusive holidays

Long before I took a five-day cooking course in Dieppe, I was a brilliant French chef. We all are, aren't we? With *Larousse Gastronomique* open on the draining board and Robert Carrier astride the mincer, I could produce the best coq au vin in Kent, and by following Elizabeth David to the letter I could produce a blanquette de veau which surprised even my friends who spend a fortnight on the Côte d'Azur every year and therefore Know It All. My bordelaise sauce was notable for its alcoholic content and I had a reputation for the cooking of Normandy, because, in the tradition of my Kent farming grandfather, I sloshed cider over everything from pork chops to duck.

But even brilliance needs constant polishing, and when Sealink offered the public a five-day cooking holiday by one of Normandy's leading chefs, I was there.

It seemed odd in those days to pick a package for such a short trip, but I soon found that it not only saved trouble in booking ferries and hotels but saved money. Tour operators, and especially the ferry companies themselves, can get cheap ferry fares and negotiate cheaper hotel rates by buying in bulk. Since then, the choice of package holidays to North France and Brittany has grown every year, so that you can choose between anything from a single day shopping trip to Boulogne to a coach tour or a fortnight in a gîte – country self-catering accommodation in anything from a converted barn to part of a manor house. People who used to say, 'I have never been on a package, thank God', as if they were saying that they had never thrown a brick at a policeman, now book packages to châteaux hotels or expensive villas. We are not supposed to call them packages. The advertising boys prefer 'inclusive holidays'.

But back to the cooking stove. I had some high-flown idea that I might be let loose in an hotel kitchen. Ridiculous, of course. Imagine the chaos which fifteen amateur cooks could create while chefs were preparing hotel meals. The Hôtel du Rhin, where the courses were held, set up a miniature kitchen alongside its main one, and here our master chef Maurice Lecourt prepared and cooked all the meals while we watched through a glass screen. We could walk in and look at what he was doing, give the sauce an experimental whisk and ask him questions.

Our group certainly asked questions. Most were confident middle-aged ladies born with a spatula in their hands who seemed to have cooked all the dishes before – from the pâté de lapin to the poulet Vallée d'Auge. Some questioning sounded like cross-examination. I sat at the back, hiding the fact that I was picking up tips which seemingly I should have known already.

Monsieur Lecourt kept his patience. He did not drop a thing for three days, then he misfielded an egg. He raised an eyebrow and said quietly: 'Accident!' His knowledge produced nonchalance. If a sauce curdled, it could be fixed. If butter began to burn, it could be fixed. A tossed pancake folded like an envelope, so with a flick of the spatula it was straight and level again.

Everything was to hand, even parsley ready chopped, milk measured, salt in a bowl to take a pinch or a spoonful.

'There is no time to cook without a plan,' he said.

I wish Barbara had seen it. She might have been persuaded that flour hidden under a handbag and saucepans full of 5p-off coupons can handicap a cook.

Frying in butter, he added a tablespoon of corn oil to stop it burning, and when melting butter, added a tablespoon of cold water. If sauces curdled, he took them off heat, poured them into a cold saucepan and whisked until they came back to a smooth paste. He deliberately curdled mayonnaise, poured in a tablespoon of hot water and whisked it back to life.

Lumps in sauces or custards did not matter; he poured the liquid through a chinoise – a conical sieve.

He failed to teach me to toss a pancake. Mine are still in orbit around Dieppe harbour. He reassured me. He tossed pancakes only for show. Normally he used a spatula to turn them.

He taught us for two and a half hours a day and packed in an enormous number of dishes. We shopped and explored the rest of the time. We had a choice of hotels: the two-star Rhin and the three-star Windsor or l'Univers mentioned in Chapter 2. All are along the front with sea views.

The cookery packages are still on offer, at the same hotels, in spring and autumn. The French found that the English ladies know more about cooking than they thought, and there is now a choice of three standards, plus one combined with visits to beautiful gardens. M. Lecourt has retired and the new teacher is my old friend Jean Tilquin, the superb chef from Hôtel l'Univers. Sealink offer group holidays, Astra Holidays cater for individuals. Astra also have two-, three- and four-day holidays to l'Universe and the Windsor hotels where you study the cuisine more simply. You simply eat the meals.

Last year, I took another package cookery course, a more expensive one offered by Silk Cut Masterclass activity holidays on which you study anything from cooking or wine to windsurfing and waterskiing. The cookery course is at the Château de Montreuil and Christian Germain not only *does* let you into his kitchen but lets you give a helping hand, like making croissants, filleting fish, skimming the stockpot and boning a chicken. He allows in eight amateurs. It is enough.

My croissant came out straight. Christian accused me, of all people, of being mean with the Grand Marnier in the soufflé. And the alcoholic touch of other dishes in my cuisine is so well known that patriots have been known to raise a bowl of my soup and say: 'Gentlemen, the Queen!'; my coq au vin deserves an appellation controllée.

But let me reassure you. If you stay at this excellent hotel, you do *not* eat food cooked by amateurs. We appeared in the kitchen in the afternoons, when lunch was over and dinner had not been started. Mind you, I did get a straight croissant at breakfast, but Christian Germain is a joker. His own croissants are famous – so rich in butter that you need to have been jogging to manage more than one.

News when we arrived was ominous. The previous course had been loaded with knowledgeable English ladies, two of whom ran a restaurant which appeared in the *Good Food Guide*. It sounded like a repeat of Dieppe. Thankfully, my fellow cooks this time were young and near to my standard – strong in enthusiasm. Christian promised to keep it to our level.

We started with a stockpot: an enormous pot containing beef bones, a few carrots and leek, one bay leaf and a handful of salt. It would simmer for 12 hours, with the lid off. A quart of thick beef stock would remain – to set to a jelly. Would we please skim it when we passed?

Though he is not a Nouvelle Cuisine chef, Christian used some Nouvelle-style dishes, but it was mostly classical cooking, with plenty of cream and butter, as befits Normandy. He does believe in boiling everything right down in order to thicken sauces, avoiding flour where possible. Six litres of red wine was boiled down with some of that beef stock to make just one litre of wine sauce. It was *superb* wine sauce.

He showed us how to make some delicious dishes during the next four days – ramekins of chicken and goose liver, crème anglaise, a superb marquise of chocolate-flavoured sponge filled with fresh strawberries and Chantilly cream and rolled, tangy grapefruit sorbet, a delicious onion and cider soup, a real chicken suprême. My favourite was filleted sea bass, stuffed with chopped vegetable fennel, button mushrooms and onion in cream and Pernod, reformed and baked, then served with a creamy sauce with Pernod. I loved his apple pie. It was made by lining a pan completely with slices of hard butter, covering it completely with sugar, sticking cored, peeled and halved *eating* apples into the sugar, heating it very gently on top of the cooker until the sugar caramelised, then covering with shortcrust pastry and baking. Simple, but delicious.

But I gained most from the tricks

I learnt. These included boning a chicken without leaving flesh for the stock pot; burning onion halves on a hotplate to colour stock brown; taking a wishbone out of a chicken or turkey to make stuffing and carving easier; filleting raw fish without leaving any flesh behind; softening butter just sufficiently to paint it on to dishes with an ordinary household paintbrush.

He put greaseproof paper under dishes in the oven to make them cook slower, opened and slammed the over door on soufflés with no ill effects, kept stirring sauces for a good minute after taking them off heat because the hot saucepan was still cooking them. He sprinkled a little icing sugar over custard and crème pâtissière to stop skin forming when cooling. He used a rubber spatula not only to get sauces out of pans but to scrape them when washing up. Dozens more useful little things he taught us.

Our mornings and lunchtimes were free. We ate magnificent six-course gastronomic dinners. And Christian took us to Boulogne to taste wine and many cheeses of the great Philippe Olivier, who took us into his holy of holies, his new maturing-cellars.

It was a memorable and amusing week. Obviously, you must book way ahead since only eight people can go on each course.

I am surprised that there are not more activity and special-interest weekends in North France and Brittany. Perhaps most people go for the food and shopping.

There are some packaged golf holidays, notably at the Hôtel du Golf de la Bretesche at Missillac, inland from La Baule in Brittany. Though it is long since I was allowed to play golf, I love this hotel. It is made from the fortified farm and stables of the Château de la Bretesche in a most magnificent position in 120 hectares of woods beside a delightful lake. Its international golf course was laid out by a Briton for a French woman champion who used to own it. My friend Cliff Michelmore called it 'one of Europe's most pleasant golf courses'. Cliff has been around a few of them. There is some good riding, too. But it is the setting which I love. The hotel is divided by a moat from the lakeside château built in the 14th century – a fairytale castle with many pointed towers, battlements, ramparts and a huge swimming pool surrounded by grass banks, made by damming part of the lake. Built by the Barons of Roche Bernard, it was sold after the French Revolution to a butcher for £400. The Marquis de Montaigne bought it in 1847, restored it, and his descendants own it. Hotel bedrooms are comfortable, the food very palatable. There are also self-catering bungalows.

Argosy (AA Travel), P&O Autostay and Astra Holidays have one-week self-catering holidays; Brittany Ferries offer three and four nights in the hotel, half-board. They have similar golfing breaks at the Château de Coatguelen at Pléhédel (see also Chapter 8).

Brittany Ferries offer inclusive

breaks of two to five nights outside summer in a choice of eighteen châteaux or manor-house hotels, including several I have mentioned, such as La Salle at Montpinchon and Château d'Audrieu, also offered by Sealink Mini-breaks with a cheaper choice of the nearby Manoir du Chêne. This is a charming 18th-century manor in two and a half acres of park, under the same management as Audrieu but not quite so beautiful nor completely restored.

Inclusive holiday costs alter yearly with inflation and market changes, but this will give you an idea. For ferry costs of car and passengers, plus two nights' dinner, bed and breakfast in Manoir du Chêne, in 1983 Sealink charged £42 in winter and £62 in summer per person with four sharing a car, £50 and £73 with two sharing. That is a bargain.

Argosy also offer a range of châteaux-style hotels, and several companies, including Townsend Thoresen Ferries and Sealink, use Hostellerie du Vert Mesnil, hidden away behind the N43 at Tilques between Calais and St Omer. It is a 19th-century mock château, with tower, in pleasant grounds and was once a seminary for priests. A few years back, a brilliant young chef from Paris and his attractive wife started the hotel, and I was a customer in its first week. The meals were a delight, the atmosphere peaceful but not dull, and it was a perfect hideaway. They left and the new management has built a fine but much bigger dining room in a barn, and improved the bedrooms. Although the cooking is not quite so brilliant, it is good. But service is scrappy outside the restaurant possibly because it is a centre for small conferences, which can always put a heavy load on staff. Also, my last dinner was interrupted by three businessmen who laid out documents and accounts around the dishes on the next table and did a business deal. Not a great compliment to the chef nor polite to other diners. They were English.

Astra have a super six-day tour of four delightful château hotels, starting from Dieppe, returning from Cherbourg. They are Domaine de Villequier down by the Seine, Manoir du Chêne, Manoir des Portes at Lamballe (see Chapter 6) and Manoir du Stang (see Chapter 8).

Domaine de Villequier is run by my friend Maurice Lalonde, who ran the Marine at Caudebec nearby for so long and is one of the best hotel-keepers in northern France. It is an early 18th-century house in a fine park with views to the Seine, big bedrooms and excellent service, although hotel additions have not improved it architecturally. All M. Lalonde's great dishes have survived his move, including the jugged duck and delicious trout pâté, but prices are inevitably much higher.

To come down to earth, many Logis and family-run smaller hotels are offered on seven-day packages, but fewer for shorter periods. Hoverspeed, the hovercraft car-ferry company, have good new off-season short breaks in Le Touquet, Honfleur, Rouen,

Deauville, Boulogne and the Champagne. They are called 'Le Weekend'.

Vacances Franco Britanniques (VFB) of Cheltenham, specialists in finding self-catering country cottages all over France and the first to market French *gîtes* in Britain, offer a few hotels within easy range of the ports and are experts at picking them. I have tried several and have not found a bad one. However, I was not too happy when they discovered my favourite little Auberge de la Durdent at Héricourt (see Chapter 5). We were rather keeping that for ourselves. But that was several years ago and they have not driven us out yet, nor from the Lion d'Or at Bayeux (Chapter 8). But when I stayed last time at Hôtel St Pierre in Villedieu-les-Poëles (Chapter 10), I got the very last room before lunch, in March.

Lesser known of their choices is the Auberge de la Selune at Ducey, just south of Avranches where the Cherbourg peninsula ends. It was created only in 1982 from an old hospice, is immaculate, and Jean-Pierre Girres the young patron-chef is a very good cook indeed. His terrine and his crab pie are excellent. Another good overnight stop, as well.

Auberge St Christophe at Pont d'Ouilly, in the Suisse Normande, is known only to connoisseurs of this land of green hills, rivers and rocks. A Logis taken over recently by an enthusiastic young couple, it has a pretty garden with a path to the river Orne, it is friendly and a good place to find peace and country air. VFB's Brittany package hotels are all good. I like especially Ar Milin at Châteaubourg, east of Rennes, built around an old watermill over a racing river, with lakes in its grounds for fishing and boating.

Townsend Thoresen's bargain winter weekends include some good touring centres. They use the excellent Du Château Hôtel at

Combourg (see Chapter 3).
Inn Tent, the big camping
operators in France, have winter-
inn off-season breaks, weekend or
midweek breaks, which include
the pleasant hotel-restaurant
Carpe d'Or at Fontainebleau, south
of Paris, and a modern but very
French hotel, La Maye, in the forest
of Crécy near where the battle was
won by Edward III, the Black Prince
and especially the yeomen-archers
of England in 1346. Another good
overnight stop for economy. It has
a menu at 45F, rooms with shower
for 65F. The locals use it for its bar
and meals.

Astra's Jours en France have
three- and four-day breaks in
spring and autumn in Brittany and
Normandy, including the Cheval
Blanc in Honfleur and l'Aubergarde
at Canapville, 5 km inland from
Deauville.

For a while, short motor touring
package holidays were sold – three
or four nights with your hotels
booked ahead. They have almost
died out because people want
flexibility. But you can still get
package rates for motor touring.
Brittany Ferries, for instance, have
four or more nights' tours in which
they will book your first night if you
wish, then they give you a map of
hotels in the scheme and vouchers
for dinner, bed and breakfast at any
of them you choose. A great
number of the hotels are in Brittany
and lower Normandy. There are
also five-night budget tours of
Brittany.

Most hotels on this Brittany Ferries tour belong to the France
Accueil organisation, similar to

Logis de France. Twickenham
Travel do similar five or more
nights' tours using Hoverspeed,
Townsend or P&O Ferries and
include hotels at Dieppe and within
range of Paris, at Maintenon and
Chartres. P&O Ferries use France
Accueil for five-night tours or more
and divide the hotels into two
areas, Brittany and Normandy.

AA Argosy Driveaway voucher
scheme is similar, but they use
Inter-Hotel and Minimotel
organisations, with more hotels
around Le Havre area, fewer in
north Brittany.

If you want a rest from your car,
Townsend Thoresen have four- and
five-night coach holidays to
Normandy, Brittany and to Paris
and the Champagne. Bed and
breakfast only are booked, so you
can go out and find yourself a nice
restaurant or bistro for dinner.

Alternatively if you want to put
your own car in for a service,
French Leave arrange ferry crossing
to Calais, Dieppe or Cherbourg,
and car hire and insurance at cut
package rates according to number
of people sharing the car from two
to seven days.

Hotels and Restaurants

Hotels with inclusive offers not
mentioned elsewhere in the book:

La Bretesche at **Missillac** (address
44160 Loire-Atlantique); 25 km NE
La Baule by N774 to Guérande, D5,
(40) 88.30.05: golf hotel, rooms and
self-catering bungalows;

international golf course; menu 80-185F; try aubergines aux moules; rooms 260-290F; half-board 320-335F each; weekends (not high season) two nights bed, breakfast, two main meals each; 720F for two people. Shut February.

Le Vert Mesnil at **Tilques**; just off N43, 19 km Calais, 4 km St Omer, 44 km Boulogne (address 62500 St Omer), (21) 98.28.99: also good overnight stop; menu 70-130F; rooms 220F; half-board 200F each per night; weekends full board two nights 660F each. Shut Mondays; February 15 to March 15.

Manoir du Chêne at **Nonant**, Calvados; 5 km Bayeux by N13, D33, 20 km Caen, 10 km from sea (address 14400 Bayeux), (31) 92.58.81: menu 70-120F (shut Mondays off-season); rooms 135-230F. Shut December 15 to February 15.

La Maye, 13 rue St-Riquier, **Crécy-en-Ponthieu**; edge of Crécy forest, 20 km N Abbeville, 32 km Montreuil, 70 km Boulogne (address 80150 Somme), (22) 29.54.35: beside river; menu 42F, 90F; rooms 60-120F; another good stopover hotel; shut Mondays; February 15 to March 15.

Domaine de Villequier, at **Villequier**, (address 76490 Caudebec, Seine-Maritime), (35) 56.75.99: menu 120–200F; rooms 200-380F; also apartments. Lovely for luxury break.

Auberge de la Sélune, 2 rue Saint-Germain, **Ducey**; 11 km S Avranches at bottom end Cotentin peninsula, 143 km Cherbourg, 65 km St Malo – astride river Sélune (address 50220 Manche), (33) 48.53.62: really good cooking; very good choice, even on 38F menu; main course choice blanquette of veal, steak, pork chop or trout; 65F menu good value; 75F menu, six courses and salad, a bargain; rooms 135-146F. Shut Mondays low season, January 15 to February 15.

Auberge St Christophe, **Pont d'Ouilly**; 48 km S Caen in La Suisse Normande (address 14690 Calvados), (31) 69.81.23: peaceful, cosy; menu 64-140F; rooms 125-155F; shut Sunday evenings, Monday evenings.

Short break holidays vary according to the time of year and also according to how business is going. Bargains can be announced at short notice. Here are the names of operators mentioned in text and some who are not. Get on their mailing list for short breaks:

A A Argosy, PO Box 100,

Halesowen, West Midlands B63 3BT; 0332 862340.

Astra, 1 Albion House, Back Hill, London EC1; 01 833 0237. Jours en France and Dieppe cookery.

Billington Travel, 2a White Hart Parade, Riverhead, Sevenoaks, Kent; 0732 460666. 'Hotels of France' – good small choice of hotels in Normandy, also Le Touquet, Montreuil, Fontainebleau, mostly five-day minimum.

Brittany Ferries, Millbay Dock, Plymouth PL1 3EF; 0752 63388.

Car Holidays Abroad, Bull Plain, Hertford; 0992 59339. Tailor-made breaks, tours – very experienced.

French Travel Service, Francis House, Francis St, London SW1; 01 828 8131. Breaks by boat, rail; separate winter programme. Very reliable – owned by French Rail.

Hoverspeed, International Hoverport, Ramsgate, Kent CT12 5HS; 0843 55555 or 01 554 7061.

Inn Tent, 26 Bank St, Wetherby, West Yorks; 0937 61314. Send for their brochure.

Just Motoring, 13 Blackheath Village, London SE3; 01 318 0921.

Page and Moy, 136 London Road, Leicester; 0533 552521. Include cookery in Le Touquet and Dinard.

P&O Ferrytours, Arundel Towers, Portland Terrace, Southampton; 0703 331431.

Rofe Travel, 17 Princes Arcade, Jermyn St, London SW1; 01 734 1398.

Sealink Travel (Inclusive Tours) 162 Eversholt St, London NW1; 01 388 6843.

Silk Cut Masterclass Holidays, Russell Chambers, Covent Garden,

London WC2; 01 240 3233.
Montreuil cookery.

Supertravel, 22 Hans Place,
London SW1, 01 584 6523.

Time Off, 2a Chester Close,
London SW1; 01 235 8070.

Townsend Thoresen Holidays,
Enterprise House, Avebury Ave,
Tonbridge, Kent; 0732 366066.

Travelscene, 94 Baker St, London
W1; 01 486 6591.

Vacances Franco Britanniques
(VFB), 15 Rodney Rd, Cheltenham,
Gloucestershire; 0242 35515.

There are too many companies
offering short breaks in Paris to list
them.

Dining rooms mean more to me than bedrooms, and companions more than beds, so it is not surprising that my choices for first- and last-night stopovers within reasonable distance of Channel ports are mostly stronger on eating than sleeping.

I really do believe in last-night stopovers on the way north in France. They add an extra dimension to a holiday. And I have often enjoyed the last supper more than any meal on a long holiday.

Making for Calais, Boulogne or Dunkirk, the Moulin de Mombreux at **Lumbres** has been one of my favourites since Jean-Marc Gaudry slipped in from L'Oasis at Napoules (three-star Michelin) seventeen years ago, converted a pretty old watermill into a tiny hotel in a tiny industrial town in the Pas-de-Calais and offered gastronomic meals. It was a revelation, in such an unlikely spot, among a mixture of paper mill and cement works, agricultural market and a trout river called the Aa.

To begin with prices were so low. Now the Moulin is very well known, prices have risen, but the meals are still a revelation to anyone new to M. Gaudry's cuisine and are worth every franc you pay.

Menus cost 120F, 150F and 185F, and as there is little choice I do not recommend it to fussy Britons who want 'our-style' dishes rather than, for instance, sole with dry vermouth and cream sauce, noisettes of lamb in old port, and rich, thick, alcoholic French sauces. I like especially the nage de Saint Jacques et de langoustines – scallops and large prawns poached in a herby wine sauce – his chicken pot-au-feu, superb vegetables and excellent dessert trolley. There are no cheap housewines and prices are high, starting around 80F for fairly simple Bordeaux and 125F for a Sancerre. Bedrooms are all pretty, some dinky to a fault. I am told that some beds are short, but I wouldn't notice. The rooms are cheap.

I have known the de Troy family's Le Chantzy restaurant-hotel at **Arras** even longer, and have come to like Arras very much.

Arras was almost totally destroyed in the First World War and fell into decay in 1940 until about 1950. Now the great 16th- to 18th-century arcaded Flemish houses in red brick and stone have been restored to glory or rebuilt in both place des Héros and Grande Place, the coats of arms of craftsmen and merchants are restored in Grande Place, and the

market famous for centuries is as bustling, crowded and interesting as ever.

The Chantzy is bustling and famous, too. The cooking, mostly Flemish, would please almost any British palate except that of a slimmer. Portions are also Flemish. Robert de Troy and his son Jean are experts on Flemish cooking: chicken in beer, lovely Flemish leek flan; wild rabbit casseroled with leeks, splendid spitroasts, including local sausages flambé in Geneva gin, hochepot (beef, mutton, pork and vegetable stew), potée flamande (bacon, ham, sausage and potato hotpot), a

splendid choice of charcuterie, and gourguinoise (a northern French version of bouillabaisse). They also serve beautiful fresh fish. Both de Troys are excellent chefs and they also have a fine chef, Hervé Mit, working for them.

The wine cellar is magnificent. A long jigsaw of caves holds well over 100,000 bottles of 1000 different appellations, dating back to 1868. The de Troys won the Laureat Mondial for the world's best wine card in 1979. If you ask nicely and the family have time, they will take you round the cellars. I was going round once with Robert de Troy and we came to a basket full of very dusty old bottles which had lost their labels. He picked up three and later, towards the end of my meal, we had a blind label-less tasting. I remember still the very old Margaux. We both agreed it was Margaux.

There's a good 65F tourist menu as well as a 120F gastronomic menu for the fit and hungry. Rooms are reasonably priced.

Arras is a good place for a final meal. It has the only station buffet with a Michelin star. Called L'Ambassadeur, it specialises in regional dishes and has two menus, at 70F and 120F.

A remarkably cheap little auberge for a stopover, a hideout or for a good cheap meal is Relais de l'Amitié, just changed into an auberge from a bed-and-breakfast *chambres d'hôte*. It is at **Salperwick**, just off the N43 on the Calais side of St Omer, and is a pleasant old house in a garden, with simple, very adequate bedrooms. According to many friends who have tried it, its 50F menu is one of the best value in northern France. Starters may include soufflé, six escargots (snails) and choice of pâtés. Main course specialities are confit d'oie (preserved goose), entrecôte or steak au poivre, beef in mustard sauce, chicken or escalope of veal. Dessert is usually fruit tart or sorbet. This meal, plus bed and breakfast, costs 95F. There is fishing only 300 m away.

Another good place for a cheap last meal for a family and, if you are there on Saturday or Sunday nights, for a rave-up, is the Catherinette restaurant at **St-**

Michel-sur-Ternoise, 2 km past St Pol-sur-Ternoise just off the N39 towards Arras. Its menus at 31-78F are remarkable value. Its specialities include veal cutlet in roquefort cheese, Flemish leek tart, frogs' legs and honest steak. It has a children's playground, so is a good spot for a long family lunch, and its weekend club-disco takes 800 people on three *pistes de danse*. I am only warning you!

A cheap restaurant nearby, with middle-priced bedrooms and no disco, is a Logis, the Lion d'Or, in **St-Pol-sur-Ternoise**. Its 48F and 85F menus are good value, its 128F menu fairly formidable. Slimmers beware – it claims to be a gourmand's delight, and its specialities are local ham braised in two local beers and guinea fowl baked in honey.

Most of the hideouts I suggested in Chapters 5 and 6 are excellent for a first- or last-night stopover. Auberge du Cochon d'Or at **Beuzeville**, for instance, has pleasant modest rooms with showers and a restaurant used by local people, with a weekday menu at 45F.50, others up to 115F. They are excellent value. Its neighbour, run by the same family, Le Petit Castel, has more comfortable and dearer rooms with bath and wc, and you can use the Cochon d'Or restaurant. Beuzeville is a nice little town with a market and is strategically placed for Deauville (23 km), Pont Audemer (14 km) and Honfleur (15 km), and only 48 km from Le Havre. It is just the sort of place where I like to stay the last night, leaving time for a leisurely breakfast and final shopping next day. Also nicely placed for a short break.

At **Corneville sur Risle**, 6 km from Pont Audemer, is an odd-looking, fake-Gothic Logis called Les Cloches de Corneville, much pleasanter inside and with very enjoyable cooking.

Because of an operetta about it by Planquette, the little town was a national joke around 1900. The unfortunate Marquis de la Roche Thulon generously gave a carillon of twelve bells to the church, then could not pay for them. They were bought by the innkeeper, who put them in his inn instead of giving them to the church. You can see them in the Logis, and even hear them by paying a fee.

The favourite dish here is rabbit cooked in cider, but there are other very good dishes, especially starters, such as skinned little tomatoes in a cream sauce with herbs.

L'Aigle in the upper Risle valley is an industrial town but with many interesting old corners and a real old-style French coaching inn, the Dauphin, which looks from the outside as if it could be fitted into any old English market town. It is furnished with solid old-fashioned comfort – lots of rich-coloured wood and warm red décor. It belongs to the international Best Western hotels association, has three stars, old-style comfort, and well-furnished bedrooms at a wide range of prices. Its restaurant has a Michelin star, so it is surprising these days to find a good 77F menu and the dearest menu at 164F. Dishes à la carte are reasonably priced. Most of its special dishes

are ones most of us know: sole normande, duckling in an orange sauce (caneton à la bigarde), kidneys in a mustard sauce. There is a touch of Nouvelle in the cooking – not many of my favourite old creamy sauces and some dishes too undercooked for my taste (deep pink kidneys). My choice would be the lobster in port wine. The special Dauphin meal for gourmets costs 273F. It is foie gras, a lobster, wine and coffee. A nice light lunch or supper!

Coming from the Brotonne bridge over the Seine past Caudebec, to the market town of Yvetôt, there are two enjoyable off-track routes. One is along the D131 to Héricourt en Caux, mentioned in Chapter 5. The other starts on the not-overcrowded N29 to 7 km past Yerville and picks up the little D2 on the left through the Saâne valley. The pretty narrow road follows the river to **Auzouville sur Saâne**, which has two very good restaurants. Be careful when map-reading – there is another Auzouville (just off the N29 before Yerville).

Of the two restaurants, Auberge de l'Orée du Bois, a thatched house in a nice garden (actually just across the river at **Lestanville**), has gone up in the world. I went a little pale when I saw its new prices last time – menus at 120-150F. Perhaps the thatcher had sent prices through the roof! In fact, patron-chef Pascal Saunier has moved into the gastronomic, luxury class, and the meals are good value. His fish, especially his escalope de saumon aux pâtés fraîches, is delicious. The auberge

is so attractive that Michelin gives it three crossed forks for atmosphere and comfort.

Perhaps M. Saunier felt that a hamlet so small should not have two restaurants in the same price range. Mme Clamaron's black-and-white Norman inn, Au Bord de la Saâne, with beamed dining rooms, still looks like the old cottage it used to be. Oddly, it does not have a bar, but pretty Madame has not hesitated to serve me wine even at 10.30 a.m. and it is very much the 'local' for eating. The main menu costs 65F, and even the alsatian dog is very friendly. Madame can arrange for you to stay comfortably in a house down the road.

Many of the Brittany hideouts I mentioned, and pleasant places like the Château hotel at Combourg and the Bresche-Arthur at Dol-de-Bretagne, are excellent for a last meal or for a stopover to give you some hours to explore St Malo or Dinan before setting off to the boat or to motor south.

Driving from the south to St Malo or Roscoff, do try to see the magnificent story-book Rohan castle at Josselin, right on the river Oust, even if it means going slightly out of your way.

In 1351, a battle with the English was settled between thirty knights from Josselin castle and thirty from Ploëmel, mostly English, who fought a staged battle with sword, dagger, battle-axe and pike, on foot. The fight went on all day, and the Josselin team finally won. It seems a better way than killing or maiming thousands, but it did not stop the Hundred Years' War.

In the same century, a really tough character, Oliver de Clisson got the castle by marrying the widow of the great De Rohan family of Josselin, who still own it. He was called 'The Butcher' and his motto was 'I do as I please'. He fought for the English first, then for Charles V of France, who made him Constable and the most powerful man in the country. He was banished to Josselin when Charles went mad.

His butchery must have been hereditary. When he was seven, his father was beheaded for allegedly betraying France. His mother, Jeanne de Belville, showed him his father's bloody head nailed to the ramparts at Nantes and made him swear to avenge it. Then she led 400 men and put to the sword the garrisons of six castles who favoured the French. When royal troops forced her to flee, she put to sea and sank every French ship she met.

You can visit the castle every day from June 1 to mid-September and Wednesday and Sunday from mid-March to May 31.

Looking straight up to the castle across the river is the Hôtel du Château, and I would always try to stay a night except in July and August, when the crowds are around. It is in a nice position by the bridge and the dining room and many bedrooms have castle views. It is friendly, offers good classical French cooking, particularly strong in fish, and, surprisingly for a popular site, has a menu at 40F as well as 72F and 130F. Rooms vary considerably but are all comfortable.

Rennes, a large industrial city, still has an old quarter near the 19th-century cathedral with some fine houses from the 15th and 16th centuries. Some have overhanging first storeys and sculptured façades. Parking is the great problem. So a good restaurant with two car parks, Le Coq Gadby in rue d'Antrain, near the cathedral, is especially useful.

Probably the most popular overnight stop for Britons on the Cherbourg peninsula is Hôtel Saint Pierre et Saint Michel at **Villedieu-les-Poêles**, the jolly God's Town of the Frying Pans which I mentioned for shopping in Chapter 6. It is right in the busy shopping street where music is played during the day.

The hotel restaurant has four menus between 36F and 78F, all excellent value. It is good old-style French bourgeois cooking, with good helpings. Patron-chef François Befort is to be congratulated on keeping these prices in a restaurant which is always full at lunchtime and mostly in the evening. His lamb pré-salé (from sea-washed salt meadows) is very good and not cooked as rare as beef, as is the fashion in France at present. I like my lamb succulent, but it should really not have an inch of pink next to the bone and run with blood. That is a Paris fashion, not one from where the lambs are produced. Many Britons were put off rabbit in recent years but his laperau (young rabbit) flambé in calvados and cooked in cider is a delight. Befort's housewine, at 22F, is very fair. His rooms are mostly simple, some have shower and bidet but no wc, and prices are low. The one snag: steep stairs.

If you are driving up or down the west coast, a restaurant I recommend highly is the De la Poste at **Marigny**, a market town east of Coutances. It has dropped its cheaper menus since I was first recommended to try it, but there is one at 75F and a very good one at 107F. Joel Meslin is an imaginative chef.

Near the east coast, between St Lô and Vire, is a hamlet called **Troisgots**, which has a population of fifty but has been a place of pilgrimage since the 12th century. It has a little auberge called De la Chapelle de Vire with a wood-fired grill, menus from 52F to 200F, a 20F housewine and adequate bedrooms. Dinner, bed and breakfast 80F.

Back on the west coast, I pulled in at the neat little town of **Lessay**'s main square early last summer to see again that Norman architectural masterpiece of an abbey founded by William the Conqueror's family in 1056. Badly damaged in 1944, it has been lovingly and magnificently restored with the original stone using old tools.

The Normandie in the main square is not old or beautiful, but it is drawing customers because it offers such good meals so cheaply. Local businessmen in dozens order the 36F menu. I had a remarkable 58F menu – four courses including half a dozen oysters and fresh strawberries in early season. It is clean and neat, has efficient service and must be one of the best Relais Routiers in France. Bedrooms are around 60F.

If you cannot get into Hubert Hardy's splendid Vieux Château hotel at Bricquebec that I mentioned in Chapter 3, make for **Valognes**, the butter market town. It was called the Versailles of Normandy until most of it was destroyed in 1944 and replaced with modern concrete, but it still has some atmosphere and two good inns. Both are cheap, good value and good enough to be popular with local people. L'Agriculture is pretty and serves enormous meals at incredibly low prices. I have not tried it myself, but local friends tell stories of four-course meals for 40F and six courses for 86F, including a large plate of shellfish with oysters. A Welsh international rugby forward – famous too as a trencherman – told me that when he tackled the six-courser, he could have done with extra time.

I *do* know the Louvre hotel, and Simone Mesnil's meals are quite remarkable value at 34F, 40F and 51F. The 40F meal is some of the best value I have found in France. I love really fresh cod, and have never had one better than her cabillaud à la crème. Choosing between her roast topside of veal and her pot-roast pintadeau (guinea fowl) needs fine judgement. Her pâtisserie is splendid, too. A bottle of vin ordinaire costs 10F, cuvée de l'hôtel 22F a bottle. Bedrooms vary in price and facilities. You can get dinner, bed and breakfast for two nights or more for 90F a night.

Arrive here very early on Friday when the huge market is held, lunch at the Agriculture with the farmers, dine and sleep at the Louvre and you have the gourmand's finish to a French trip.

With these two hotels in Valognes, the France et Fuchsias at **St Vaast** and the Vieux Château at **Bricquebec**, who wants or needs to eat or sleep in Cherbourg?

Hotels and Restaurants

Lumbres, 51 km E on N42 from Boulogne, 42 km SE Calais (address 62380 Pas-de-Calais) –

Moulin de Mombreux, route Bayenghen, (21) 39.62.44: see also page 134; menu 120-185F; room 130F with bathroom. Shut December 20 to February 1; Sunday evenings, Mondays.

Sapinière, at **Wisques**, on D208e, 8 km E Lumbres, 4 km W St Omer (address 62500 St Omer), (21) 38.14.59: changed hands; simple, useful; cheap; menu 50F, 70F, 95F; housewine 13F.50; rooms 65F (single), 125-170F (double); shut Sunday evenings.

At **Salperwick**, off N43, 3 km before St Omer (address 62500 St Omer) –

Relais de l'Amitié, near church, (21) 38.11.91 (to become 93.41.91): see also page 136; Jean-Etienne Cossart, chef, has joined his parents; menu 50F; remarkable value; rooms 76F; half-board two nights 190F each; full board two nights 250F each. Fishing, pedaloes 300 m; shut Thursdays.

Arras, 90 km SE Boulogne on D341, 117 km SE Calais (address 62000 Pas-de-Calais) –

Chantzy, 8 rue Chantzy, (21) 21.02.02: see also page 135; tourist menu 65F, for gastronomic menu 120F and carte; wines 100,000 bottles, 1000 appellations; rooms 85-150F; open all year.

Ambassadeur (Buffet Gare), pl. Foch, (21) 23.29.80: menu 70F, 120F; shut Sunday evenings.

Moderne, 1 bd Faidherbe, (21) 23.39.57: by station; comfortable old hotel, bed and breakfast, all rooms with bath; 150-250F (four people); brasserie below. Shut December 24 to 31.

Béthune, 29 km N Arras, A26 motorway 2 km; on N43, 81 km Calais, 75 km Boulogne (address 62400 Pas-de-Calais) –

Vieux Beffroy, Grand'Place, (21) 25.15.00: in beautiful square of Flemish-style buildings, 12th-century belfry; old favourite with *Travellers' France* readers; well run; excellent cooking; super gastronomic menu 125F including wine; small menu 60F including wine; rooms 132-142F; half-board 160F each per night; weekends half-board, with dinner, wine, 300F for two people per night. Shut November.

Les Tourterelles at **Noeux-Les-Mines**, 3 km from Béthune S on N374 (address 62290 Pas-de-Calais), (21) 66.90.75: charming old house, old panelling, nice furnishings; candlelit dinners; fine regional dishes; menu 65F,

120F; Muscadet 48F; Blaye claret 60F; rooms 100-200F; shut Sunday evenings, but hotel open if booked ahead.

St-Michel-sur-Ternoise, on N39, 34 km W Arras, 69 km Boulogne, 120 km Calais (address 62130 Pas-de-Calais) –

Catherinette, in a suburb of St-Pol-sur-Ternoise, (21) 03.12.42: see also page 136; menu 31-78F; disco Saturday, Sunday evenings – 50F includes supper; shut Mondays.

St-Pol-sur-Ternoise –

Lion d'Or, 14 rue Hesdin, (21) 03.10.44: see also page 136; locals eat here; menu 48F, 85F, 128F; wines from 13F.50 (open), 28F bottle; rooms 130-192F; shut Sunday evenings in winter.

Crécy-en-Ponthieu (see also Chapter 9), in forest 19 km N Abbeville, Montreuil 32 km N, battlefield of 1346 where 20,000 French fell and Black Prince commanded English (address 80150 Somme) –

Canon d'Or, ave Gén.-Leclerc, (22) 29.51.14: old post inn; Mme Janine Vigeant-Grand'Eury cooks beautiful meals served in charming old-world dining room; classical cuisine; excellent fish; try lobster quenelle, lotte à l'armoricaine; menu 39F, 58F, 72F, 120F; rooms 80-120F; half-board 120F each per night. Shut Saturdays, Sundays (winter only).

Azouville-sur-Saâne,

Lestanville, 25 km S Dieppe by N27, D23, D149, D2, 74 km Le Havre, 22 km NE Yvetôt (address 76730 Bacqueville-en-Caux) –

L'Orée du Bois, (35) 83.27.16: see also page 137; very attractive; menu 120F, 150F; wines from 50F; no rooms. Shut Wednesday evenings, Thursdays.

Au Bord de la Saâne, (35) 83.20.12: black-and-white Norman inn; menu 75F; rooms possible in village.

Guimerville, 8 km SE Blangy-sur-Bresle on D49 or just off N15 bis, 55 km W Dieppe (address 76340 Seine-Maritime) –

Auberge de la Gare, (35) 93.55.30: outstanding cooking from Joel Levasseur in little white village inn; try civet of goose in Chambertin; game in season (hare, venison, boar); menu 57F, 86F, 140F; housewine Bordeaux 33F; shut June 20 to July 10; Sunday evenings, Mondays.

Brionne, built on islands where river Risle divides, 6 km from Bec Hellouin, historic abbey, 41 km S Tancarville bridge over Seine, 28 km SE Pont Audemer on D130, 76 km Le Havre (address 27800 Eure) –

Logis de Brionne, pl. Saint-Denis, (32) 45.77.22: excellent Logis; favourite of my readers; Alain Depoix cooks Norman dishes according to what is fresh in season; so I recommend his 55F menu 'suggestion of the week'; try stuffed quail normande; menu 40-135F; rooms 87-128F; weekends 10% reduction to bill. Shut

January; also Sunday evenings (summer); Friday evenings, Sunday evenings, Mondays (winter).

At **Bec Hellouin**

La Tour, (32) 44.86.15: attractive little restaurant; cheap; menu 42-55F; housewine 24F; cider 18F.

Auberge de l'Abbaye, (32) 44.86.02: Michelin star; Gault guide ignores it. Mme Sergent cooks delightfully in Norman manner; try rabbit in cider, lobster in cream, apple tart. Carte only; meals around 170-200F; housewine 55F; rooms 180-215F; three lovely old buildings converted.

Bernay, 38 km S Pont Audemer, 86 km Le Havre (address 27300 Eure) –

Angleterre et Cheval Blanc, 10 rue Gén.-de-Gaulle, (32) 43.12.59: another readers' favourite; Jean Cabourg patron since 1948; menu 69F; carte; try trout, guinea fowl; much farm produce; good value; rooms 84-105F; half-board 230F each, weekend half-board 380F for two. Always open.

Conches-en-Ouche, 18 km SW Evreux, between two forests, 34 km SE Bernay, 120 km Le Havre (address 27190 Eure) –

Grand'Mare, ave Croix de Fer, (32) 30.23.30: attractive old Logis opposite little fishing lake; Jean Dubois an excellent cook; try apple and calvados soufflé, mussels in cream, chicken in cider, tart flambé in calvados; menu 55F, 85F (Sundays); carte around 150F; rooms 65-110F; half-board 120-150F each per night.

La Toque Blanche, 18 pl. Carnot, (32) 30.01.54: old Norman cooking in old Norman house, served by staff in old Norman dress, with a trou normand of calvados to help your appetite; calvados available from ten to 100 years old; menu 78F, 90F; shut Mondays; no rooms.

Beuzeville – see also page 136; ideal for Deauville, Honfleur, 48 km Le Havre (address 27210 Eure) –

Cochon d'Or, (32) 57.70.45: see also page 136; try sole normande, chicken Vallée d'Auge (very good), duck in orange sauce; menu 42F.50 (weekday), 65-115F; rooms 72-90F (showers); half-board (min. three nights) 105F each per night. Shut Mondays.

Also rooms at *Petit Castel*, 50 m away, (32) 57.76.08: rooms 130-184F (bath, wc); always open.

Vieux Logis at **Conteville**, 14 km E Honfleur on D312, (32) 57.60.15: Michelin star; old Norman house with delightful old Norman furniture; inevitably pricey but very good. Carte only around 130-200F; wines from 65F; shut Wednesday evenings, Thursdays; January 15 to February 15.

Corneville sur Risle, 6 km Pont Audemer, 45 km Le Havre (address 27500 Pont Audemer, Eure) –

Cloches de Corneville, (34) 57.01.04: see also page 137; very nice cooking; don't know why we missed it for so long; must have been preoccupied with Pont Audemer; menu 75-115F; housewine 42F, Bourgueil 54F;

rooms 105-220F; weekends two nights bed, breakfast, shower, wc, two main meals 300F each; restaurant only shut Wednesdays.

L'Aigle – see also page 137; 46 km S Bernay, 132 km Le Havre, 250 km St Malo (address 61300 Orne) –

Dauphin, (33) 24.43.12: Michelin star; super fin-de-siècle décor; Bernard family have run it over sixty years. Menu 77-164F; housewine 16F; rooms 117-294F; half-board for two people 386-484F per night. Always open.

Argentan, 45 km N Alençon, 23 km SE Falaise, 14 km W of superb horse stud Pin au Haras, 198 km Cherbourg, 57 km Caen, useful for stopover or exploring l'Orne's beautiful country (address 61200 Orne) –

France, pl. Gare, (33) 67.03.65: pleasant, neat one-star hotel; try feuilletés of salmon, sole normande, nice desserts. Menu 40-100F; housewine 21F; rooms 67-159F; shut Sunday evenings.

Saint-Hilaire-du-Harcouët, in a convenient place for Cherbourg and routes from it, St Malo and north Brittany, Calvados, 75 km E St Malo, 27 km SE Avranches, 29 km SW Vire, 34 km E Mont-St-Michel, 148 km Cherbourg (address 50600 Manche) –

Cygne, rue Waldeck-Rousseau, rte Fougères, (33) 49.11.84: very popular with readers of *Encore Travellers' France*; Henri Lefaudeux's cooking praised; menu 45-145F; housewine 30F;

modern hotel, old-style terrace; rooms 120-165F; half-board each 140-160F; open all year.

Josselin – see also page 138; castle, very beautiful, on river Oust, 75 km Dinan, 105 km St Malo, 72 km W Rennes (address 56120 Morbihan) –

Du Château, rue Gén.de-Gaulle, (97) 22.20.11: lovely riverside position; book; menu 44-130F; housewine 22F; rooms 80-180F; half-board 145-205F each.

Rennes – see also page 139; cathedral, 69 km S St Malo, parking dodgy, but this restaurant has two parkings –

Le Coq Gadby, 156 rue d'Antrain, (99) 38.05.55: elegant; menu 70-98F; shut August 1 to 21.

Villedieu-les-Poêles – see also page 139; on Cotentin peninsula, 112 km Cherbourg, 87 km St Malo, 22 km NE Avranches N176 (address 50800 Manche) –

St Pierre et St Michel, pl. République, (33) 61.00.11: wonderful value; deservedly popular; book; menu 36-78F; rooms 50-135F; housewine 22F, fair Bordeaux 32F; weekends autumn, winter only, Friday evening to Monday morning, half-board 250-300F each.

Le Fruitier, 17 rue Gén.-de-Gaulle, (33) 51.14.24: had its head off when I last saw it; totally renovated; all rooms now wc, bath or shower; good old dishes like coq au vin, trout in almonds, tripe mode de Caen, beef tongue in port. Menu

herbs); menu 38-90F; rooms
71-130F; half-board 105-130F each.

Troisgots – see also page 140;
hamlet 30 km N Vire, 12 km S St Lô,
just off D28, 87 km Cherbourg –

Auberge Chappelle de Vire, (33)
56.32.83: simple, welcoming
auberge; excellent value; open
country; menu 52-200F; cooking
over wood fire; housewine 20F;
rooms 80-120F; half-board 80F
each.

Marigny, just off D972, halfway
between Coutances and St Lô
(address 50570 Manche) –

La Poste, pl. Wesport, (33) 55.11.08:
see text; menu 75-190F; good
Norman dishes – crêpes
normandes flambées, St Pierre
(John Dory) in cider; shut Sunday
evenings, Mondays.

36F.50-55F; housewine 28F; rooms
112-129F. Shut February school
holidays 15 days.

Vire, Cotentin peninsula – south
end, rebuilt after war damage,
unexciting, 117 km Cherbourg, 115
km St Malo, 39 km St Lô (address
14500 Calvados) –

Voyageurs, ave Gare, (31) 68.01.16:
simple family hotel; good cheapish
overnight; nice trout in red wine,
ham in cider, scallops in cider;
menu 44-120F; housewine 35F;
rooms 85-150F; half-board 120F
each. Shut Sundays.

France, 4 rue d'Aigneaux, (31)
68.00.35: one star; reasonable
prices; try vire sausages –
andouillette (chitterling and

Coutances, 13 km east
Coutainville on W coast Cotentin
peninsula, lovely little hillside
town; 11th- to 13th-century
cathedral with fifteen windows
showing St George, St Thomas à
Becket and St Blaise, 75 km
Cherbourg (address 50200
Manche) –

Au P'tit Homme, 4 rue Harcourt,
(33) 45.00.67: pleasant little corner
restaurant; try brochette of
scallops or of lamb, desserts with
crème Chantilly base; menu 40-
80F; shut Sunday evenings,
Mondays.

Relais du Viaduct, 25 ave Verdun,
(33) 45.02.68: Logis and 'casserole'
Relais Routiers; big enclosed
pavement terrace in town centre;

menus change daily; good straightforward regional cooking; excellent value; 100F menu has four courses, could include lobster; menu 35-100F; housewine 25F; rooms 58-85F; demi-pension 95F each; weekends Friday dinner to Sunday lunch full board 180F each.

Lessay – see also page 140; 21 km N Coutances, 56 km Cherbourg (address 50430 Manche) –

Normandie, 3 pl. St Cloud, (33) 46.41.11: excellent value meals; menu 36-58F; rooms 70F; shut Saturdays; mid-January to mid-February.

Valognes – see also page 140; 20 km Cherbourg (address 50700 Manche) –

Louvre, 28 rue Religieuses, (33) 40.00.07: very good value; recommended; menu 34-51F; open wine 10F; cuvée hotel 22F; rooms 55-120F; half-board 90F each; shut December; restaurant shut Saturdays in winter.

Agriculture, 15 rue L.-Delisle, (33) 40.00.21: menu 40-86F; complicated shutting times; restaurant sometimes shut Sunday evenings, usually Mondays; phone to check, rooms 75-134F.

11 Hideouts within range of Paris

My favourite motorway in France is the A1 from Lille to Paris. Not that I ever drive on it, but it carries the big lorries and hurrying car drivers from Germany, Belgium and the Channel ports to Paris and leaves whole beautiful forests and charming villages free for people like me to explore in peace.

And in the countryside north of Paris, where for centuries French kings and emperors had lodges and estates on which they hunted wild animals and women, there are still lovely woodlands, hills and hamlets with fine country inns where knowledgeable Parisians hide away on weekends. Few other Frenchmen know and Britons almost totally ignore such places. Britons go south of Paris to see Fontainebleau or belt down the motorway, round Paris on that bewildering *périphérique* and on to the motorway again to the south.

In *Travellers' France* I routed readers through the Compiègne forest and the little-known, attractive forest of St Gobain to Laon and south to Epernay. I had effusively grateful letters from travellers who had never thought of going to these delightful spots before.

The motorway has an advantage. If you decide to spend a short holiday in this pleasant part of France, you can now nip down the motorway for a bit of shopping in Paris. You could jump in your car after lunch, buy your Aunt Maggie a little souvenir from Yves St Laurent or Printemps, and be most of the way back to the quiet forests before that appalling 6-7 p.m. Parisian rush-hour traffic jams the ring road and the entrances to the motorways.

To the east of the town of Compiègne, through the smaller forest of Laigue, is the village of **Blérancourt**, where the château was rebuilt and turned into a museum to symbolise Franco-American friendship. At its gate, in the old lodge, is a hideaway I found twenty years ago. From the outside Le Griffon looks like an attractive old village auberge – creeper-clad, with a large village green in front where, if it were in Kent, the local cricket team would be playing. Inside, it is a hostelry of individuality, charming décor and good cuisine.

Franco-American friendship may have worn thin, but there is nothing shoddy with the welcome at Le Griffon. It is a fine place for a country weekend, with a sortie into Paris if you wish. The bedrooms are nicely furnished with period pieces

– simple and comfortable. The food is very good, although I do confess that it has not reached the standards set a few years back by Yves Chanterau and his wife when they ran it. It still serves a good Flemish leek and cream tart, and also an interesting sabayon of salmon, with a sort of zabaglione sauce of wine, egg yolks and cream.

The food is good enough to entice Parisians to drive 110 km each way for Sunday lunch, and Parisians are outstandingly finicky about Sunday lunch. On summer's evenings or at lunchtime in spring or autumn you can sit under the trees in the garden with a bottle of pétillant dry and fruity Blanc de Blancs from nearby Champagne and wait in utter peace for your meal.

Blérancourt's museum in the château has interesting relics of the First World War. One I find fascinating is the Model-T Ford ambulance, which used to be driven under shellfire over potholes and corrugated muddy tracks by volunteer girl students from the US and England. Most modern drivers would hardly be able to cope with it on a motorway.

The château was built in 1612 by the son of a Paris furrier who had risen to power at court, and designed by Mansard on the model of the Luxembourg Palace in Paris. Ruined in the French Revolution, it was not entirely rebuilt when an American field ambulance unit set up a hospital in its grounds in 1917. After the war, two rich women who had been with the ambulance unit, Ann Murray Dike and Ann Morgan (sister of the banker J. Pierpoint Morgan), who had shown great energy in helping local people rebuild their lives, were the driving force behind the restoration of the château as the national museum of Franco–American cooperation. One of the American volunteer ambulance drivers, Edward Seccombe of Derby, Connecticut, bought the ambulance, had it restored at his own expense and shipped it to the château.

There is a superb drive along route Eugénie through the oak and beech forest to **Compiègne**, which dates from Charlemagne. Off the N31, along the D546 is an historic glade containing a railway coach. Here Marshal Foch, commander of Allied Forces, received the German surrender in 1918. So in 1940 Hitler insisted on receiving the French surrender here. The original carriage was taken to Berlin and destroyed as the Allies approached. A replica coach stands in the glade, with genuine objects inside.

To the south is the 'feudal' castle of **Pierrefonds**, perched on a spur of rock, with tall pointed towers simply designed for imprisoning fairytale princesses. In fact, the feudal castle was destroyed in the 11th century. In 1857 the Emperor Napoleon III had a copy built by Viollet-le-Duc, the architect who rebuilt the medieval city of Carcassonne.

I am very fond of Compiègne, for it stands beside one of the most beautiful forests in France. The forest covers 38,000 acres, and 50,000 acres with the forest of Laigue across the river Aisne. Used for hunting by every French sovereign from Clovis to Napoleon III, it is criss-crossed by avenues, some for driving, others of grass for walking or horse riding. They cover 625 miles. Park your car and follow yellow-marked walking tracks for a couple of hours and you can reach the rugged heart of the forest and still find your car again.

The castle at Compiègne rates behind only Versailles and Fontainebleau as a royal palace. Charles V had it built as a country retreat within the protection of the city walls. Louis XV rebuilt it in a severe but elegant style, Louis XVI received his fiancée here – Marie Antoinette, youngest daughter of Marie-Thérèse, Empress of Austria, and due to die as Queen under the guillotine. Some of the rooms in Compiègne are still decorated and furnished as she designed them. But most of the rooms were redecorated by the artists Redouté and Girodet for Napoleon, who had the furniture specially made. Napoleon used it as a safe hideout, Napoleon III and Empress Eugénie for extravagant hunting parties and balls.

In the Grand Hall and old kitchens is a most interesting transport museum. There are 150 vehicles from a Roman chariot to a Citroën chain-track car, including a mail coach, horse-drawn bus, transports used by Napoleon on his retreat from Moscow, a De Dion car which reached 100 kph in 1899, and a little 4CV Renault of 1900. There is also a collection showing the evolution of the bicycle.

In the town hall is the museum De la Figurine with 80,000 lead, wood and cardboard soldiers, many of whom are refighting the Battle of Waterloo. I wonder if the result will be the same.

Hôtel de France in Compiègne, a charming old hotel, has a restaurant called Du Chat Qui Tourne which serves good meals. In 1665 a mountebank walked in with a cat and set it to turning the spit where the meat was cooking. The locals were so impressed that they changed the name of the inn. Electricity has replaced feline power but the name has stuck.

To see Compiègne, I would be tempted to stay at **Elincourt Sainte Marguerite**, 15 km along the D142. Château de Bellinglise is a delight. A 15th-century château in pink, with turrets and a grey-green roof, it stands in a big park with a lake in which the house is reflected among water lilies. And now it is one of the Châteaux Hôtels Indépendants. The chef, Luc Macaigne, produces some really excellent dishes, such as suprême de turbot au Champagne, duck in calvados, and selle d'agneau aux girolles (saddle of lamb with an unusual and delicate fungus, girolles). Menus start at 80F, and there are some tempting gastronomic weekends at cut prices.

A charming old creeper-clad house with cosy bedrooms, and beamed dining room with warm red tablecloths, all among trees and greenery, is the Bon Accueil, in the forest at **Vaudrampont**, on the D332 road to Crépy en Valois. Chef Jean Edouard Lacroix, one of the family who own it, used to be a chef at the Connaught in London.

In 1981 he won the Meilleur Cuisinier de l'Oise award. So, for the best cooking in the area, 110F is not excessive for a meal.

There is another old favourite of mine down the road at **Crépy en Valois**, but there was a certain amount of internal building work going on in 1983. Hôtel des Trois Pigeons is known for its fish. It is comfortable, its prices are reasonable, and what I like is that you meet the locals in the bar before and after dinner.

My very favourite place to stay is **Laon**, capital of France in the 9th century when Paris was a village and Charlemagne's mother, Berthe 'Au Grand Pied' (Bertha of the Big Feet), made this her seat.

The old part of Laon stands on top of a steep hill, with the newer town on the plain below. As you enter the town, you see tree-lined boulevards rising steeply among buildings to the old walls of the fortified medieval town and a superb 12th-century cathedral which became a model for several cathedrals in Europe. It has impeccable symmetry – a strong but gentle building. From the terrace alongside views stretch across country for many miles.

Laon is 129 km from Paris and near to the edge of the Champagne. A fine way to reach it is from Compiègne on minor roads through the forests of Compiègne, Laigue and St Gobain.

We stay at a fine old coaching inn here dating from 1685, Bannière de France, comfortable, excellent cooking, very nice atmosphere and most reasonable prices. There is an excellent-value menu at 60F,

including wine, and very good menus at 100F and 150F, with good housewine at 20F a carafe and a good cellar.

Around here and in the Champagne wine district are several hotels which are rather pricey but have a reputation for outstanding food. One is the Hostellerie du Château at **Fère-en-Tardenois**, 108 km east of Paris and 46 km west of Reims. It is in a lovely park and has a strange history. It was built in 1206 and owned by the Valois-Orléans family. When Henry II got the chop, it was confiscated, then given back to the wife of the Prince of Condé. It came into the hands of the Duke of Orléans who took part in the French Revolution, called himself Philip Egalité, and knocked down part of his château to show he was almost as equal as the man in the street. He was still guillotined.

It is beautiful, superbly furnished, has immaculate service and two Michelin stars, which the Blot family and chef Patrick Michelon richly deserve. The cheapest menu at 160F is excellent, the dégustation at 270F is gorgeous.

For drinking champagne, I prefer quieter Epernay to Reims. That is no insult to Pommery or Heidsieck, and especially not to the Widow Cliquot. I just happen to have friends at Mercier and Moët et Chandon in Epernay. But **Reims** has two trump cards – its magnificent cathedral and Gérard Boyer's restaurant. Though many of Reims' greatest treasures were destroyed in the First World War, and it took twenty years to restore the cathedral, it is back in true splendour now – one of the greatest, and I think the most beautiful church in the world.

For me, it has improved in recent years. To the 13th-century stained-glass windows, restored so beautifully by the local workshop of Simon after war damage, have been added the absolutely magnificent colourful windows by Marc Chagall. The Simon workshop made these to Chagall's design, too. Not only their colour and beauty move me. They remind me so vividly of a tiny village church at Tudeley in Kent where smaller but equally lovely windows by Chagall shine in memory of a beautiful girl we all knew and who died when only nineteen.

Gérard Boyer's Restaurant Boyer is in a Napoleon III château in a superb park right in the centre of the city, in view of the cathedral. It has three Michelin stars and is without doubt one of the greatest restaurants in the world, and suitably pricey. M. Boyer has only just moved to this sumptuous spot from his old La Chaumière. Rooms are beautiful but cost 500F to 800F a night for two people – still, you could pay that for being a room number in a modern city hotel.

To visit many champagne cellars, you need a letter of introduction. But not for Mumm (34 rue de Champ de Mars, 45-minute tour) nor Veuve-Cliquot-Ponsardin (pl. des Droits de l'Homme).

On the road to Epernay is a superbly positioned, beautifully furnished luxury hotel with views across the vineyards. Called Royal Champagne, it is at Champillon. Meals cost about 260F, the cooking is traditional, with rich sauces and much flavour, and I love it. The French Gault Millau guide, bible of Nouvelle Cuisine, is not so keen. Michelin gives it a star.

Don't be frightened by all these high prices for meals. You will find one in Reims with a full menu for 42F listed below!

You can visit Moët et Chandon caves in **Epernay** (20 ave Champagne, 51.71.11). The company was founded in 1743, not long after that local monk Dom Perignon, to whom we all owe so much, perfected champagne making. Moët cellars are the largest in the world, with seventeen and a half miles of maturing bottles, all of which are turned gradually and tilted by hand. The caves' museum has the record of Napoleon's visit and his hat. Presumably he forgot it after an enthusiastic tasting session. There is a bigger champagne museum of interest at the end of avenue Champagne. At Hautvilliers, 4 km north on the N386, are the Benedictine abbey and vineyards where Dom Perignon performed his miracle. Moët own the abbey.

You can get a list of times of visits for champagne caves in Reims, Epernay and nearby towns from Comité Inter Professionnel du Vin de Champagne, 5 rue Henri-Martin, 51200 Epernay, (26) 51.40.47.

West of the A1 motorway and much nearer Paris than Compiègne is another Condé château, **Chantilly**. Its history was for long the story of the French court, the kings and their powerful favourites. Greatest of these was Le Grand Condé, friend and relative of Louis XIV. He held a party lasting three days for the king and court in 1671. There were 5000 guests. Marquees were put up, inns and villas in the area requisitioned for guests.

The great chef Vatel had to feed them in courtly manner – sixty tables of eighty people three times a day. Vatel did not sleep for twelve days before. First night, two tables had no roast for dinner. He was upset all night. Next morning the fish failed to arrive from the coast. Exhausted, Vatel went to his room and ran a rapier through his heart.

The present château, which you can see, was built in 1875 in Renaissance style. It is crammed with treasures, has beautiful gardens, and nearby are a great forest and the Chantilly racecourse.

Chantilly is only 49 km from Paris, so quite a good place to stay and make sorties into the capital. I can well recommend the restaurant mentioned below, Relais du Coq Chantant, for value and cooking. You could stay 6 km away beside the forest at **Gouvieux**, where there are two very nice hotels at medium prices. Château de la Tour, in a wooded park, is elegant and very pleasantly furnished in the style of its period, the end of the last century. Hôtel Pavillon Saint Hubert was originally the dog kennels for the princely hunts of the Chantilly forest and where the whippers-in and such lived. It is the sort of dog-house I would not mind being sent to; comfortably and warmly furnished, with a terrace overlooking the river and good food. Move over, Rover!

Even nearer Paris (35 km) is the comfortable Hostellerie du Lys, in its own grounds in the forest at **Lamerlaye**.

Beauvais is a superb little old town; animated, plenty to see, and only 76 km from Paris. The cathedral, begun in 1227, was never quite finished but is magnificent in its new town setting, has a superb and awesome Gothic choir and even more superb windows, some from the 14th to 16th centuries, some recent by Max Ingrand and Braque. I wish Braque had been asked to design more church windows. The few that exist are magnificent.

In St Etienne church there are some lovely Renaissance windows by Angrand le Prince. Next to the cathedral is the new national tapestry museum, with gorgeous tapestries from the 15th century to today. Tapestry weaving started in Beauvais by order of Louis XIV. The art has been revived in the last fifty years, mainly through the great modern artist Jean Lurçat, who died about ten years ago – friend of Cocteau, Picasso and Matisse. Strange that the great Bayeux tapestry was woven for the French by the English and the biggest tapestry in the world, designed by Graham Sutherland for the reborn Coventry Cathedral, was woven by the French.

In Beauvais, you could stay near the cathedral at the Palace hotel, eat in the reasonably priced and good La Cremaillère.

South of Paris, the **forest of**

Fontainebleau has survived miraculously the invasion of tourists from all over the world and the weekend invasion of millions of Parisians. It is a massive forest, of course, and the invaders mostly stick to the area around the great palace and places fairly easy to reach, like Barbizon, the little village which lured so many artists in the last century to paint landscapes that Napoleon III classed the area as an 'artistic reserve'.

The forest can be as beautiful in winter as in spring and autumn or midsummer shade, especially when the snow falls. Cézanne's *Neige Fondant en Forêt de Fontainebleau* is a superb winter scene – memorable rather than depressing.

Crowds make for the area just north of Fontainebleau village off the N7, and for the route Ronde, a lovely half-circle drive round the village, made by Henry IV of France so that the more delicate members of the court could follow the hunt without getting their boots dirty.

A lovely drive along a fairly big road is to **Milly-la-Forêt**. It passes through quite wild-looking forest of pine, oaks and beech. In fact it is so carefully tended that you will find notices naming trees as if they were pets. I like the notices warning me 'Stag and Boar Crossing'.

Milly is a pleasant old town with a superb 15th-century market made entirely of oak and the 12th-century chapel of St Blaise-des-Simples – a tiny chapel dedicated to a saint who used the multitude of herbs which grow around this area to heal the sick. Jean Cocteau, who is buried in the chapel, redecorated the inside with frescoes which I find delightful, especially those of herbs round the nave. There is a bust of Cocteau – to me one of the greatest writers, artists and above all playwrights of all time. He died here in 1963. Behind the chapel is a garden where some of these 'simples' (medicinal herbs) grow.

Château de Courances, 5 km north and approached by a fine avenue lined with trees, is a handsome 17th-century house which you cannot visit. But do see its huge park and gardens, with waterfalls, lakes, fish ponds and grand canal, hallmark of the man who designed it, the great Le Nôtre.

He laid out the original gardens of Fontainebleau Palace, too, but not the informal Jardin Anglais. Do find time to see these, as well, when visiting the palace.

The palace at Fontainebleau is not so breathtaking or dazzling as Versailles but has great charm. Many kings and their queens and mistresses lived there and left their mark. Originally a fortified château of Louis VII, it was made into a beautiful palace by Francis I, the true Renaissance king who loved grandeur and art and hired the greatest men to provide it. Among the many artists and craftsmen he brought from Italy to decorate it were Rosso, Primaticcio and Benvenuto Cellini, the artist who left us not only masterpieces of sculpture and silverwork but his autobiography, a masterpiece of line-shooting. Francis bought the *Mona Lisa* to decorate a room – all for love of his mistress, Anne de Pisseleu.

For love of *his* mistress, Diane de Poitiers, Henry II had Delorme design the absolutely magnificent ballroom. He also had a garden made for her. When Henry was killed accidentally in a tournament by Captain Montgomery of the Scots Guards, his wife Catherine de Medici kicked Diane out and sacked Delorme. She brought back the Italians. She was also the queen who thought French cooking so primitive that she sent for the Medici chefs and recipes from Florence, thus, say the Italians, giving birth to French cuisine.

Henry IV, who loved the palace, got rid of the Italians and did a lot of redecorating in the Flemish style. He also made the grand canal in the gardens, which was left as a feature by Le Nôtre when he redesigned the gardens for Louix XIV. Despite his love of Versailles, Louis, a great hunter, came here often to chase game and Louise de la Vallière; later in life he brought Mme de Maintenon.

Marie Antoinette had time to alter the Queen's Apartments before she lost her head.

Napoleon loved Fontainebleau. He built himself some new special apartments alongside to be occupied by his wives, Josephine, and then Marie Louise. His furniture survives. Earlier furniture was stolen in the Revolution. He imprisoned a Pope here, abdicated in the Red Room, and said goodbye to his Old Guard in Cour de Cheval Blanc on his way to internment in Elba.

The guided tour of the palace Grands Apartments takes about an hour, but you can follow yellow signs and go round yourself. The tour of Napoleon's Petits Apartments is on Saturdays and Sundays only.

Fontainebleau village has many hotels and restaurants, but gets crowded with tourists and you may like to stop outside. We have found a Logis and Relais du Silence 8 km away, on the edge of the forest and only 3 km from the A6 motorway to Paris (60 km). Auberge Casa del Sol is at **Récloses**, near Ury, and is a family-run hotel with family-style cooking of all fresh ingredients from the market.

Everyone should see **Chartres** cathedral. It has been called the world's most beautiful church, and even if you disagree, you will surely rate it one of the most beautiful. Built in the 12th century, it is a mixture of Gothic and romanesque styles, is vast (130 m/ 143 yd long) and I find it rather dark and sombre inside, but that only accentuates the rich colours of the unsurpassed windows made 700 years ago. The building of it was a remarkable story. A barely finished cathedral was burned down in 1194, and everyone in the area, from paupers and the old to lawyers and high-born ladies, gave money and came to work on it with their own hands.

But I think Chartres is worth a few days' visit in its own right, especially in autumn or winter. It is a little town with a warm feeling with many old buildings and streets. The museum in the bishop's palace has some fine Flemish paintings, including

Erasmus by Holbein, enamels by Limosin, and tapestries. St Pierre's church has some magnificient Renaissance glass windows, and the old bridge and houses by the river Eure are delightful.

Here, too, I have listed a restaurant and an hotel-restaurant with low prices. Chartres is only 89 km from Paris but is outside the Paris price-belt into the prices of a country market town.

Hotels and Restaurants

Blérancourt – see page 147; D66, D130 NE from Compiègne, through Laigue forest, then right on D934 at Cuts (33 km), 115 km Paris (address 02300 Chauny, Aine) –

Le Griffon, (23) 39.60.11: menu 65F, 80F, 120F; housewine 35F; rooms 90-170F; half-board only during week. Shut Sunday evenings, Mondays.

Compiègne – see also page 148; 82 km Paris (address 60200 Oise) –

Hôtel de France et Rôtisserie du Chat qui Tourne, 17 rue Eugène Floquet, (4) 440.02.74: charming old hotel; Logis 'casserole' for good local cooking; menu 45-195F; rooms 55-196F.

De Flandre, 16 quai République, (4) 483.24.40: solid comfort and reliability near the river; menu 54F; rooms 80-160F; shut December 15 to January 15.

Le Picotin, pl. Hôtel de Ville, (4) 440.04.06: traditional cooking; good value; menu 46-75F;

housewine 27F.50; good wine list; shut Tuesday evenings, Wednesdays except June, July, August. No rooms.

At **Elincourt Ste Marguerite**, 15 km from Compiègne N by N32 and D142 (address 60157 Oise) –

Château de Bellinglise, (4) 476.04.76: see also page 149; lovely grounds with lake; menu 80-165F; rooms 210-270F; half-board 250F each; weekend gastronomique (includes gastronomic meals, wine, coffee) depart after lunch Sunday, arrive Friday dinner 775F each; arrive Saturday lunch 555F each; arrive Saturday dinner 450F each. Shut Sunday evenings.

At **Vaudrampont**, heart of forest, 10 km S Compiègne on D332 to Crépy, 80 km Paris (address 60127 Morienval, Oise) –

Bon Accueil, (4) 442.84.04: see also page 149; delightful forest hideaway; I have had wonderful meals; I must stay next time; menu 110F, 195F; wines from 55F; rooms 118-190F; shut February; Monday evenings, Tuesdays.

At **Choisy-au-Bac**, in forest 3 km E of Compiègne –

Auberge des Etangs du Buissonnet, (4) 440.17.41: restaurant in nice park with own lake; wild fowl; carte only 150-200F for meal; wines 40-500F; shut Sunday evenings, Mondays.

At **Vieux Moulin**, 9 km E Compiègne by D973, white road D14 left, deep in forest (address

60350 Cuisse-la-Motte, Oise) –

Auberge du Daguet, 25 rue St-Jean, (4) 441.60.72: famous restaurant in lovely surroundings; fine ambience; menu 125F. We had ris de veau Vallèe d'Auge (calvados, cream, herbs); sorbet of marc de champagne, superb salmon, gorgeous smelly, sharp, cooked goats' cheese called crotin (dung!) de chavignol and superb chocolate profiterolles; wines from 35F; shut Wednesdays.

Crépy en Valois, 70 km NE of Paris, 24 km SE Compiègne (address 60800 Oise) –

Trois Pigeons, 4 pl. Paon, (4) 459.11.21: see also page 150; following alterations, Francis Garnier, fish fanatic, promises to treat his British clients to some fine fish dishes, like his fish ragoût; he also makes a nice perigourdine mix of kidneys and sweetbreads; menu 60F, 80F, 148F; rooms 90-130F; half-board 225F for two. Shut February; Sunday evenings, Mondays in winter.

Laon – see also page 150; do see it – a superb place, 129 km NE Paris, 47 km NW Reims, 30 km NE Soissons (address 02000 Aisne) –

Bannière de France, 11 rue F.-Roosevelt (old high town), (23) 23.21.44: Paul Lefevre keeps up his standards and delights my readers; Dominique Havot cooks beautifully; try St Jacques (scallops) flambées au noilly, escalope de veau aux écrevisses and mouthwatering chocolate profiterolles. Menu 60F (includes wine), 100F, 150F; rooms 60-220F; half-board (three nights min.) 175-190F each per night. Shut December 20 to January 20.

Angleterre, 10 bd de Lyon (lower town), (23) 23.04.62: modern, pleasant furnishings; comfortable. Good cooking; huge shellfish platter; menu 55-195F; rooms 99-195F; half-board 155-220F each; shut December 24 to January 24.

Fère-en-Tardenois, 26 km NE of Château Thierry motorway exit, 108 km NE of Paris, 45 km W Reims (address 02130 Aisne) –

Hostellerie du Château (N 3 km by D967, then forest road), (23) 82.21.13: see also page 150; try canard au cassis, seabass (bar) with truffled butter; menu 180F; menu dégustation 270F (you will need the sorbet au marc to make a hole for you in the middle); lovely pricey wines – Chardonnay from Champagne or Bouzy red from Champagne 160F. Shut January 1 to March 1.

Reims – see also page 150; 141 km E Paris (address 51100 Marne) –

Boyer, 64 bd Henry-Vesnier, (26) 82.80.80: I will cheerfully part with 250F (if I have it) for one of Gérard Boyer's meals; I did not know a suprême de volaille could taste so splendid; housewine 95F without service, but it *is* a rather splendid Bisseul from just east of Epernay; rooms 500F, 800F.

Le Forum, 34 pl. Forum, (26) 47.56.87: down-to-earth; simple grills, brochettes at prices to please your bank manager; choice, and daily changes; menu 43F, 65F; housewine 29F. Shut Sunday nights, Mondays.

Hôtel La Paix, Restaurant Le Drouet, 4 rue Buirette, (26) 40.04.08: new box building but comfortable, efficient; all bedrooms with bath, wc; indoor garden with pool; menu 85F, 109F; housewine 24F; rooms 269F. Restaurant shut Sundays.

At **Champillon** – see also page 151; on N51, 18 km S Reims, 6 km N Epernay on edge of Forêt de la Montagne (address 51160 Ay, Marne) –

Royal Champagne, (26) 51.25.06: see also page 151; surroundings, views, service, old-style cooking with rich sauces, ambience, all suit me; inevitably very pricey; menu 260-270F; rooms 260-430F; always open.

Sept-Saulx, 166 km NE Paris, just off A4 motorway and N44 between Reims and Châlons-sur-Marne (address 51400 Mourmelon-le-Grand, Marne) –

Cheval Blanc, (26) 61.60.27: I have forgotten when I had my first plate of crayfish in champagne here, or seabass in Bouzy red wine, but the Lefevre-Robert family have been here since 1870 and Bernard Robert is now assisted at the cooker by his daughter, making six generations; pricey and worth it; menu 130F, 195F; lovely gardens, heart of countryside; nice rustic décor; rooms 130-260F. Shut mid-January to mid-February.

Chantilly – see also page 151; 40 km N Paris in Chantilly forest (address 60500 Oise) –

Coq Chantant, 21 rte Creil, (4) 457.01.28: see also page 152; very pleasant restaurant, pleasant décor, good value; try canette de barbarie (wild duck), bavarois de tourteau, superb desserts. Menu 77-109F; housewine 36F; shut part February, early September. No rooms.

Relais Condé, 42 ave Mar-Joffre, (4) 457.05.75: near the racecourse, in an old chapel converted to worldlier matters; but it is run by Michel Luck, so you can enjoy a good meal and pray for a win on the 4.30. Luck will at least be with you at the table – very good restaurant, with fine wine list; the housewine at 50F is a Cahors with lots of body and strength; menu 85F; shut mid to end January, mid to end July; Mondays, Tuesdays. No rooms.

At **Gouvieux**, 3 km W from Chantilly by D909 (address 60270 Oise) –

Château de la Tour, (4) 457.07.39: see also page 152; another gorgeously furnished château; menu 69F, 98F; rooms 150-291F; half-board 200-280F each.

Pavillon St-Hubert, just past Gouvieux, 6 km W Chantilly by D909, D162, (4) 457.07.04: see also page 152; beside Lys forest on banks of river Oise; known for freshwater and sea fish; carte only, allow at least 100F; rooms 105-150F. Shut August (restaurant only).

At **Lys-Chantilly**, 7 km S Chantilly

on N16 (address 60260 Lamorlaye, Oise) –

Hostellerie du Lys (4) 421.26.19: see also page 152; spit-roast over wood; eat on terrace in good weather; wood fires in winter; try confit of duck; menu 95-115F; wine Côte de Rhône 38F; rooms 160-230F; shut December 20 to January 6.

Bazainville, 60 km W of Paris by N12, 5 km E Houdan, edge of Rambouillet forest (address 78550 Houdan, Yvelines) –

Relais du Pavé, on N12, (3) 487.61.52: another pricey, extremely good restaurant with Michelin star; fine old country inn with flower garden and terrace; pricey bedrooms; Claude Marguerite is called a 'disciple of Escoffier', and to anyone who is too young to know who Escoffier was, he invented lovely rich sauces; Claude's steak de canard au rhum won a Poêle d'Or award in 1974, a Maître Cuisinier de France; wines from 50F; superb cellar of wines from 1872; rooms 310F. Shut February; Monday evenings, Tuesdays. Lunch menu weekdays 100F; carte 200-250F with wine.

At **Pontchartrain**, on N12, 40 km W Paris, 15 km Versailles (address 78760 Yvelines) –

La Dauberie, 3 km by D13 at Mousseux, (3) 487.80.57: beautiful pricey old auberge in hideaway hamlet of trees and flowers; one of three superb attractive restaurants here, but other two, *L'Aubergarde* and *Chez Sam*, are on busy N12 and have no rooms; cost around 160F

minimum to 250F for a meal, but the cooking is delicious – even rabbit is a different dish as rillettes de lapin sauce à la grain de moutarde; try fillet of beef in sabayon de vin rouge (egg yolk, cream and red wine 'zabaglione'), duck served with mango and grapefruit; delicious desserts, and crotin rôti (that super smelly goats' cheese called 'manure'); rooms 300F.

Grigny, remarkable hideaway in Paris suburbs, beside the Viry-Châtillon lakes, like an oasis in suburban desert, between N7 and A6 motorway only 26 km S of Paris centre (address 91350 Essonne) –

Château du Clotay, (6) 906.89.70: for the rich, for celebrations or for lovers; or for a new-style honeymoon in Paris; total peace in a 19th-century manor with superb Louis XVI furnishings and colour TV in bedrooms, huge bathrooms to each bedroom. 'Light-traditional' cooking by Christian Antoine; nice touches like Breton lobster on a bed of haricots verts; menu 130F, 190F; wines from 80F (Brouilly, Château Beau Rivage); rooms 250F (single), 350-450F (double); shut Sunday evenings, Mondays.

Beauvais – see also page 152; 76 km NE Paris on N1, 98 km E Dieppe, 165 km SE Boulogne (address 60000 Oise) –

Palais, 9 rue St-Nicolas, (4) 445.12.58: quiet, comfortable bed-and-breakfast hotel near cathedral; sleep here, eat in Crémaillère (below); rooms

100-160F; shut August 1 to 15.

Crémaillère, 1 rue Gui-Patin, (4) 445.03.13: fine regional cooking at very reasonable prices; try ficelle picarde (rolled pancake, creamy savoury stuffing), guinea fowl, tripe in cider, fresh fish daily, super desserts; Renée-Marie Lémenager's son Daniel cooks now; comfortable, warm; menu 61F.80; housewine 28F; well-chosen cave, especially Bordeaux, Burgundy; good value; shut Wednesdays except for reservations.

Warluis, 7 km S Beauvais on N1 (address 60430 Oise) –

Des Alpes Franco-Suisses, (4) 402.01.21: looks and is run like a mountain hotel in Savoy; very good value; mini Alpine zoo in garden, with small goats, deer, St Bernard dog; savoyardes dishes – fondue, raclette, desserts flambé in William pear liqueur; menu 35-86F; restaurant shut Mondays.

Chartres – see also page 154; 80 km Paris by N10 or A11 motorway (address 28000 Eure-et-Loir) –

L'Ecu, 28 rue Grand Faubourg, (37) 21.34.59: rustic; very good value, excellent normande (cream sauces) fish dishes, sea and freshwater; smoked pork, pheasant, good cheeses, menu 53F, 80F; housewine 24F; rooms 60-120F; half-board, including wine, 110-140F each. Shut December 20 to January 5; Sunday evenings.

Auberge St Maurice (Banquetti), 20 rue St-Maurice, (37) 21.13.89: 'casserole' Relais Routiers; local dishes, plus Mediterranean dishes to order – paella, bouillabaisse marseillaise; menu 35F, 45F; housewine 18F; shut Sundays.

Fontainebleau – see also page 153; 64 km S Paris (address 77300 Seine-et-Marne) –

Ile de France, 128 rue de France, (6) 422.85.15: much work done to improve hotel over five years; dining room elegant, nice garden; rooms include family rooms sleeping three to five people. Known mostly for Chinese chef from Hong Kong, Yam Kwong Leung, who cooks French dishes but more Chinese; his Chinese fondue famous – it costs 100F; good Chinese fish dishes. Promotional menu with drinks only 35F, other menus 50F, 80F; wine from 28F, carafe 33F litre; rooms 170-230F.

At **Récloses**, 8 km S by N7 and D63 E (address 77116 Ury, Seine-et-Marne) –

Casa del Sol, (6) 424.20.35: see also page 154; nice gardens, terrace, friendly atmosphere; all fresh products from the market; good family cooking; menu 95F, 125F; housewine 30F; rooms 160-265F; half-board 230F; shut Monday evenings, Tuesdays.

12 Paris for beginners

Almost every month, Paris becomes a different city.

Spring means café tables and chairs back on the pavements, girls wiggling a little faster, men rediscovering their smiles and courtesies, shopgirls awakening from their ritual nail-filing and hurrying forward to serve, even traffic policemen smiling sometimes.

July and August mean that any Parisian who can raise the cash and the time is away out of the city, leaving it to the poorer citizens, public servants, shopkeepers and invading tourists.

But with the late autumn mists enshrouding the Seine and that ugly but symbolic Eiffel Tower alongside dripping water like a long, lean, sad man just saved from drowning, cosiness returns to Paris. Look around you at the signs: no blossom on the chestnut trees in the Champs-Elysées and the last leaves falling, but hot roast chestnuts on sale from barrows. Girls in trousers of tantalising cut, with sharp creases, and raincoats tightly belted to accentuate the positive. Apéritif drinkers snuggle in warm bars, lights shine invitingly from restaurants and superb shop windows. Taxis hurry beautifully dressed women and elegant escorts to parties and cabarets.

There is a Paris for every man – and two for every woman . . . one for shopping, one for loving. *My* Paris is really an open-air city. Springtime and early autumn especially – peering at the paintings and drawings of never-to-be-known painters on the banks of the Seine, eating cheaper meals outside little restaurants in St Germain or the Latin Quarter, watching the intelligent girls from what Parisians still call the Sorbonne but bureaucrats now call the University of Paris Three and Four combining flirting with putting the world right. Their dancing eyes and expressive mouths do more for me than the suspender-clad thighs and professional smiles of cabaret girls.

But winter in Paris has great compensations.

You can spend longer in the Louvre, or especially in Jeu de Paume, enjoying paintings in peace and warmth, or mooching round department stores such as Galeries Lafayette or Printemps. Outside, the women on Faubourg St Honoré look chic in winter wrappings – not like shapeless parcels fighting the weather, as in London. Cold winds bring colour to the cheeks of students looking for books in the

jumble of shops of 'Boul-Mich' –
Boulevard St Michel. There is ice
on the pool where little boys sail
boats in Luxembourg Gardens and
droplets on the royal noses of the
statues of queens of France. And if
the Latin Quarter cafés look
crammed, someone will move over
for you to make room.

Paris is a city to *savour* at all times
of year – not a city for timetables.
No good rushing around with a big
list of things to see in a short time.
You will not get around to half of
them and you will leave yourself no
time for the greatest pleasure of all
– contemplating the passing scene.

If this is your first time in Paris,
take a few old-timers' tips. Avoid
taxis when you can. Denis Norden,
radio and TV writer, said once that
for anyone learning speed-reading,
there is no better exercise than

watching a Paris taxi-meter
clocking up the francs.

First time, I would take a tour of
the city in one of those panoramic
buses with commentary in English.
This is touristy and a bit pricey, but
there is no better way to get your
bearings when time is short. The
trip probably includes a quick tour
of the Louvre, Notre-Dame and
Sacré Coeur cathedral on the hill at
Montmartre, and stops at such
places as the Eiffel Tower, Arc de
Triomphe and the Panthéon. No
way to *see* Paris, but a good
reconnaissance.

Ordinary buses are much
cheaper, but walking is best –
almost the *only* way to see Paris. To
get from one walk to another, use
the Métro. No part of the city is
more than 400 yards from a Métro
station, but you may well have to

climb several staircases and stump long corridors before you get to the platform.

There is a flat rate for a journey, however long, but second- and first-class fares. Buy a carnet of ten tickets which can also be used on buses. There are maps in every station and it is best to note the terminus of your line, for that is what is shown on the centre of each platform.

Bus travel is not at a fixed rate for a journey. Bus stops list routes and how many tickets are needed for your journey. All routes run from 7.30 a.m. to 10.30 p.m., some until midnight, and some suburban routes run every hour all night, which is why Parisians can go to the theatre or a disco when Londoners cannot. You can get off for a while and rejoin a bus journey on the same ticket, which helps with sightseeing.

Two-day and four-day tickets called *billets de tourisme* give you freedom of the Métro, buses and funicular up the hill to Sacré Coeur, including first-class travel on the Métro – helpful in rush hours, when second-class carriages are jammed with people.

A good bus route is No. 24 from **Gare St Lazare**. Every day except Sundays. It goes round **place de la Madeleine**, with luxury food stores, into **place de la Concorde**, called Europe's most beautiful square, and along the Seine beside the **Tuileries gardens**, past the **Louvre**. There's a view across the river, of fine buildings, including the Mint, called **Hôtel des Monnaies**, and the **Institut de France** which is

headquarters of the Académie Française – society of the greatest artists and writers, known as the Immortals. It crosses by **Pont Neuf** to **Ile de la Cité**, the island in the Seine where there are a lot of important buildings, such as the law courts (**Palais de Justice**) and **Notre-Dame** cathedral. It goes over **Petit Pont** to the Left Bank, turning left along quai St Bernard to the edge of the 400-year-old **Jardin des Plantes** – formal and botanical gardens, and the Natural History Museum. It goes on to the **quai de Bercy**, with wine warehouses. On the way back, it sticks to the Left Bank, providing a good view of Notre-Dame, crossing the river by **Pont Royal** into **Concorde** and the superb **rue Royale**. **Maxim's** restaurant is at No. 3.

For newcomers to Paris, **Concorde,** the **Louvre** (not just a picture gallery but the world's biggest museum, housed in a royal palace built between 1200 and the 1880s) and **Notre-Dame** are essential viewing. And you will probably want to fit in a wander through **St-Germain-des-Prés** district, not quite so Bohemian as of old but still pleasurable, the **Arc de Triomphe**, built by Napoleon to celebrate victories of his army, **Champs-Elysées**, not quite so elegant as of old but still one of the world's most attractive and impressive streets.

I am sure you will want to see **Sacré Coeur**, a truly lovely church. Built as a symbol of hope after the French disasters of the Franco-Prussian war of 1870, its whiter-than-white dome splits the

Montmartre skyline; inside it is gold and crimson, Paris of the turn of the century – fin de siècle; outside, among gnarled old trees and old white houses just about kept together with loving care, **place du Tertre** throngs with visitors and hopeful artists who will never make it, sadly oblivious to the fact that the art centre emigrated to Montparnasse back in the mid-1920s. Toulouse-Lautrec, Utrillo, Picasso, Modigliani all lived here, so did Baudelaire and many great writers. **Abbesses** Métro station is the nearest to the funicular up to Sacré Coeur but the shops and stalls at the bottom are splendid for wandering around.

Everyone has to go up the **Eiffel Tower** once. Lifts which could frighten the life out of the fainthearted, but have been safe so far, will take you up the three stages but there are usually queues for each lift. There are also bars alongside. One platform at the top is enclosed in glass usually too dirty to see through clearly. The other gives a wonderful view over Paris, though not so attractive to me as that from Montmartre, nor more interesting than that from the new arts centre at Beaubourg. You can climb the 1652 steps to save a few francs. But unless you are a mountaineer in training, don't.

The tower was built for the Exhibition of 1889, was 984 ft (300 m) high – now 1051 ft (320 m) with TV masts – weighs 7000 tons, has 12,000 pieces of metal joined by 2½ million rivets, was meant to be pulled down after twenty years but stayed as a radio, then TV transmitter. The Germans considered pulling it down for scrap during the occupation but Parisians, many of whom had thought little of it until then, were suddenly prepared to defend it with their lives.

I am sure that you will want to see the **Left Bank**, the Seine-side quays where you can buy books on any subject, and more hopeful artists sell their work to tourists, the **Latin Quarter**, and its very cheap restaurants of which three out of four sell couscous, the North African semolina dish which can be great or a soggy mess swimming in fat. You could hear any language; the **Sorbonne**, Paris University, is not the best looking in Europe, but one of the most international. And in vacations, when students go home, courses in French culture and literature are held, mostly for foreigners. At least, that is what they are supposed to be about, though friends tell me they are often more about close international friendships.

Hard by is **place de St-Germain-des-Prés**, with the oldest church in Paris, built in the 11th century, and the **Café des Deux Magots**, where Sartre and the Existentialists met after the Second World War. Writers, journalists and artists still meet, eat and drink round here, but no longer the rebels and true eccentrics.

There is a new place to see in Paris – something I would not miss despite its scaffolding and coloured pipe architecture which puts it, with the Eiffel Tower, as an enemy of Parisian elegance. It is called **Centre Nationale de l'Art**

et de Culture Georges Pompidou – a mouthful reduced by the Parisians to **Beaubourg**, the name of a village engulfed centuries ago. This collective name is used for the centre plus the site of Les Halles, the old market beloved by all Parisians and now moved to the suburbs to become efficient and faceless. The old streets around are mostly now turned into pedestrian walks.

Beaubourg is modern Paris. Not only the magnificent modern art collection with works from almost every great painter of this century, but for all its other shows. Many are free. The big free escalator that snakes up the front of the building gives you views to rival those from the Eiffel Tower. At the centre of the old market is the Roman-style Forum in glass, four floors, with sixteen enclosed walking streets of banks, shops, restaurants, two cinemas, two theatres. It has 160 boutiques run by some of France's most famous houses, including Pierre Cardin, Ted Lapidus, Yves St Laurent.

At the Pompidou Centre, the modern paintings are on the second, third, and fourth floors. The second offers mostly drawings – by Picasso and Matisse among others. The third floor shows the Fauvist and Cubist painters, including Braque and Picasso. On the fourth floor are works of Matisse, Dufy, Chagall, Paul Klee, Max Ernst and some contemporary painters. Entrance to this museum is on rue Saint Martin; the Forum entrance is on rue Sebastopol. For either, take the Métro to **Les Halles** or **Rambuteau**.

The museum is closed on Tuesdays. You pay 9F to go in but it is free on Sundays. For 16F you can go into the museum and whole Beaubourg centre. These fees could rise by the time you read this – France has inflation, too. You pay for nearly all museums and such in France, except on Sundays. The average is 9F.

For a free show, just hang around the vast courtyard of Beaubourg and see mummers, fire-eaters, clowns and student musicians. Don't begrudge them the odd coin – they like to eat.

I have two favourite walks round Paris which take in a lot of these places I have mentioned, but not Sacré Coeur, the Eiffel Tower or Beaubourg. One takes us round elegant Paris and its world of fashion, the other round the Latin Quarter, the quays on the Left Bank of the Seine and St Germain. The great point is to make them flexible – wander off at a tangent if something takes your fancy.

Our Walk of Elegance begins at **Etoile**, now called place Charles de Gaulle by the bureaucrats but not by Parisians. If you are fit, do climb the Arc de Triomphe's 164 steps for a fine view of the twelve roads radiating into Paris. Beneath the arch lies France's Unknown Soldier from the First World War. The Eternal Flame is rekindled at half-past six each evening.

Walk down Champs-Elysées to **Rond Point**, where all the cars in Paris seem to meet in evening rush-hour. Don't worry about Champs-Elysées itself – we shall be back. Go left down **avenue Matignon**, past some well-known art galleries into **rue du Faubourg St Honoré**. This is where the rich and elegant still shop. True, some great fashion houses have gone round the corner into other streets but in this little area you will see many great names of fashion houses, jewellers and perfumiers – Cartier, Hermès, Chanel, Lancôme, Lanvin, Lapidus. Pop round the corner into the **avenue de Marigny** and there is Cardin. The inspiration and artistic talent in their window displays is awe-inspiring.

We go left through **rue Royale** to **place de la Madeleine**. Frankly, we are not here to see the church but Fauchon, the greatest food shop in Paris. In joyous displays are terrines and pâtés – seen best early morning before they are mutilated by buyers – meats and gelées, superb fish, magnificent pâtisseries and a remarkable display of breads of dozens of types, shapes and sizes. A few years back, Fauchon burned down. I could not believe it as I saw the desolation. Happily it is all rebuilt, and as Denis Norden said: 'What a marvellous **smell** it must have made when it was burning.'

Place Madeleine is a good place to take a morning coffee.

Go round the church through **rue Tronchet** to **boulevard Haussman**, named after the baron who rebuilt Paris with wide boulevards to make room for Napoleon III's cavalry to attack the people if they dared to revolt, and incidentally made Paris beautiful.

This is where we actually go *into* the shops to mooch around and perhaps buy something to wear, to take home or to use in the kitchen.

Turn right, and across the road on the left is Au Printemps, the departmental store which sells most things from books to wigs and pots, pans and good handbags looking suspiciously like the top fashion bags until you look closely. Clothes, too, of course. The Primavera Boutique is useful for small presents. On Saturdays you could find some real bargains on the stalls outside. Further down on the right is Galeries Lafayette, where some of the leading fashion designers have boutiques selling at prices well below their haute couture houses, and there is the biggest perfume store in France.

Almost alongside is **L'Opéra** – the Opera House. It is difficult to get a seat for a performance but by going into the Opera Museum you can see inside the hall and it is very colourful – a gilded baroque palace in white, blue, pink, red and green marble, with a dome decorated by Chagall.

And here let us grab a seat at Café de la Paix and order a glass of healing wine after all that shop mooching. All right – Café de la Paix is a tourist cliché. But in all my travels I have found few better places to just sit and watch the passing scene, and Parisians feel the same, for they still go there to sit and stare.

Next we can follow avenue de l'Opéra to a little street on the right called **Pyramides** which takes us to one end of the **Louvre**. Apart from Greek, Roman, Egyptian and Oriental antiquities, the Louvre has probably the biggest collection of paintings in the world. It also has many surprises – like Constable's painting of Hampstead Heath. Sculptures are on the ground floor, but the magnificent Venus de Milo statue, stolen from the Greek isle of Milos, is among Greek antiquities.

Lying back across the road from the side of the Louvre, away from the river, is the **Palais Royal**, never the same since burned during the Commune revolt of 1871 and now a civil service building. Its gardens are open – one of the city's quieter hideouts. And at No. 1 is Louvre des Antiquaires – three stories of antiques offered for sale by the best-known dealers of Paris. You can walk around.

Now we can follow the attractive arcaded **rue de Rivoli** past the Tuileries gardens to **place de la Concorde**, made from a rubbish dump to show off a statue of Louis XV and the spot where his successor, Louis XVI, and Marie Antoinette, were guillotined. The 75 ft (23 m) stone needle is twenty-three centuries old and stood before a temple in Luxor until given to the French in 1829.

On the Rivoli corner is my favourite Paris museum, the **Jeu de Paume**, with its magnificent Impressionist paintings – Degas' ballet dancers and laundrywomen, *Le Moulin de la Galette* by Renoir, Manet's *Déjeuner sur l'Herbe*, surely the greatest of all picnic paintings, Gauguin in Brittany and Tahiti, hundreds more by Sisley and Van Gogh, Monet, Pissaro, Toulouse-Lautrec, Cézanne and Boudin. Even if we see only a few, let us stop here. It was built for a game between tennis and fives.

Like the Louvre, it closes on Thursdays.

Go into **Tuileries gardens** and wander up to the Louvre. The statues round the ponds and lawns are from the 17th and 18th centuries. The **Terrace du Bord de l'Eau** on the Seine side gives good views of the Left Bank.

Champs-Elysées is really two streets – divided by Rond Point. The first stretch from Concorde goes through attractive gardens under those famous horse-chestnuts. They muffle the traffic noise. In spring and summer Parisians bring their families to play here, and there are stalls selling ice-cream and coke, swings, roundabouts, donkey and goat carts, and Punch and Judy. On the south side, the gardens extend to the Seine. At rue Winston Churchill (rue Alexander III when I was a boy) are two pavilions built for the 1900 Paris Exhibition – **Petit Palais**, with a permanent exhibition, modern and medieval, and **Grand Palais** for temporary exhibitions. Past Rond Point the boulevard is bustle and liveliness. Elegant 19th-century houses are now banks, restaurants and cafés with pavement tables and, alas, more and more quick snack bars and take-aways. 'America,' a Parisian told me scathingly. But Parisians still meet here. It's a great place to sit and stare, but not to eat.

I usually begin my tour of the Left Bank on the right – at **Sully Morland** Métro station, then cross by **Pont Sully** to little **Ile St Louis** in the Seine. Here we can walk along quai de Béthune to cross to the Left Bank by **Pont Tournelle** and turn right along the quays by the Seine. You will soon find yet more artists offering their works to tourists. At the second bridge we can nip over to **Ile de la Cité** to see **Notre-Dame** cathedral. It was started in 1163. Outside, its elegant flying buttresses, rose windows and delicate lacy stonework are stunningly impressive, and inside, the hundreds of candles burning for the sick and the dead look like a strange fiery forest.

Back on the Left Bank, where we meet **boulevard St Michel**, is a narrow street called **rue de la Harpe**. Here are cheap restaurants where students go in the evenings – hardly gastronomic, but good value and good fun. Bookstalls line the quays. We continue along the river bank to the Mint and the Institut de France, then turn left on **rue Bonaparte** which leads us into **place St-Germain-des-Prés**. Take a coffee or an apéritif here, just to see what is happening, though it is more interesting at night.

A short way down **boulevard St Germain** cross the road past **St Sulpice** church and turn right to **Palais de Luxembourg**. Built by Marie de Medici out of the war reserve which she stole from the Bastille. She made better use of it. Her palace is now the Senate (upper house) of the French Parliament and is open only on Sundays. Luxembourg Gardens have a delightful informal atmosphere, with children playing, students strolling. Nice to know that they still walk hand in hand.

Take **rue Medicis** outside the palace, then left into Boul Mich and

right soon into **rue Soufflot** to the **Panthéon**. Here are the tombs of famous men – Voltaire, Rousseau, Zola, Victor Hugo, Braille, inventor of the Braille system for the blind, and Jean Moulin, French Resistance leader against the Nazis.

Walk round **Lycée Henri IV**, and we are in the real old Latin Quarter – **rue Descartes**, leading to **rue Mouffetarde**. Descartes has small shops, nice pâtisseries and cafés by day, some musical bars and restaurants for fringe night life. It was always a haunt of artists, writers and students. **Mouffette** means skunk in French and Mouffetarde got its name from old-time smelly skinners, tanners and dyers. A remnant is **Gobelins factory** nearby where tapestries and carpets have been woven since Louis XIV's reign. You can visit it on Wednesday, Thursday and Friday afternoons. Mouffetarde is narrow, winding and lively, with food shops, a market open every day selling everything from skirts to shirts to aubergines and cabbages, and some bargain restaurants used by working people and students – many serving Greek, Arab, Chinese or Vietnamese dishes. It is fun at night. From here either wander down **rue Censier** and **rue du Buffon** to **Jardin des Plantes** botanical gardens and catch the Métro from **Austerlitz**, or continue down **avenue des Gobelins** to **place d'Italie** with some dearer restaurants and cafés, and another Au Printemps store.

Bargain shopping in Paris is not condensed into one area. But **rue Ste Dominique**, a colourful and lively street of good little restaurants and a street fruit market, on the St Germain side of the Les Invalides, has several good value stores – La Clef des Soldes for sportswear and a bargain annexe opposite with clothes for men, women and children; Milsoldes, with a jumbled mixture from clothes to ornaments; Paris Pas Cher in nearby rue Jean-Nicot, with bargains in cooking pots to umbrellas. **Latour-Maubourg** is the Métro station.

A trick Parisian girls know is to buy shoes, clothes and handbags in resale shops. Be warned – these are not cheap. But they sell fine couture clothes worn three or four times by the rich or famous who dare not be seen in the same things for long. And you could even pick up something unworn but left over at the season's end. The nearest Métro for the right area is **St Philippe-du-Roule**.

Real Paris markets are great fun. Most flea markets have become dull and touristy, with small chance of finding a bargain or anything unusual. The flea market at St Ouen is biggest, best known, dearest and not worth the journey.

Night Life? It's entirely a question of taste. Go to the famous cabarets like **Moulin Rouge** and the **Lido** and you will see the slickest show and feel regimented. Don't ask a taxi driver. He will take you to a clip joint. On balance, avoid anything with flashy lights. And don't forget the café-théâtres – often with fair-priced meals and a small show, possibly a one-man or -girl show. **The Crazy Horse Saloon** on avenue George Cinq is expensive but is said to have the best strippers in the world.

Don't go to the **Bois de Boulogne** at night. You will be mugged, beaten up or mistaken for a mugger, junky or no-gooder by the police, and arrested. However, it is great in the daytime – especially Sunday morning. It has two lakes, many gardens, restaurants and cafés and two racecourses.

Do take a boat trip on the Seine by Bateau Mouche. This is another tourist cliché, but a lovely way to see Paris – especially at night, when you can have a gastronomic meal aboard. It's pricey but delicious – especially in the right company.

I should like to thank Hoverspeed for letting me repeat the routes I wrote for their guide cassette which they give to their Paris Break clients. They are my way of seeing Paris.

13 Camping and caravanning

When our daughters were small, we used to go to Brittany to stay with Comte de Massol de Rebetz at Château de Lanniron by the river Odet near Quimper.

Let me put it another way: we used to go camping in the delightful, peaceful grounds of the count's château, and hold polite conversations in the mornings with his sister when we bought fresh farm produce from the barn. We only joked about staying with the count to snob neighbours who in those days regarded tents as fit only for Boy Scouts, bedouins and homeless vagabonds.

Odd, because many of them owned caravans. Belonging to the Caravan Club was almost as snob as belonging to the MCC.

Then the British discovered that camping was *très snob* in France, and we met the Jaguar, Rover and even Rolls drivers on the better French camp sites. 'The children love the freedom. We go to the Caribbean in the winter,' they told us.

Now inflation threatens to make bedouins of us all. The biggest revolution in the holiday industry over the last ten years has been the boom in tents resembling canvas bungalows waiting fully equipped, on site. People who would never

have *dreamed* of camping use those. To think that it is only about seventeen years ago that Jim Cuthbert, then of Thames TV, started this fashion by forming Canvas Holidays and I gave him my considered opinion that it would never catch on!

The camping boom is international, and the French tourist authorities announced two years ago that in midsummer there were three campers seeking every one official pitch and that there was a real hazard from people camping *au sauvage* – in fields, woods or even on the roadside. That is mostly in the South of France, the Ardèche and Dordogne. But sites in Brittany and near coasts in Normandy and Pas-de-Calais get very booked up in July and August, and we have found that the best way to find a pitch is to go along when people are leaving, between 10 a.m. and noon. Some sites take no reservations. Others reserve a pitch only for a week or more and only if you send a substantial deposit. The answer is the same as with hotels – if you want a short break near the sea, do your very best to avoid July and August.

We were delighted recently to find that the count's site in Brittany, called **L'Orangerie de Lanniron**, is not only still tranquil and yet popular, but now has an all-weather tennis court, a swimming pool and children's pool, and in July and August serves hot take-away dishes, which can be a delight when you don't want to cook but fancy more than a salad. If you smell full-scale meals being cooked on a French camp site, you can bet it is from British tents or caravans. The younger French tend to eat out, unlike their parents, who would spend all the morning preparing and cooking a vast three o'clock lunch and until late evening sleeping it off.

The joy of the Orangerie site is its sanitary arrangements. Washing facilities are excellent – hot water for all basins, sinks and showers, individual basins in private cabins with mirrors and lights. There are sit-down 'British' loos, too. Most Britons are not so used to standing on their own feet as the French. For us, loos can make or break a camp site. The only time Barbara has smoked in the last twenty-five years has been a Gauloise in a camp site loo, though now she swears that lighting matches does the trick.

L'Orangerie also has washing machines – another boon. It is one of the great Castel et Camping sites of France – best for people who put plumbing, space and peace first. Others prefer livelier sites with more facilities, like one we have known even longer quite near to L'Orangerie – **La Pointe St Gilles**, beside a small beach in the very lively and pleasant family resort of Benodet. This has many more electrical connections than most sites, a very comprehensive take-away meal service, butcher's shop, children's playground, driers and ironing rooms as well as washing machines, hot showers and a hot tap (but only cold water in its washrooms). It was one of the first used by Canvas Holidays, and many British tents-on-site companies now use it.

Some French sites have big playrooms, dancing, full restaurant and snack bars, drinking bars, boutiques, TV room, tennis and supermarkets. Others are football fields and their pavilions pressed into service for the midsummer rush. Sites are officially graded into one- to four-star. In 1984 you would pay about 65F a night in a one-star site to 100F in a four-star for tent, car and family of four. Tighter control over site grading has brought a big improvement to French sites, and public demand for more comfort has helped, too.

You may camp on farmland providing you ask the farmer's permission first. In some areas, farmers are not keen because campers have become a nuisance by leaving gates open, asking constantly for water or to use toilets and so on. It is possible to camp in forests if you apply on the spot to the local Office National des Eaux et Forêts. You may not camp by the roadside or overnight in a lay-by, and the police are getting tough about this.

There are also some farm and open-field camp sites with simple toilets, water points, basins, showers and sinks, usually listed in area camping lists. The Camping Bretagne list for Brittany, for instance, marks them as AN (open air) CF (farm sites). Some Fermes-Auberges in Brittany serve typical Breton meals and have a few camp pitches.

For a very few sites, including one near Paris, you need an international camping carnet, which you can get from the AA or RAC if you are a member of these, or from the Camping Club of Great Britain, Caravan Club or Motor Caravanners' Club if a member.

Most sites in the north of France are open from May 1 to the middle or end of September only. Some site take-aways or shops do not open until June 1.

Though the number of pitches on a site is much more strictly controlled these days, some do have their tents or vans too close together for our liking. It may be amusing or educational to overhear your neighbours arguing about the washing up, putting the world right or making love, but remember – it is a two-way traffic.

We once stayed on a site called **De la Plage** at **La Trinité** in south Brittany, a lively little fishing port with a harbour where you can hire boats. The site had a lot to offer – direct access to dunes and a sand beach, excellent toilets, shade and a really good food take-away outside the back entrance. Alas, the tents were too close for our liking. We could hear sounds of pop from one side and Scrabble from the other into the night.

One of our favourite sites in Brittany is near to **Cleden-Poher**, an unprepossessing place on the N164, just west of Carhaix-Plouger in the centre of Brittany. We found it because I had driven too far and

my children were tired and hungry. We followed a notice to a camping site called **Le Moulin Vert** along a rough little lane and found ourselves in a lovely spot. The setting is superb, in meadows, with trees and hedgerows and the river Aulne running fast through it, rich in salmon and trout. The green and mauve hills of the Noires range are its backcloth and by the river is an old mill with its main building turned into a shop, café and rest room. I could have spent weeks there.

We found a beautiful uncrowded but more sophisticated site near Dol-de-Bretagne, 24 km SE of St Malo, at **Epiniac**. In 250 acres of woods, meadows and lakes, the **Château des Ormes** site has a nice rustic bar in a barn, heated swimming pool and children's pool, nice restaurant, good take-away, a shop, free fishing in the three lakes, dancing twice a week, pedaloes, tennis, riding; also good sanitation blocks, plenty of hot water and showers. A mobile butcher's shop calls twice a week. It is near some delightful places, including the oyster beds of Le Vivier sur Mer and Cancale, Combourg, its castle and good cheap restaurants, and Dinard, the beautiful medieval town on the river Rance. It is the only site in Brittany to get the top accolade of four red tents from the Michelin camping guide. We have stayed here twice with one of the best on-site camping companies, Eurocamp; once we used a tent, the second time a caravan. I confess that I gave up tents for caravans two years ago because of a very dodgy back, although I admit that the beds I have been given by Canvas Holidays and Eurocamp have been better than many in hotels, if smaller. My tenting is now done for me by two daughters, one of whom really prefers canvas walls to brick when travelling, and who have been camping since they were a year old. What I especially like about caravans at my age is the more civilised facilities in most on-site vans.

These on-site operations are great value but you need at least a week; except for a few special offers in winter, they won't book you for less. If you don't own a tent, you can very occasionally hire one at French sites, but I found only one in the official Nòrmandy list of sites, though plenty of caravans. The Brittany list lumps them together, so it is impossible to tell. Picardie marks only caravans; the Michelin guide gives only caravans or bungalows.

You can hire all camping equipment in Britain from **Black's Camp Hire**, 146 The Grove, Stratford, London E15, 01 519 1313. They have several pick-up points.

AA Argosy Tours will hire you full camping equipment or one of those superb camping-trailers which convert into a super tent. You pick them up at Dover. But the lower limit is one week and you must let the AA book your ferry crossing.

Finding a site near Channel ports can be difficult in high season. **La Bien Assise**, a new Castel et Camping site at **Guines**, the historic little town 10 km S of Calais, will be a boon, as is **La Ville**

Mauny, 2 km from Dinard, for people using St Malo. The **Forêt de Montgeon** in a wooded park in Le Havre is a good one of the municipal sites, which are usually cheap and useful. At **Le Portel**, the fishing village almost attached to Boulogne, is an Airotel, picked for outstanding facilities, called **Le Phare**, with fine sea views and a restaurant. Dieppe's site, **Du Pré Saint Nicolas**, is only two-star. It is on the way to Pourville.

For Cherbourg, there is a site by the sea eastward at **Bretteville** called **Du Fort**.

The original **Paris camp site** beside the Seine and Bois de Boulogne, and only ten minutes by car from Etoile, has always been full when I have arrived, though I expect it is emptier in winter. The **Airotel Maisons-Laffitte**, in that greeny posh suburb beside the river, is a fine site, with ultra-modern sanitation. From a station 1 km away you can get a train into Paris – Gare St Lazare, taking eighteen minutes, and the last one back goes at 12.30 a.m. It has self-service shop, restaurant, launderette, bar, all heated in winter. There are super mobile-homes here which you can hire on a ferry package with AA Argosy Tours for five days or more, or in winter for three days: a good way to see Paris on a budget. Paris is fun in winter. You can also hire vans there.

A new caravan-only site has opened at **Issy-Les-Moulineaux**, 4 km west of central Paris, with buses into the city.

Hotels and Restaurants

Here is a short list of useful camp sites which we know. You will find a good list in Alan Rodgers' *Selected Sites* (Deneway, £1.85). Not so extensive as some, but he has inspected all of them himself and we have never yet disagreed with his comments.

Michelin's *Camping Caravanning France* (£3.50) gives 3500 sites, graded and facilities shown, but with no description. The official French *Camping and Caravanning Guide* lists 8400 sites (in French – £3.95 by post from FFCG, 6 The Meadows, Worlington, Bury St Edmunds, Suffolk). Letts' *Campsite Guide* (£2.50) lists 5000 sites.

Also apply for lists from:
Brittany: Comité Régional du Tourisme, 3 rue d'Espagne, 35022 Rennes; **Normandy: Comité Régional du Tourisme**, 34 rue Josephine, 27000 Evreux; **Castel et Camping**, Mme Qidou, BP32, 56470 La Trinité-sur-Mer; **Fermes-Auberges de Bretagne**, CER, rue du Tumulus, 56340 Carnac, Brittany; **Comité Régional du Tourisme de Picardie**, 9 rue Allart, BPO342, 80003 Amiens; **Airotel**, 7 rue Elise Arramendy, 64500 St-Jean-de-Luz.

Sites discussed in this chapter

Quimper – *L'Orangerie de Lanniron*, 29000 Quimper, (98) 90.62.02: May 1 to September 15.

Benodet – *Pointe St Gilles*, 29118 Benodet, (96) 91.05.37: April 1 to September 30; also *Letty*, (98) 91.04.69: by beach with dangerous tidal race; good facilities. June 25 to September 10.

La Trinité-sur-Mer, Morbihan; off D186 coast road between Trinité and Carnac – *Plage*, 56470 La Trinité, Morbihan, (97) 55.73.28: May 15 to September 15.

Cleden-Poher, Finistère – *Le Moulin Vert*, 29270 Finistère, (98) 93.82.05: Whitsun to September 15.

Dol-de-Bretagne, at Epiniac – *Des Ormes*, 35120 Epiniac, Ille-et-Vilaine, (99) 48.10.18: May 20 to September 15.

Guines – *La Bien-Assise*, 62340 Pas-de-Calais, (21) 35.20.77: May 1 to September 30.

Le Havre – *Camp Municipal Forêt de Montgeon*, 76600 Le Havre, (35) 83.45.90: April 1 to September 30.

Dinard – *La Ville Mauny*, 35800 Dinard, (99) 46.94.73: Easter to October.

Le Portel – *Airotel Le Phare*, 62200 Boulogne-sur-Mer, (21) 31.69.20: April 1 to September 30.

For **Cherbourg**, at Bretteville – *Fort de Bretteville*, 50840 Fermanville, (33) 43.30.90: open all year.

Dieppe – *Pré St Nicolas*, rte Pourville, 76200 Dieppe, (35) 84.11.39: open all year.

Paris – *Parc de Camping Paris Ouest*, Bois de Boulogne – open all year, no reservations but get there very early; minibus to Métro station.

At **Maisons-Laffitte** – *Airotel Caravanning Maisons-Laffitte*, 78600 Maisons Laffitte, 962.43.27: always open.

At **Issy-les-Moulineaux**, Paris Ouest, Ile St Germain – *Parile Campexel*, caravans only, 67-73 rue Pierre Poli, Issy-les-Moulineaux, (1) 555.58.24.

Other recommended sites

Dinan, at **Taden**, NE just outside, Côte-du-Nord, Brittany – *La Hallerais*, Taden, 22100 Dinan, (96) 39.15.93: outstanding site; February 15 to November 15.

Martragny, SE Bayeux, Calvados – *Château de Martragny*, 12 km from sea, 14740 Bretteville-l'Orgueilleuse, Calvados, (31) 80.21.40: May 1 to September 15.

Blangy-le-Château, W Cormeilles, NW Lisieux in Calvados countryside – *Le Brevedent*, 14130 Pont-l'Evêque, (31) 64.72.88: super country site by lake with pool; reservations min. three days; May 1 to September 15.

St Valéry-sur-Somme, W Abbeville, S of Berck, Le Touquet – *Château de Drancourt*, 80230 St Valéry-sur-Somme: useful for Boulogne or Dieppe; 8 km from beach; popular; open all year.

Honfleur, near Le Havre – *La Briquerie*, 3½ km at Equesmauville, 14600 Calvados, (31) 89.28.32: good restaurant; April 1 to September 30.

Near **Hesdin**, for Hesdin forest, Canche valley, 24 km SE Montreuil – *Camping La Loge*, attached to popular *Auberge de la Forêt*, (21)

86.86.52: auberge has super 65F menu and carte (try trout in cream, guinea fowl, snails, frogs' legs, charolais beef, fine lamb).

Forêt-Fouesnant, south Brittany – very many sites around here in lovely countryside; we used to stay at *Saint Laurent*, Kerleven, 29133 La Forêt-Fouesnant: with seawater swimming pool in rocks, shallow bit for children; interesting site; May 15 to September 15.

Inland from **Trebeurden**, north Brittany, – *Le Cleuzio Holiday Centre*, attached to holiday hotel with facilities you can use; restaurant, bar, swimming pool, tennis, pony trekking; bookable three nights or more on package with ferry by Brittany Ferries, Milbay Docks, Plymouth, 0752 751833.

Companies offering tents and/or caravans on site in Brittany, Normandy or Pas-de-Calais include:

AA Argosy, PO Box 100, Halesowen, West Midlands, **Canvas Holidays**, Bull Plain, Hertford, **Carefree Camping**, 41 St Stephyns Chambers, Banks Court, Hemel Hempstead, Herts, **Eurocamp**, Edmundson House, Tatton St, Knutsford, Cheshire, **French Travel Service** (by train, boat), Francis House, Francis St, London SW1, **Fresh Fields**, 441 Oxford St, London W1, **InnTent**, 26 Bank St, Wetherby, West Yorkshire, **Townsend Thoresen Holidays** (mobile homes), Enterprise House, Avebury Ave, Tonbridge, Kent.

14 Shopping - duty-free and souvenirs

On Boulogne's quai Gambetta, at the end of rue Faidherbe beside the bridge to the car ferries, a retail fish market is held each morning. Stalls are piled high with cockles and mussels, clams, crabs, the ugly monkfish (lotte) which the French adore, sea bass and the odd fierce-looking lobster.

On my way home I try to reach here before midday, when it starts to close, to take home my favourite souvenirs of France – two dozen oysters, a kilo of little mussels which come usually from Etaples down the coast and a few expensive but beautifully fresh langoustines for Barbara. Popped into a plastic bag, they keep fresh until I get them home to the fridge that night.

Since we joined the EEC, I have not been such a great souvenir hunter. You can get most things at home, often cheaper. So I stick mostly to food and wine. But souvenirs and duty-free loot are part of the British way of travel. I have known people fail to catch a plane trying not to miss buying their spirits and cigarette ration at an airport for a bit less than they could get it aboard. Those magazine articles and radio and TV programmes about 'best buys' for duty-free make me smile. It is no good telling me that I can save a quid on a bottle of Scotch in Bahrain if I'm heading for Dublin, nor even that I save 50p on a Dunkirk boat when I am heading for Cherbourg. I heard a TV programme discussing at length whether it paid you to fill your car tank with petrol in Britain or France. It hardly seems worth much fuss. The price wanders in both countries, and even a whole tankful won't save you all that much at a price difference of 10-20p a gallon. You can't keep popping home to refill. What speed you do makes more difference.

I have often met Britons shopping for souvenirs on their first day abroad, and I feel so sorry for schoolchildren with little to spend agonising on day trips to Calais and Boulogne on what to take home to Mum. I have nothing against souvenirs but I do not believe that any of us should run short of money because we feel committed to taking back a little something to Aunt Agnes.

More of us are settling for food – unusual cheese which even the gourmet delicatessens do not sell or which will be cheaper and fresher in France, coffee (much cheaper in France – buy it in those plastic-covered bags and keep it in the deep freeze), cans of olive oil (also much cheaper), charcuterie (sausages, cooked meats, smoked jambon cru – expensive, but four *tranches* or slices with salad make a summer meal for two), pâtés (different and better than at home), lovely tiny thin French beans, luscious fruit such as peaches (cheaper and fresher in France).

Ministry of Agriculture orders and Customs and Excise attitudes are very tolerant about importing foodstuffs in reasonable amounts. Customs told me recently that there is no problem about shellfish of the usual types, from oysters to sole, nor about cooked meats, cheese or pâté. Reasonable amounts of vegetables, such as a kilo or so, are tolerated but not potatoes at present because of the Colorado beetle scare. A kilo or so of fruit is allowed, too. I have often brought home trays of peaches. But I do declare them – just in case.

Unless the weather is very hot, we take home butter, preferably bought in the market from farmers, cut off a huge slab and not done up in fancy paper. We prefer farm-made butter to factory butter, but it is dearer.

Liquor rules are laid down by the EEC, agreed by us, and I think it is foolish to bring even one bottle more without declaring it. If you buy spirits aboard ship or at any other duty-free shop, you can bring back 1 litre. If you buy them in a wine shop or supermarket in an EEC country, you may bring back 1½ litres (two bottles). You may also bring back from an ordinary shop – not duty-free – 4 litres (six bottles) of table wine. Instead of the spirits (not in addition), you can bring from an ordinary shop 3 litres of champagne or of fortified wine under 22 per cent, such as port, vermouth, sherry, crème de cassis. You can bring 200 cigarettes, 100 cigarillos, 50 cigars or 250 grams of tobacco. Also about 2oz (50 grams) of perfume (which would cost you a pretty penny) and 9oz (¼ litre) of toilet water. It does pay to buy these in duty-free shops, even if the price is hardly a bargain.

We ran into a lady in distress in Boulogne's Auchan supermarket recently. She could not find any wine in plastic bottles. Her friend who had been over before had advised her to stick to plastic-bottled wines because they were cheaper and best value. Cheaper, perhaps; but best value?

Very cheap wine, for lapping in litres, in France can be a bargain, or can be like battery acid. Far better to pick up the special offers, such as a pack of six bottles of a good Vin de Pays or a VDQS (Vins de Qualité Supérieure) of Tarn, Touraine or Corbières, costing about 20p a bottle more and much kinder to your palate and stomach.

Middle-priced wines such as Pouilly Fuissé, St Emilion, Sancerre (going up because fashionable in Paris), Muscadet (gone up), a good Beaujolais or a Brouilly or Fleurie (better version of Beaujolais), and that heavy strong Cahors, are all usually bargains at a half to a third the price we would pay at home. For instance, I bought a good '79 St Emilion for £2 in France when it was around £4.50 here, and Muscadet-sur-lie for £1.15 when it was £3.40 here.

It pays to buy these from a specialist wine merchant. You might get them a little cheaper in a hypermarket but not usually from the best vineyards or bottlers, nor so well kept. A French restaurateur told me: 'True, hypermarket wines have not been standing on the shelf so long. They have been shaken around and stood outside in the sun or snow.'

When experts say that good wines are as cheap at home as in France, they mean *great*, expensive wines like Château Latour.

Clothes, of course, are usually cheaper in Britain but French clothes for women and children still *do* have flair – if you pay enough. Swimsuits, delightful raincoats which can make a girl look chic or sexy, beautifully cut shorts and, of course, undies. We saw a delicious pair of red silk French knickers, cut slanting for the long leg look and trimmed with lace, in Boulogne and rushed in to ask the price. 540F! Barbara said that they would do wonders for a girl's morale if only to enable her to say to any man trying to get into her life: 'Careful – that's fifty quids' worth of knickers you are pulling at.'

Our other special souvenir is traditional kitchen equipment, such as conical whisks, spatulas that bend, cone-shaped sieves called chinoises – ideal for clearing lumps from sauces or the humble gravy and, when we can afford them, super saucepans. Kitchen knives, too. You can buy kitchenware quite cheaply at supermarkets but if you want the real things which chefs use, strong and lasting, pay more in a specialist shop. It will be cheaper in the end. Whisks, for instance, need strong metal handles, not wooden ones which fall off. Despite the wonders of electric aids, real French chefs think you cannot cook without conical hand whisks. Saucepans should have thick-gauge steel bottoms welded in, not welded on to the pan as an afterthought.

In some supermarkets and particularly department stores such as Prisunic, you can buy nice cheap drinking glasses, packed in boxes for transport, ideal for bouncing at parties. I have found some unusual rough large wine goblets going cheaply in florists. They are intended for flower arranging. For me, red roses look better in my garden, red wine in my goblets.

For children, we hunt the stationery counters of department stores, especially at the beginning of term. French and Italians have a flair for school equipment and you can buy both in French shops. Exercise books are splendidly covered in pretty patterns and car or cowboy designs, so are cases of pencils and instruments. The French equivalent of the long-departed school satchel still survives, looking more like a smart shopping bag. Our children took them home as Christmas presents for friends. They are lightweight, pretty or smart, with plenty of room for the usual schoolgirl clobber. My wife once used one as a shopping bag. Often you can get pencil cases and exercise book covers to match these bags, making a fashionable ensemble. Boys' pencil cases are often gimmicky – shaped like Grand Prix cars, veteran cars, animals or ukeleles!

Boulogne

Boulogne still has small individually run shops, unusual in modern towns so big, as well as Prisunic and Nouvelles Galeries department stores and the usual run of chain shoe shops. Most of the best shops are in **rue Faidherbe**, a one-way street coming down from the old town to the quai Gambetta and bridge for the ferry, **rue Thiers** at right angles about 200m up it, **rue Victor Hugo**, also at right angles. These last join Faidherbe to **Grande Rue**, a one-way street going up from the dock to the old town. The extension of Victor Hugo towards the station is called rue Nationale.

Leave your car on quai Gambetta or in the first-storey car park behind the Champion supermarket and walk.

On the left up Faidherbe is a good rather posh-looking bakery and cake shop, almost next door to a fashion shop, *Griff*, which sells clothes by Ted Lapidus, Pierre Cardin, and other top chaps of fashion. Good men's shirts. On the next corner is *Eram* shoe shop where you can buy some good value shoes from Italy as well as dearer fashion shoes; Lecoq, further along, sells more luxurious shoes. The popular bakery *Moderne* has a splendid bakers' smell. *Carole Imper*, on the opposite side of Faidherbe, sells

superb rainwear; next door is *Aux Bonnes Choses*, old-style grocers with good charcuterie, wines and cheeses. *Florence* is a leather and handbag shop usually with special offers.

Nouvelles Galeries is in rue Thiers. So are *Magaine*, the shop with the £50 knickers and nice, more popularly priced dresses, swimwear and undies, *Pommou* and *PimcKie*, boutiques for younger people.

But the real treasure cave in rue Thiers is *Philippe Olivier*'s cheese shop. It gets crowded. To enjoy it, wait until the latest wave of Britons has just left. Olivier matures his cheese in special caves under the shop and you can arrange to see them. He has over 200 cheeses. His own Camembert, labelled Olivier, is the best I have tasted. He sells Maroilles, the cheese with the reeling smell and lovely taste when cooked. He wraps it well for your car's sake. But all his cheeses are splendid because he does not buy them from cheese factories but from farmers and small local producers. It makes all the difference. People who snootily tell me that they never bother to take cheese home because their own local shop has a fine selection should really try his cheeses. They are a revelation.

Caprice in rue Nationale has beautiful, often expensive, gifts, like superb dinner services or something small in porcelain.

My very favourite shop in Boulogne is intended for sailors. It is an old-fashioned ship's chandlers, with anything for sale from a rope to fenders, compasses and cabin lights, to everything the good ship's cook needs in the galley: pots and pans, huge soup ladles, roasting pans of many sizes, stewpots. Any of them would do splendid service in a landlubber's kitchen. And some of the sea-going clothes would do good service ashore, too. Called *Angelo*, it is behind Hôtel Faidherbe in **rue Pot d'Etain**. There is a copper fish fryer I want from there when I have £30 to spare.

The car park for *Champion hypermarket* is in **boulevard Dounou** behind the market and Hôtel Ibis. It is almost opposite the bridge which you take to cross the river after leaving the ferry.

Champion is a smallish hypermarket with some interesting outer shops, including some selling good-value leather handbags. Another sells fish – you could get your oysters here if they have not run out. The foodstore has a good charcuterie counter and fair wine prices.

Boulogne has a super wine shop for those who want to take their liquor ration home in wine – ten bottles, or take more and pay the difference. You still get your allowance, then you pay an average of 80p to £1 a bottle, and if you get a good claret or a Pouilly Fuissé at around £3 a bottle less than in Britain, that is worth it. You reach the wine store, *Le Chais*, by driving up boulevard Dounou under a railway bridge, then immediately turning left down a narrow road, **rue des Deux Ponts**. From the other end you can reach it from rue Nationale, an extension of rue Victor Hugo.

Le Chais sells no plonk, but it has some very good special offers, usually sold by the bottle. A nice Loire dry white cost us 6F.50 a bottle (end of 1983), a fair Muscadet 9F a bottle, a good Muscadet 12F and a very nice '79 Bourgueil red from the Loire 23F. Mostly the wines are sold in sixes or cases of a dozen, very safely packed – some in wooden cases. You really start gaining when you buy something like a '79 or '81 St Emilion, a Pouilly Fuissé (so dear in Britain now because of American and Japanese buyers competing at auctions) or any claret. I have bought good clarets for £3 to £4 a bottle which would have cost £6 to £7 in Britain. Stock up for special occasions and Christmas, like I do. Beware: they take no credit cards: old-fashioned cash or travellers' cheques.

Calais

Shopping in hypermarkets has nothing like the appeal of shopping in streets. I prefer to drift around, window-shopping, to rushing with lists from one department to another. Hypermarkets are for keeping out of the rain or shopping after 7 p.m. Most keep open until 10 p.m. Monday to Saturday. But the *Continent hypermarket* at Calais Marck is one of the best in the north of France. It has a very wide range of goods, including wine, and their charcuterie and their cheese counter offer a far wider choice than any of the smaller supermarkets. Furthermore, because of the

Britons on day trips shopping there, these foods are sold quicker and are often fresher.

Calais is, frankly, not such an interesting place for shopping or window-shopping as Dieppe, Boulogne or Le Havre, though as good as St Malo and Cherbourg.

There are two distinct shopping areas – that around **place d'Armes** and the old tower, near the port, used mostly but not entirely by tourists, and the older shops up the hill past the station and town hall. I have always found a reasonable choice of charcuterie and vegetables at *Gro supermarket* on a corner in place d'Armes. *Au Gourmet* stocks fewer items but often better quality and dearer – also Nicolas wines. Two fairly good wine shops here are the new caves under Eric Hamiot's *La Feuillandine* restaurant and *Le Cellier*, right across the place and main road, beyond *Maison du Fromage*. This cheese shop is not quite in the class of Olivier's in Boulogne, but sells over 200 cheeses including Maroilles – washed in beer and smelling like a pub toilet but delicious when cooked.

There is a good fish shop in **rue de Mer**, just past place d'Armes. This street becomes rue Royale, leading towards the station. Here are *Outhier* (good bread and cakes), *Bellyneck* (charcuterie), *Descamps* (children's clothes, linen, beach/bath robes – good quality, pricey).

You will find clothes shops and more food shops on **boulevard Jacquard** – straight up from rue Royale past the station. A turning off it to the left, **boulevard La Fayette**, has the posher shops, such as *Croissant Chaud* (guess what? croissants), *Cupillard* (good, expensive copper saucepans), *Au Fin Bec* (super charcuterie), *Huitrière Calaisienne* (best place for oysters and mussels).

Keep plodding up Jacquard past the post office and you may ultimately find **place Crêvecoeur** where a market is held on Thursday and Saturday mornings – good for butter, cheese, veg and fish. The earlier you get there, the better value you will find.

Dieppe

A few yards from Gare Maritime where Sealink boats dock, right opposite the beginning of **Grand'Rue**, is a small fish market selling fish brought in that morning to the Port de Pèche just down the quayside and auctioned there before breakfast. Fishermen bring in mostly turbot, brill, bass, sole, nearly all shellfish but especially small mussels and Dieppe's speciality – coquilles St Jacques (scallops). *Armorique*, on quai Henry IV where passengers leave the ferries, has a very good fish restaurant upstairs and sells best-quality shellfish downstairs and a superb fish soup in plastic containers to take away. You can buy high-quality fish, too, at Quenouille's *A la Marée du Jour* at the corner of Grand'Rue and place Nationale.

Since Grand'Rue became a pedestrian street, it has taken over even more of the shopping trade.

The Saturday market there is one of the best I have found. Most of the produce really does come direct from the farms and the fishing boats. Stalls and baskets are filled with oysters, mussels and coquilles St Jacques. You can sometimes buy oysters incredibly cheaply if they are too small for the restaurants. I once bought them for 2F (about 20p) a dozen. There are tubs of butter, huge farm cheeses, big terrines of pâté, too. Stalls are spread into all the side streets, particularly **rue St Jean**, where from one of the smaller farmers I buy the best butter I have ever tasted. In **place Nationale** stalls sell clothes and handbags. I have seen little electric cars on offer. They take two people and you can drive them without a test or licence. There are herbs for sale on some stalls on Grand'Rue, but you can buy a wonderful variety of these, cheaply, by the ounce, in **rue St Jacques** very near Des Tribuneaux, the historic inn. The herb shop is called Λ. *Ferment*, and its perfume as you enter is as intoxicating as in an Eastern market.

Grand'Rue starts with small branches of the famous department stores *Printemps* and *Prisunic*, and after that you find at least one example of almost any shop you could want. Across the road at *Royal Fruit*, carefully handpicked fruit in season is sold. Down the other end at No. 105 is *Tout Pour la Maison*, where you can buy kitchenware such as those conical chinoise strainers, knives you can really sharpen and slicers for tomatoes, onions and meat.

The best shop for kitchenware is *Magdalene* in **rue Barre**, a continuation of Grand'Rue. It supplies restaurants. *Terpin* (rue Barre) and *Bergeret* (Grand'Rue), ironmongers, also sell a lot of kitchen items.

In rue Barre and Grand'Rue are six jewellers, four boulangeries-pâtisseries (bakers and cake shops), five pâtisseries (making fancier cakes and mostly dearer), a super épicerie (grocer) selling everything from pâté and biscuits to chicken, wine and tinned meats, and another in place Nationale, and two confiseries (even more expensive and beautiful cakes and sweets). There are three good charcuteries, too, for your picnic snacks or to buy smoked country ham, pâté and sausages to take home.

There are five shoe shops, from *Bally-France* selling high fashion, to *Bata* selling cheaper versions and bargains in such things as Italian mules or beach shoes. There are all sorts of clothes shops, from those with gorgeous gowns lying around the window with no price tags, to boutiques which seem to change their name with changes of fashion but are always with us, and shops dripping jeans even from their lampholders.

Le Roy-Delepouille sells good-quality clothes for beach, town or sportswear, including the famous Hermès fashions. The really smart fashion shop is *BDT*. Here they sell elegant, cool numbers which you see French women wearing on TV but never seem to see on living, walking girls. Maybe I mix in the wrong French circles. For glamorous, expensive French undies, Barbara has been seduced by *Au Dé d'Argent* and *Feminités*, both in Grand'Rue. Feminités has beachwear, too. Even the babies have style: *Duquesne-Layette* offers clothes 'from birth to twelve years old – exclusivité Pierre Cardin'. And *Bébé-Styl* is just that.

Locals of Dieppe do a lot of their shopping in rue St Jacques, leading to the church. Here are two good bakers, *Devaux* and *Lanchon*, and my favourite grocer's shop in Normandy – *Claude Olivier*, who sells almost as many cheeses as his namesake in Boulogne, matures them in his own caves and also does a nice line in wine special offers. He sells Nicolas wines – dull but cheap and reliable. But I buy my wine at the *Co-op* in **rue Duquesne** between Grand'Rue and the sea front.

Tutti-Frutti in St Jacques is a super fruit shop, despite its name.

My own secret favourite shop is in Grand'Rue – *Techni-Loisir*, selling beautiful true models of racing cars, trains and jets that really fly.

A *Mammoth supermarket* is 4 km away on the Rouen road. But I shall stick to Grand'Rue.

Cherbourg

Cherbourg is going through a change of life. By the time you read this, I hope, the demolitions and erections in **place du Géneral de Gaulle** will be completed and it will have returned to its schizo role

of a restful grandstand of pavement cafés for watching fountains spray and the world go by on Monday, Wednesday, Friday and Sunday and a splendid market for fruit, vegetables, butter, cheese and clothes on Tuesday, Thursday and Saturday morning. This is still the best centre to start shopping trips.

Parking is hell in Cherbourg, so you can park on the **quai de l'Entrepôt** across the harbour basin, walk over the bridge and you are nearly there.

Streets on one side of place de Gaulle are for pedestrians only, so inevitably have a fair sprinkling of boutiques and shoe shops. In the streets beyond are the real shops for buying cooked meats, bread, cakes. The department store *Magazins Réunis* is on **rue Gambetta** alongside the place, and in a turning off here, **rue Portes**, is a branch of *Arthur Martin*, the ironmongers – useful for presents, kitchenware, cheap crockery and glasses. This leads towards **Grand'Rue**, best for food – especially *Le Pottevin* for smoked jambon de campagne – the chewy, country ham. *Ledsos* further along sells top-grade oysters.

The new shopping area is in **rue au Blé** near the fish market. Old shops have been refaced and smart shops now flourish. Boutiques abound. If you have won the pools, make for *Infinitif*, where labels have familiar names like Yves St Laurent and Lapidus, not to mention Cardin. This street is something of a tourist trap: antique shops and pricey gift shops alternate with clothes.

My favourite shop is in **rue**

Fourdray, by place de Gaulle. It is called *Croissant d'Oré* and you can see and smell croissants being made.

Continental hypermarket is across the harbour bridge on **quai Entrepôt**, and sells all the usual hypermarket items in abundance. It has a good car park, is convenient for the ferry down the quai and sells cheap petrol.

Le Havre

Being an industrial and fishing port rather than a holiday centre, Le Havre has good genuine French shops, though some of its streets seem to have strayed from fashionable parts of Paris, with prices to fit.

Place de l'Hôtel de Ville is the planners' centre of the rebuilt town. Smart shopping starts here and goes through **place Gambetta** and down **rue de Paris** to **quai de Southampton** – convenient for Townsend-Thoresen customers, whose boats leave from there. Shops for food and clothes are good and pricey. *Gervais* in rue de Paris sells excellent fish – a bit of a risk on an overnight boat perhaps in midsummer, but you should be all right. *Rôtisserie Gambetta* sells very good pâtés, cheeses and a fair selection of wines, and is open on Sundays.

Northwards from place Hôtel de Ville, **avenue René Coty** takes you to the few older parts of Le Havre still left, and the ordinary folks' shops like *Monoprix*, a sort of French Woolworths, and *Printemps*, almost a French Marks & Spencer but with classier items in household linen, china and saucepans, and more fashionable undies. Printemps branches vary. This is better than the one in Dieppe.

Take **rue Voltaire** from place Gambetta and you find the covered market halls very soon on the right. The usual stalls are there: fish, vegetables, meat, cooked meat and a very good cheese stall. There are fresh herbs in season.

The hypermarket *Auchan* is up in the high town, about 4 km out. Take the **Cours de la République** NE (Fécamp road) under the tunnel and follow the sign to the commercial centre at the roundabout. It is a real, original style hypermarket, selling almost everything and with many individual shops as well as a food hall.

St Malo

I like shopping in the walled town of St Malo. It is random shopping, with little order, mostly small shops and many pleasant surprises, especially in cheaper clothes, special offers of shoes, ties or jeans, and plenty of bakers, grocers and wine shops.

Just walk up **Grande Rue** or **Puits aux Braies** next to it and you will find them all round, including a *Monoprix*.

There are street markets on Tuesday and Friday, selling everything from fish and beans to clothes. Other street markets are at

place Rocabey, at the end of **quai Duguay-Trouin**, outside the walls, on Monday, Thursday and Saturday, and at *La Découverte* shopping centre on **ave Géneral-de-Gaulle** (D301) on Wednesday and Saturday. The hypermarket is at La Découverte, too.

At **St Servan**, near the ferry terminal, are open markets on Wednesday and Saturday.

15 Briefly Belgium

The Belgian coast used to be the cheapest holiday area in Europe. Before coach-camping holidays started, those of us who could not afford a holiday abroad could still manage a few days in Belgium. That stage has not yet been reached again, but despite inflation, holidays in Belgium were actually cheaper in £s in 1983 than 1982.

When we started to buy a house and rear a family, we were in the condition then known to polite bank managers as 'temporary financial embarrassment', now called 'cashflow problems'. In basic English, we were broke.

So we took our £60 drop-head Nash Metropolitan, called the 'Yellow Peril', to a chalet on the Belgian coast at Bredene, a simple resort with no promenade, little laid-on entertainment, enormous sands backed by huge dunes, with remains of bunkers from Hitler's West Wall skulking under them – all blessedly a ten-minute tram ride from the genuinely bright lights and shops of Ostend.

The chalet was basic, with no running water in the kitchenette. Water was twenty yards away, lavatories were clean but thirty yards away. But we had great fun. We went to beautiful Bruges by train (Belgian railways are very useful), to the swinging family resort of Blankenberge and elegant Knokke-Heist just along the coast, lunched on shrimps or superb Belgian frites (the best chips in the world) from street stalls, and took most of our evening meals in cheap cafés, dining on shrimp croquettes made from shrimps landed that morning, écrevisses à la liègeoise (crayfish boiled in onions, herbs, carrots and wine), tomatoes stuffed with shrimps and mayonnaise, and bellekes (balls of minced pork or veal roasted in the oven).

Holiday chalets are still there, but are now bungalows with full plumbing, and Metropolitans are now 'collectors' cars'.

This coastal area, easily reached by boats to Ostend, Zeebrugge or Dunkirk just over the French border, is splendid for families and for teenagers – lively, fine sands, entertainment of every sort from children's amusements to discos, music bars, casinos and horse racing. Apart from Ostend, a working port as well as the second most fashionable resort, the season lasts from about Easter until early September, and the other resorts are virtually shut down off-season. Resorts are fun but far from beautiful. For beauty you must go inland to Bruges, Damme or Ghent, for scenic beauty to the lovely hilly Ardennes – rather far for a short break, but worth it.

Quietest and poshest of the resorts is **Knokke**, partly because it has a lot of private villas owned by well-to-do Belgians and Germans from the industrial cities. This is the seaside for Germans from the Rhur, who can reach it quickly by motorway. But Knokke can hardly be called a quiet retreat, for it has joined with three neighbours to make a resort with 120 hotels, a casino, plenty of entertainment, one of the largest golf courses in Europe and even several camp sites. This is very much a campers' coast, and in Bredene nearly everyone stays in a holiday village chalet or camp site.

Knokke has one of the great restaurants of Belgium. Mme de Spae and her daughter Rita cook well enough in their Aquilon restaurant to please both Michelin (two stars) and Gault (two red toques), so there is no need for me to tell you how good they are with combined traditional and Nouvelle Cuisine. They serve superb fish mousses, scallops in wine, various lovely shellfish dishes, including delightful hot langoustine terrine, and mouthwatering pastries a fat man should go without. Not cheap, of course – around 1500 Belgian francs (about £20) for a meal. Good cooking can be cheap. Great cooking, never.

Belgium is a country of gourmets as much as France, and of hearty eaters, like many French people. When a Belgian is defending his rights he is said to be 'defending his beefsteaks'. The French cuisine here is almost as good as in France; the Flemish is mostly better than cooking in Germany or Holland, specially in **the Ardennes**, where forests and hills produce superb wild boar, venison, hare and wildfowl, served spit-roasted or in a pot with delicious sauces, or smoked like the wonderful Ardennes ham and smoked boar ham; there is jugged hare and game pâté. The fish of the coast is outstanding. Belgians swear that Dover sole feeds on chalk, Ostend sole on shrimps! But their famed and beloved oysters were often bred in Whitstable or Helford and taken across to be fed until fat and succulent.

Vegetables are very good, too, and they use a lot of endives (chicory). Some fine dishes are Flemish karbonaden (beef stewed in beer), roast goose à la visé (boiled, then roast, making it less fatty – cream and egg sauce), endives à l'ardennaise (braised with pork and ham), waterzooi (prime pieces of chicken in vegetable broth, thickened with cream). Some old dishes seem very modern: hare with onions and prunes, rabbit with plums, pigeon breast on a bed of gratinated leeks. Some were obviously invented to fill peasant bellies: potato purée with black pudding, stewed apples.

Unlike the French, Belgians usually take a snack lunch and eat their main meal in the evening. They drink a lot of wine, imported mostly from France, Germany and Luxembourg, and make very good beer. It is strong and they drink more beer per head than any other people. Don't stick to light Pils. Try the double-fermented beers which taste different from place to place: Trappist (abbey beers), Geuze and Goulden Carolus are good ones. To warm up in winter, take a couple of pints of these with hutsepot (beef, mutton, pork and veal mixed with potatoes and several vegetables in a super-stew).

Gastronomic and gourmet weekends are held on the coast in winter at De Panne, Koksidje, Knokke, Ostend, Middelkerke and Blankenberge. You can get a list of interesting special weekends in Flanders, mostly off-season, from the Belgian Tourist Office, 38 Dover St, London W1, 01 499 5379. There is even a pubbing weekend in Antwerp.

Blankenberge in season is a family resort in the old sense, putting children and their play ahead of motorists, with areas on the promenade for pedal cars, bikes or just running and playing. Parents can play in the casino. There are 3 km of fine sand, a fishing harbour, yacht marina and a real old-style pier.

I like **De Haan**. It is a pleasantly mature resort which seems to have changed little in forty years. It does have a fine but pricey restaurant, Le Coeur Volant, where they serve good lobster and oysters. Also the Townsend Thoresen holiday village, which shows how far these have come since we stayed in Bredene: bungalows, swimming pool, shop, restaurant, lounge-bar and a camping site attached.

Middelkerke I like too, because it has nice farms and villages around it. **De Panne**, near the French border, has dunes 2 km

wide and arrowed pathways through them. It has a distinct French atmosphere and a lot of French visitors.

All have wonderful sands, safe bathing and seasonal amusements, but none is like **Ostend**, the busy seaport, big fishing port, ferry terminal and resort, all pushed into a lively area between sands and docks. Ostend is not elegant or beautiful, it is crowded and it is fun. It has good shops at fair prices and all sorts of entertainment much cheaper than in most parts of Europe. The bathing is good, you can catch a quick train to Bruges, one of the finest living medieval cities, or to Brussels, the cosmopolitan, pricey capital of Europe.

You can handpick your eating places in Ostend as in Dieppe, for there are plenty at reasonable prices. Most offer the Blegian national dish: steak and chips, and in season superb local asparagus cheaper than in Britain.

The fish, especially shellfish, is superb, too. You can lunch from stalls on the fishing quai, **Visserskai**. They will open oysters for you, make you the freshest of crab or lobster sandwiches, or just sell you a pint of whelks.

Then you can dine across the road at one of the many quayside restaurants – Lusitania, where you try not to make jokes about sinking a dozen oysters and where they serve superb lobster bisque and sole; La Crevette, which was my old favourite; Le Grillon, much cheaper than either; Kwinte, cheaper still; and Hoeve, where I had a good meal recently for £5 and could have had an unusually good one for £10. Top of them all is Prince Charles, where a meal costs around £20 and is worth it.

The best fish restaurant in Ostend is Hostellerie Bretonne, in **Vindictivelaan**. Patron-chef is a Norman, Jacques Marriere, who leans slightly towards Nouvelle Cuisine. His hot oysters in champagne, his fish stew (soupe de la mer du nord) with garlic mayonnaise (aïoli) spread on croutons, his fish steamed over algues (a sort of seaweed) are all superb. The menu is £18 – gourmets are rich in Belgium. But there are dozens of good restaurants serving fairly cheap meals. One is Café Gloria on **promenade Albert I**, where shellfish is excellent.

From May to September, Ostend has trotting races by floodlight at the Wellington racecourse, where you can sit and drink while you watch the racing. It is as much a social occasion as a race meeting.

Ostend's casino is not only a reliable place to have a flutter but has good entertainment, including a weekend night-club with floorshow. Its Périgord restaurant, one of the best on the coast, has pleasant ambience and reasonable prices. Meals cost from £6 to £12. For the more energetic there are many discos.

One of the best lively weekends we have had abroad was at the Ostend Carnival, held at the end of February or beginning of March. It starts with a lantern parade through the steets, on Friday night, builds up to Saturday night's Ball of the Dead Rat – a masked fancy-dress rave-up at the casino. It is named after a notorious cabaret in Paris at the time of Toulouse-Lautrec and the great days of the Moulin Rouge. Carnival groups come from all over Europe. Five thousand guests dance to six bands in different rooms and drink in many bars until breakfast time. Masks are compulsory, but shed at midnight.

The first time we went to the Ball of the Dead Rat, Barbara went appropriately as a black cat, in a lace catsuit. There were several other cats there. At midnight I grabbed, kissed and demasked the wrong blonde cat! That sort of 'mistake' is frequent during the carnival. Barbara was busy dancing with a sheik.

After breakfast of beer or champagne and shrimps, the action continues all day in the streets. It is quite a party.

A superb Flower Festival is held at the end of August. On Saturday you can go to the little village of **Lochristi**, near Ghent, for the begonia festival. This is where most of the begonias and azaleas are grown, and during this weekend you can see great carpets of flowers against a floral background. On Sunday **Blankenberge** holds its great Parade of Flowers, with flower-bedecked floats which even make Jersey jealous.

Belgium has more festivals and carnivals even than Germany. It is worth finding out from the tourist office before you go if any are taking place while you are there. One of the best known in Britain is the **Wieze** Beer Festival at the end of September and beginning of

October. It is not quite on the scale of the Munich festival, nor so dear, but there are thousands of chickens roasted on spits, tens of thousands of frankfurters and hamburgers, and the beer is piped direct from Van Roy brewery. A smaller but just as jolly beer festival is held a little later at **Diksmuide**, near Ostend.

Bruges is one of my golden cities; I never tire of it. When midsummer visitors are there in daytime for coast resorts, it is crowded. But often it is a haven of tranquility.

It was one of the largest commercial cities in north Europe from the 14th to 16th centuries. Then the sea retreated, waterways silted up, leaving a perfectly preserved medieval city. In quiet corners it is difficult to believe that you are in the 20th century. Everything is done to conserve it. When the Holiday Inn was built in 1970 on the site of a Capucin convent, the gabled convent façade was removed, then restored to blend with neighbouring gabled buildings. The chapel was restored at the back of the hotel and is popular for weddings, with receptions in the same building.

In the city you may hear it called Brugge, not Bruges. This is west Flanders, and the language is mainly Flemish, not French. There is still strong feeling in Belgium about the differences in language and culture between the Flemings and the French-speaking Walloons as historic as the differences between English- and French-speaking Canadians, and includes old religious divisions. Not thinking, I asked the way of a man in Ostend (Oostende) in French. In perfect English he said: 'I don't understand French.' Then he told me the way!

If you are new to Bruges, take a

canal trip. Boats run every day from March to November between 10 a.m. and 6 p.m. The trip takes thirty-five minutes, costs about £1, and although it covers only a fraction of the canals which lace the city, it passes some of the most delightful treasures of Bruges and reaches the romantically named **Minnewater**, meaning the Lake of Love. This was originally Bruges' commercial dock. You can get off at **Huidenvettersplein**, by the lovely old Duc de Bourgogne, an hotel in an incredible canalside setting and with almost flamboyantly picturesque 16th- and 17th-century décor and furnishings. Its cuisine is a fine mixture of French traditional and the best of Flemish. Sole walewska and waterzooi de poissons are especially good.

You can sightsee by boat or on foot in Bruges. Fifty canal bridges and narrow streets make driving a chore. Cross the canal from the Duc and walk up **Wollestraat** and you are in the **market square** and real centre of old Bruges. The market is held on Saturday mornings, but the square is always fun. The restaurants and cafés in the old buildings lure me. Le Panier d'Or, in the old roofmakers' hall, was for long the most famous. In his autobiograhy *The Moon's a Balloon* David Niven tells a wartime story of sitting there wining and dining after the Canadians had freed Bruges, to realise, as he left, that all had become silent: the Canadians had left again; the Nazis were coming in at the other end.

La Cività d'Or restaurant, in the old fishmongers' hall, is popular

now. They are both rather pricey. We use Sint-Joris, sandwiched between them – simple, well-cooked three-course meal for around £5. Or the Central.

All are in view of the 13th-century **Belfry**, about which Longfellow, the American poet, wrote a long and very bad poem. It rises 266 ft (81 m) above two wings of the medieval market building to a stately octagonal tower. If you spend half an hour climbing its 366 winding steps you will see right across the city over the beautiful old patrician houses and tree-lined canals to the new industrial city beyond. Or sit outside a café in the square and listen to the forty-seven bells of the carillon playing a different tune every quarter of an hour. They are played automatically these days, of course. But about four times a week the town carilloneur plays popular and classical melodies for about an hour, a wonderful free concert you can hear across the town. The **tourist office** in the Belfry building will tell you the times. One is always at a quarter to twelve on Sunday mornings.

Bruges has a wealth of beautiful old public buildings. But it is the old houses which I love most, and many are now hotels or restaurants. There is the delightful Hôtel Bourgoensch Hof on **Woollestraat**, with a terrace looking down the canal and some splendid beds upstairs. And the delightful new Navara Hotel in a 16th-century palace on **Sint-Jacobsstraat**, 100 m from the Belfry. It was the home of the Prince of Navara, and two centuries later Napoleon stayed here. His cypher is on a large window. It has no restaurant, as yet, but is good value for such elegance. There are rooms or suites for one to five people. An inclusive mini-break to the Navara by boat and rail from London, three nights' bed and breakfast in June and September 1983 cost £64 to £67 each person (Transeurope Holidays – see page 194). Meal vouchers for a choice of restaurants were £6.

The Ardennes is one of Europe's best-kept secrets – a land known mostly to walkers, animal lovers and hunters, where the air is still clean and traffic so sparse that you can hear the birds sing. It is an area of forests rich in wild boar, roe-deer and foxes, rivers with clear waters running below giant cliffs, and near-empty roads. Old villages have little inns where you will find the lovely game, ham and trout special to the Ardennes and possibly a boar turning on a spit for dinner. You can walk the hills, climb, canoe or laze.

Strange that this little-known land of hills and valleys makes up nearly a third of Belgium, a country we imagine to be flat. At the old town of **Namur**, known as the 'gateway to the Ardennes', the gentle undulating fields of central Belgium stop suddenly and you are in the deep valley of the rocky-banked river Meuse. Namur is dominated by a rocky cliff where the Sambre and Meuse rivers meet. Inevitably, a citadel sits on top. You can reach it by cable car, tram or car. Views are superb.

The old town is over the river Sambre. It has interesting medieval and lovely Renaissance buildings. In the convent are some of the most prized treasures of Belgium: works in gold and silver of the monk-goldsmith Brother Hugo of Oignies. One shows men on stilts jousting. That sport lasted until quite recently, when it was stopped because of nasty injuries. Stilts were popular because the Meuse flooded its banks, leaving a treacherous slimy bog. That is the logical explanation. I prefer to believe the story in ancient chronicles: the people of Namur rebelled against the harsh rule of their lord, Jehan, so he besieged the city and starved the people. Emissaries were sent to plead for mercy, but he said he would see no one, whether they came by foot, horse, carriage or boat. So they went on stilts, and their lord laughed so much that he relented.

The Gothic cathedral, by the Italian, Pizzini, has a Jordaens painting and a memorial to Don John of Austria, who beat the Turks at the sea battle of Lepanto and saved Christendom. He was a great lover, too. The dreaded Philip II of Spain gave him the nasty job of Governor of the Low Countries, keeping the rebellious Dutch and Belgians in order. While he was camping outside Namur, a lady sent him some gloves. They were poisoned and he died. He was only thirty-one. Historians still argue whether the gloves came from a Belgian resistance patriot, a double-crossed lover or by order of Philip II, who was jealous of his half-brother's prowess in battle and bed.

The wooded uplands of

Ardennes begin beyond **Dinant**, 28 km south of Namur – a pretty little town, despite destruction through the centuries. It was conquered by the Duke of Burgundy, called Philip the Good, in 1466. He was no good for Dinant. He razed the city, tied 800 locals back to back and had them drowned in the Meuse. Dinant was attacked several times, until in 1914 the Kaiser's Germany Army, trying to cow the Belgians, shot 695 civilians and burned 1100 houses. In 1940 and 1944, poor Dinant was again bombarded and much destroyed by Hitler's armies. But its setting is beautiful and it is a happy town – lively, with good watersports, from water skiing and canoeing to fishing and swimming in a riverside pool. It has good restaurants. Hostellerie Thermidor in the station road is very good value, especially for local crayfish dishes.

Dinant is probably the best centre for exploring the Ardennes. I believe that Britons searching for beautiful country and good food are missing a lot by not exploring this land, and I am glad that, as I write, Hoverspeed are planning mini-breaks there for motorists.

The gem of the forests is **Bouillon**, on both banks of the river Semois. The ruins of its historic castle perched above the town and curving river are a grand sight. From the dining room of the old Poste hotel, which overlooks the river beside a small bridge, you can see the castle across the water.

The scenery is wonderful from almost all the roads around Bouillon. Eastward, the Semois is twisting and turbulent, running through a great oak forest. About 1½ km outside **Herbeumont** is a most attractive restaurant in an 18th-century abbey by the riverside – Hostellerie du Prieuré de Conques. The cooking is excellent, the trout and other river fish superb, and you can pay anything from £10 to £30 for a meal. The honest wild woodland game and river fish dishes of the Ardennes may not win many French accolades, but I would take a break in Ardennes just to taste them, even if the scenery were not so beautiful and tranquil as it is.

Hotels and Restaurants

Knokke-Heist, 8300 West-Vlaanderen –

Aquilon, Lippensiaan 306 (050 601274): see also page 186; carte 1200-2000FB*; closing times very seasonal.

Rogier, Lippensiaan 249 (050 601530): good local fish; tourist menu 450-550FB. Shut Monday evenings, Tuesdays; October.

De Haan, 8420 West-Vlaanderen –

Coeur Volant, Normandielaan 24 (059 233567): see also page 187; carte 1500-2000FB.

Ostend (Oostende), 8400 West-Vlaanderen –

Admiral Hôtel, Langestraat 72 (059 708656): popular with Britons;

*FB = Belgian francs. Autumn 1983 rate: 80FB = £1.

rooms 1400-2500FB; restaurant.

Prado, Leopold II laan 22 (059
705306): nice modern
bed-and-breakfast hotel in flowery
square; rooms 1200-1600FB.

Lusitania, Visserskai 35 (059
705066): see also page 187; carte
1550-2000FB.

La Crevette, Visserskai 46 (059
702130): carte 810-1500FB; shut
Thursday except midsummer;
November 20 to December 20.

Le Grillon, Visserskai 31 (059
706063): menu 700-800FB; shut
Thursdays.

Kwinte, Visserskai 28 (059 701343):
see also page 187; shrimps and
shellfish au gratin; cod with leeks;
menu 500-700FB; shut
Wednesdays.

Prince Charles, Visserskai 19 (059
705066): see also page 188; try
North Sea bouillabaisse; Ostend
sole with mussels, shrimps,
scallops; scallop terrine;
fisherman's sauerkraut; carte
around 1500FB.

Hoeve, Visserskai 27 (059 702677):
menu 400-720FB; shut Mondays.

Gloria, Albert I Prom 60 (059
706811): known for good scallops,
North Sea fish soup, brill; carte
800-1500FB.

Hostellerie Bretonne,
Vindictivelaan 23 (059 704222): see
also page 188; carte around 1500FB.
shut Wednesdays.

Koksidje-Bad (Coxyde), 26 km S of
Ostend, 8460 West-Visanderen –

Aquilon, Koninklijkebaan 318,

Sint-Idesbald (058 512267):
excellent restaurant in pleasant
little resort, lovely imaginative fish
dishes and superb North Sea
bouillabaisse (for two); menu
870-1950FB; shut part October,
January; Sunday evenings,
Mondays except midsummer.

Bruges (Brugge), 8000
West-Vlaanderen –

Duc de Bourgogne,
Huidenvettarsplaats 12 (050
332038): see also page 190;
beautiful; carte 1500-2000FB;
rooms 2000-2500FB; shut Sunday
evenings, Mondays except July.

Bourgoensch Hof, Woollestraat 39
(050 331645): bed and breakfast;
rooms 1350-3050FB.

Navara, St Jacobsstraat (050
340561): see also page 191;
beautiful; bed and breakfast;
rooms for one to five people;
prices seasonal; 750-4900FB (five
people).

Sint-Joris, Markt 29 (050 336062):
menu 400-450FB.

Civière d'Or, Markt 33 (050 331793):
see also page 190; tourist menu
400FB plus carte.

Pandhotel, Pandreitje 16 (050
334434): charming small bed-and-
breakfast hotel with bar in city
centre; pretty furnishings; rooms
for two, with bathroom, and
breakfast 1650FB.

Dinant, 5500 Namur –

Hostellerie Thermidor (082 223135):
outstanding value; menu 400-
875FB; rooms 460-810FB; shut

Tuesdays; Monday evenings low season.

Bouillon, 6830 Luxembourg belge –

Poste, place St Arnoud 1 (061 466506): tourist menu 425FB; carte 920-1250FB; rooms 1400-1515FB.

Aux Armes de Bouillon, rue Station 11 (061 466079): menu 425-1250FB; rooms (with breakfast) 600-1800FB; shut Mondays off-season; part August.

Herbeumont, 6803 Luxembourg belge –

Hostellerie Prieuré de Conques, rte Florenville 176 (061 411417): see page 192; menu 950-1500FB (shut Tuesdays); rooms (with breakfast) 1250-2400FB; open mid-March to January 1.

Tour operators specialising in trips to Belgium

Belgian Travel Service, Bridge House, Ware, Herts – (0920) 61171; **Hoverspeed**, Hoverport, Ramsgate, Kent – (0843) 54881; **Sealink** (Belgian Mini-Breaks), 163 Eversholt St, London NW1 – (01) 388 6843; **Townsend Thoresen**, Enterprise House, Avebury Ave, Tonbridge, Kent – (0732) 365437; **Transeurope**, Southend Airport, Southend-on-Sea, Essex – (0702) 351451.

Index

Names of hotels, restaurants, and camping and caravan sites are printed in *italic*.

Fiction

☐	**Options**	Freda Bright	£1.50p
☐	**The Thirty-nine Steps**	John Buchan	£1.50p
☐	**Secret of Blackoaks**	Ashley Carter	£1.50p
☐	**Hercule Poirot's Christmas**	Agatha Christie	£1.50p
☐	**Dupe**	Liza Cody	£1.25p
☐	**Lovers and Gamblers**	Jackie Collins	£2.50p
☐	**Sphinx**	Robin Cook	£1.25p
☐	**Ragtime**	E. L. Doctorow	£1.50p
☐	**My Cousin Rachel**	Daphne du Maurier	£1.95p
☐	**Mr American**	George Macdonald Fraser	£2.25p
☐	**The Moneychangers**	Arthur Hailey	£2.50p
☐	**Secrets**	Unity Hall	£1.75p
☐	**Black Sheep**	Georgette Heyer	£1.75p
☐	**The Eagle Has Landed**	Jack Higgins	£1.95p
☐	**Sins of the Fathers**	Susan Howatch	£3.50p
☐	**The Master Sniper**	Stephen Hunter	£1.50p
☐	**Smiley's People**	John le Carré	£1.95p
☐	**To Kill a Mockingbird**	Harper Lee	£1.95p
☐	**Ghosts**	Ed McBain	£1.75p
☐	**Gone with the Wind**	Margaret Mitchell	£3.50p
☐	**Blood Oath**	David Morrell	£1.75p
☐	**Platinum Logic**	Tony Parsons	£1.75p
☐	**Wilt**	Tom Sharpe	£1.75p
☐	**Rage of Angels**	Sidney Sheldon	£1.95p
☐	**The Unborn**	David Shobin	£1.50p
☐	**A Town Like Alice**	Nevile Shute	£1.75p
☐	**A Falcon Flies**	Wilbur Smith	£2.50p
☐	**The Deep Well at Noon**	Jessica Stirling	£2.50p
☐	**The Ironmaster**	Jean Stubbs	£1.75p
☐	**The Music Makers**	E. V. Thompson	£1.95p

Non-fiction

☐	**Extraterrestrial Civilizations**	Isaac Asimov	£1.50p
☐	**Pregnancy**	Gordon Bourne	£3.50p
☐	**Jogging From Memory**	Rob Buckman	£1.25p
☐	**The 35mm Photographer's Handbook**	Julian Calder and John Garrett	£5.95p
☐	**Travellers' Britain**	⎫ Arthur Eperon	£2.95p
☐	**Travellers' Italy**	⎭	£2.50p
☐	**The Complete Calorie Counter**	Eileen Fowler	80p

All these books are available at your local bookshop or newsagent, or can be ordered direct from the publisher. Indicate the number of copies required and fill in the form below   10

....

Name_____
(Block letters please)

Address_____

_____

Send to CS Department, Pan Books Ltd, PO Box 40, Basingstoke, Hants
Please enclose remittance to the value of the cover price plus:
35p for the first book plus 15p per copy for each additional book ordered
to a maximum charge of £1.25 to cover postage and packing
Applicable only in the UK

While every effort is made to keep prices low, it is sometimes
necessary to increase prices at short notice. Pan Books reserve
the right to show on covers and charge new retail prices which
may differ from those advertised in the text or elsewhere